EMPIRE, ECONOMICS, AND THE NEW TESTAMENT

EMPIRE, ECONOMICS, AND THE NEW TESTAMENT

Peter Oakes

WILLIAM B. EERDMANS PUBLISHING COMPANY
GRAND RAPIDS, MICHIGAN

Wm. B. Eerdmans Publishing Co.
4035 Park East Court SE, Grand Rapids, Michigan 49546
www.eerdmans.com

26 25 24 23 22 21 20   1 2 3 4 5 6 7

ISBN 978-0-8028-7326-2

Library of Congress Cataloging-in-Publication Data

Names: Oakes, Peter (Peter S.), author.
Title: Empire, economics, and the New Testament / Peter Oakes.
Description: Grand Rapids, Michigan : William B. Eerdmans Publishing
    Company, 2020. | Includes bibliographical references and index. | Summary:
    "A collection of essays about the New Testament world through archaeologi-
    cal and textual lenses"—Provided by publisher.
Identifiers: LCCN 2020021682 | ISBN 9780802873262 (hardcover)
Subjects: LCSH: Bible. New Testament—Social scientific criticism.
Classification: LCC BS2545.S55 O35 2020 | DDC 225.9—dc23
LC record available at https://lccn.loc.gov/2020021682

Unless otherwise indicated, Bible translations are by the author.

Contents

FOREWORD

The study of the early Jesus movement has been enhanced by significant developments in the past generation of scholarship—with one particular development being well represented by the research of Peter Oakes. Characterized in particular by a turn to the material culture of the Greco-Roman world, this development involves interpreting the New Testament (and "Christian origins" in general) by means of nonliterary data from that foreign world—data discovered buried in the dirt and sand (and sometimes the volcanic debris) of ancient sites, but now often housed in museums and special collections.

This form of ancient data is normally studied in departments of archeology, art history, classics, ancient history, and the like; and in previous generations, such data were not regularly accessed in order to shed programmatic light on the early Jesus movement of the first century and beyond. Of course, occasionally a voice would rise to prominence that powerfully articulated the relevance of aspects of the material cultural of the Greco-Roman world for the study of the origins of "early Christianity," and there was always a recognition that scholarship needed to be open to that dimension of research. But the main currents of New Testament scholarship seemed happily to trudge along under the pretense that the material culture of the Roman world was somewhat peripheral to what really mattered. Even when the early Jesus movement was specifically studied in relation to the Greco-Roman world, scholars often prioritized the texts of the Greco-Roman literary canon as the primary *comparanda* against which to interpret the theological discourse of the early Jesus followers.

In the year 2020, this long-standing perception of things looks noticeably outdated. New Testament scholarship no longer suffers under the impression that material culture is an interesting but relatively insignificant tributary stream that only occasionally might flow into the mainstream. There is now the recognition that engagement with material *realia* is itself a powerful current within the mainstream of scholarship. In the process, the texts of the Greco-Roman elite are now regularly studied in relation to (and sometimes in contrast with) the material artifacts of the ancient world—artifacts that often shed light not only on the lives of the elite but also the lives of "ordinary" people. In the literature of the Greco-Roman elite, those "ordinary" lives are often invisible or are depicted through lenses heavily filtered by the power structures and value systems of the elite themselves. Focusing on Greco-Roman material culture enables scholarly conversations about the world of the earliest Jesus followers to be more sensitive to the conditions and contours of the everyday lives of the ancient sub-elites while bypassing the biased filters of their much more powerful contemporaries.

This is where Peter Oakes has made some of his most significant contributions—conceptualizing how forms of Jesus devotion might lie across a heavily contoured map of various first-century sub-elite identities and, in the process, capturing glimpses of how "the good news" of the early Jesus movement might have been processed by diverse members of early Jesus groups. What emerges from Peter's work is an intriguing exhibit of how that "good news" may have seeped into the folds of everyday first-century lives—the lives of sub-elite Jews and gentiles, free and slave, males and females, in various overlapping mixes. In the process, we more easily observe the potential force of New Testament texts in relation to the pressing concerns of first-century audiences—not the profound theological experts of later centuries, but people "on the ground" trying to get by in their everyday lives. Representing a kind of reception history of the first audiences of these important texts, this dimension of Peter's research lies along a trajectory with strong connections to the feminist/liberationist agendas of the late twentieth century and into the "people's history" of the twenty-first century. Along the way, Peter offers a highly nuanced approach, sorting through a variety of forms of relationality in accordance with a broad range of prosopographic differences (avoiding, for instance, the tendency to imagine all of the earliest Jesus followers as being at or below subsistence level, as is sometimes done).

The essays contained in this book (especially those in its first two sections) flow from Peter's main wheelhouse—listening for the way New Testament texts might have set off various resonances for people variously embedded within the world dominated by Roman structures of value. Whether he is setting out space-distribution modeling, or engaging in socioeconomic modeling, or exploring attitudes toward the Roman Empire, Peter doggedly earths the reading of theological texts in the historical realities of the ancient world. Few are as attuned to matters of Roman social history and cultural conventions as Peter Oakes. In this regard, Peter is one of the best representatives of contemporary New Testament scholarship—as testified to by the essays collected within this volume.

BRUCE W. LONGENECKER

PREFACE

Although it rapidly became obvious that engineering was not the degree I should have signed up for, I remained fascinated about how things worked—what bits were in them, how they fitted together and functioned—and about how best to analyze things in view of what we can find out about how they work. In many ways, most of the chapters in this book try to do that, for various aspects of the world that the New Testament writers and early audiences inhabited. Engineering also made me see the world in terms of models (for instance, in a course on measuring things, we were asked: How do you model the idea "is equal to" when your aim is to give manufacturing instructions that will result in producing two components that will fit together?). Another boon of the particular engineering syllabus that I was studying was that I could take two finals papers in less engineering-y subjects, economics and industrial sociology. Also crucially during the period of my first degree, I heard the chaplain of Downing College Cambridge, one N. T. Wright, giving a long series of Christian Union talks such as, "Here comes the King!" (on the triumphal entry in Luke).

Six years of inner-city school teaching and youth work were then followed by a BA at London Bible College (now London School of Theology), with Conrad Gempf and others compellingly contextualizing the biblical texts. Then Tom Wright again, for doctoral study, with many conversations about Christ and Caesar. At Oxford I also met Simon Price, who generously took on guiding my reading in the archeology and economics of Roman colonies. Alongside this, his *Rituals and Power* was a further major influence.[1] In the graduate New Testament seminar led by Chris Rowland, he and fellow students generously joined in role-playing to indulge a fascination I had developed in the

---

1. S. R. F. Price, *Rituals and Power: The Roman Imperial Cult in Asia Minor* (Cambridge: Cambridge University Press, 1984).

differences we could expect between how texts sounded to various types of ancient hearers.

Through the British New Testament Society, I met Philip Esler, who cemented my interest in models through Thomas Carney's *The Shape of the Past*.[2] On arriving at Manchester, I got to know Roger Ling and to engage with his fabulous project on the Insula of the Menander at Pompeii. Many other encounters since then—in Manchester, at Society of Biblical Literature, in the Context Group, and elsewhere—have helped shaped this volume.

Chronologically, the first is an early expression of my interest in expected differences of hearing, in particular where there would be economic disparity among early Christians receiving Paul's letters. "Jason and Penelope Hear Philippians 1:1–11" explores this, using Paul's ambiguity, in the opening of his letter, about the nature of what he appreciates about the Philippian Christians.

Four papers on New Testament and empire were published next. "God's Sovereignty over Roman Authorities: A Theme in Philippians" expands work on Christ and the emperor in my *Philippians: From People to Letter*.[3] The paper broadens from a focus on these two key figures onto consideration of the portrayal of the authorities throughout the letter: for instance, on their role and limitations in relation to Paul's imprisonment.

A pair of articles then develop a model of the complexity and inherent tension in Rome's reputation among various types of people in the empire. The articles then map that onto complexity and tension in the depiction of Rome in the New Testament. "Christian Attitudes to Rome at the Time of Paul's Letter" constructs the basic model and applies it to Romans. "A State of Tension: Rome in the New Testament" considers the model across the range of New Testament texts, in critical dialogue with scholars who have diluted some of that tension, especially by assigning some New Testament texts very firmly to the "positive" or "negative" camps in relation to empire.

The fourth article, "Remapping the Universe: Paul and the Emperor in 1 Thessalonians and Philippians," was written in response to James Harrison's "Paul and the Imperial Gospel at Thessaloniki."[4] In reaction to claims that appeared sometimes overstated, my article proposes a fourfold model of types of relationship between particular early Christian texts and elements of Roman imperial ideology. The article then uses that framework in analyzing key in-

2. Thomas Carney, *The Shape of the Past: Models and Antiquity* (Lawrence, KS: Coronado, 1975).

3. Peter Oakes, *Philippians: From People to Letter*, SNTSMS 110 (Cambridge: Cambridge University Press, 2001).

4. J. R. Harrison, "Paul and the Imperial Gospel at Thessaloniki," *JSNT* 25 (2002): 71–96.

stances in two of Paul's letters, concluding with the idea of early Christians "re-mapping the universe," an adaptation of one of Simon Price's key proposals.

The socioeconomic modeling of Philippi in *Philippians: From People to Letter* led to an invitation to contribute a brief response to what turned out to be Steven Friesen's hugely influential "Poverty in Pauline Studies."[5] This in turn led to an invitation to contribute to Bruce Longenecker and Kelly Lieben-good's major international project that produced *Engaging Economics*.[6] I took the opportunity to try to think through how to approach economic issues in New Testament studies, producing the chapter that leads off the economics section of this collection: "Methodological Issues in Using Economic Evidence in Interpretation of Early Christian Texts." Methodological concerns are also central to "Economic Approaches: Scarce Resources and Interpretive Oppor-tunities." However (as well as representing a few further years thinking), this essay is refocused for a student textbook audience, including provision of a compact worked example. The same type of audience is in view in "Urban Structure, Patronage, and the Corinthian Followers of Christ." In that case, the textbook was produced by the Context Group for Biblical Research, seeking to apply sociological and anthropological approaches to biblical studies in the classroom.

Since publication of *Reading Romans in Pompeii*,[7] much of my thinking on economic and empire-related issues has been expressed in exploring the implications of the early Christians meeting and hearing New Testament texts in various types of first-century space, especially houses and workshops. This leads to "Nine Types of Church in Nine Types of Space in the Insula of the Menander," which considers socioeconomic aspects of the implications of var-ious choices of space for early Christians to meet in. The same interests lead to the piece that opens this collection: "A House-Church Account of Economics and Empire." The occasion of producing the collection led me to reflect on what implications a first-century house-church context would have for how economic and empire-related issues would impact on the lives of various types of group members and, consequently, how that would relate to the handling of such issues in New Testament texts.

5. Steven J. Friesen, "Poverty in Pauline Studies: Beyond the So-called New Consensus," *JSNT* 26 (2004): 323–61; my response was "Constructing Poverty Scales for Graeco-Roman Society" (367–71).

6. Bruce W. Longenecker and Kelly D. Liebengood, eds., *Engaging Economics: New Tes-tament Scenarios and Early Christian Reception* (Grand Rapids: Eerdmans, 2009).

7. Peter Oakes, *Reading Romans in Pompeii: Paul's Letter at Ground Level* (London: SPCK; Minneapolis: Fortress, 2009).

I would like to thank the various publishers for permission to republish articles. They are republished in their original form except for some stylistic harmonization. I also thank Roger Ling, for permission to reproduce his plans, and the Archaeological Superintendency at Pompeii for permission to reproduce Janet's photographs. I thank Michael Thomson, who got this project going at Eerdmans, and Trevor Thompson, Jennifer Hoffman, and the rest of the Eerdmans team for all their help in bringing it to fruition. Thanks also to conveners and colleagues in all the events and collaborations that were involved in the creation of the various articles. Thanks to Sam Rogers for help with the indexing. Finally, thanks particularly to Janet for the photography, for endless other help, and for making it all worthwhile.

Unless otherwise indicated, all Bible translations are my own.

Abbreviations

CIL	*Corpus Inscriptionum Latinarum.* Berlin, 1862–
JSNT	*Journal for the Study of the New Testament*
JSNTSup	Journal for the Study of the New Testament Supplement Series
NIV	New International Version
NRSV	New Revised Standard Version
NTS	*New Testament Studies*
SNTSMS	Society for New Testament Studies Monograph Series
WUNT	Wissenschaftliche Untersuchungen zum Neuen Testament

PART I

HOUSE CHURCH

1 | A House-Church Account of Economics and Empire

"Anyone of you who does not give up all their own possessions cannot be my disciple."

—Luke 14:33

"If someone is hungry, let them eat at home."

—1 Corinthians 11:34

"Let every person be subject to the governing authorities."

—Romans 13:1

"And the ten horns that you saw, and the beast . . . will burn her up with fire . . . the great city that has kingship over the kings of the earth."

—Revelation 17:16–18

The surprising disparity among New Testament texts such as these has had a range of explanations. One is to argue that New Testament books have differing views on economic and imperial subjects. We can see this, for instance, in the work of Klaus Wengst.[1] A second explanation that has had long-term influence is Gerd Theissen's classic sociological conclusion on the economic texts. He ascribes the differences to the effects of different groups among the Christians: itinerant charismatic preachers of the early Palestinian Jesus movement and settled Hellenistic house-church communities. He sees the economically radical texts as relating to the former groups, while many of the less radical

---

1. Klaus Wengst, *Pax Romana and the Peace of Jesus Christ*, trans. J. Bowden (Philadelphia: Fortress, 1987), compare 89–104 (on Luke) with 55–88 (Jesus and Paul), 118–35 (Revelation), and note the conclusion on p. 137.

ones relate to the latter.[2] A third explanation that has been prominent uses James C. Scott's concept of "hidden transcripts." It argues that many of the apparently conformist and subservient New Testament texts mask a radical underlying agenda, designed to be invisible to the authorities.[3]

This chapter argues that most of the diversity of New Testament rhetoric on economic and imperial issues can be satisfactorily accounted for by the situations of members of first-century house churches. Each end of the rhetorical spectrum on both economic and imperial issues makes considerable sense in first-century house-church contexts. Although not denying that there is some diversity of views among New Testament texts, some diversity of lifestyle among early Christians, and some textual presence of hidden transcripts, the diversity of New Testament rhetoric can be accounted for with far less need to appeal to such factors than has often been the case. Circumstances in the house churches make sense of both the more radical and the less radical rhetoric on economics and empire.

We will begin with an economic account of situations within first-century house churches, as represented by the model craftworker house church developed in *Reading Romans in Pompeii*.[4] We will move from there to considering what relationships the members and groups would have to the Roman Empire. We will use these analyses to consider economic and empire-focused New Testament texts in relation to members of the Christian groups. We will end by considering structural issues underlying our arguments and conclusions.

ECONOMIC SITUATIONS IN THE MODEL CRAFTWORKER HOUSE CHURCH

The model craftworker house church is a device to help us understand socio-economic locations, diversity, and potential hierarchies within first-century

2. Gerd Theissen, *Sociology of Early Palestinian Christianity*, trans. J. Bowden (Philadelphia: Fortress, 1978), 10 (on wandering charismatic preachers), 115 (on Paul's letters to Hellenistic communities). An intermediate group for Theissen is early Palestinian Christian communities that were sympathizers to the charismatic preachers, providing their financial support and following their teaching. He sees some Synoptic sayings as relating to these groups (17–18).

3. E.g., Warren Carter, *The Roman Empire and the New Testament: An Essential Guide* (Nashville: Abingdon, 2006), 12–13, drawing on James C. Scott, *Domination and the Arts of Resistance: Hidden Transcripts* (New Haven: Yale University Press, 1990).

4. Peter Oakes, *Reading Romans in Pompeii: Paul's Letter at Ground Level* (London: SPCK; Minneapolis: Fortress, 2009), 1–97.

Christian groups, and to use that understanding for analysis of various issues and texts.[5] The starting point for modeling a house church is the host's household. Even just the exercise of writing down the list of people one might expect in the household of someone with space to host a reasonable-sized group immediately makes us aware that there is quite a range of social situations within a household, and hence within even the most basic house church. This itself should affect the way in which we analyze New Testament texts, alerting us to the fact that, for every New Testament text, there are important issues to consider about how it intersects with the lives of various types of people within the hierarchy of a first-century household.

The model then builds on the host's household by asking both how many others could fit into a meeting in the house and who these others are likely to be. If the host has the largest house in the group, the other members (maybe typically two to three times the number in the host household: anything beyond about that implies an amount of unallocated space unlikely in a non-elite household) will predominantly come from families poorer than the host family: any odd group members from wealthier families would, on these assumptions, not be householders. The host household would probably all, to some extent and in some sense, be members of the Christian group meeting there. Other households joining the group could be complete or partial.

The above produces the essential shape of the model house church. Adding details from studies of housing and households from any of the parts of the Mediterranean world where we know of first-century Christian groups would produce a model of the same general shape as that below (with the main variations probably being in the social level of the host, the ratio of host household to others, and the presence or absence of slaves). *Reading Romans in Pompeii* gives specific substance to the model by focusing on craftworker house churches, a category directly evidenced by Rom 16:5 (cf. Acts 18:3), supported by, for example, 1 Thess 4:11. It then uses evidence from a town where there is direct evidence of craftworker housing and where scholars have been able to make some useful estimates relating to the socioeconomic structure of the population.[6] Our model comprises forty people, as follows:[7]

---

5. For general discussion of models, see John H. Elliott, *Social Scientific Criticism of the New Testament* (London: SPCK, 1995), 40–48.

6. Especially Andrew Wallace-Hadrill, *Houses and Society in Pompeii and Herculaneum* (Princeton: Princeton University Press, 1994).

7. This Pompeian model craftworker house church is based on Oakes, *Reading Romans in Pompeii*, table 3.6.

1. craftworker, wife, children, a few (male) craftworking slaves, (female) domestic slave, dependent relative
2. several other householders (smaller houses), some spouses, children, slaves, other dependents
3. a few members of families with non-Christian family heads
4. a couple of slaves with non-Christian owners
5. a couple of free or freed dependents of non-Christians
6. a couple of homeless people

We will take the six sets of members in turn.

Group 1: The Host Craftworker Household

Many of the larger Pompeian craftworker houses could have been used to con-struct the model. Drawing on the major analysis of the Insula of the Menander led by my Manchester colleague, Roger Ling, and others, especially Penelope Allison,[8] *Reading Romans in Pompeii* took the instance of the *Casa del Fabbro* (House I.10.7) as the focus for construction of the model. Although the Italian archeologists' name for the house means something like "House of the Smith," the very large number of loose finds of woodworking tools and furniture parts suggests that the principal activity there was cabinetmaking.[9]

The ground-floor plan size is 310 square meters, including a rear garden. There are also several upstairs rooms. Comparing this house with others in Andrew Wallace-Hadrill's survey of housing in Pompeii and Herculaneum, the House of the Cabinetmaker has a larger plan size than 70 percent of other houses.[10] On the other hand, it is only about 30 percent of the size of houses at the lower end of elite housing.[11] Most rooms are reasonably but fairly simply decorated. Two rooms have very high-quality decoration, probably predating the house's use by the cabinetmaker.[12] The loose finds include a few pieces

8. Roger Ling, *The Insula of the Menander at Pompeii*, vol. 1: *The Structures* (Oxford: Clarendon, 1997); Roger Ling and Lesley Ling, *The Insula of the Menander at Pompeii*, vol. 2: *The Decorations* (Oxford: Clarendon, 2005); Penelope M. Allison, *The Insula of the Menander at Pompeii*, vol. 3: *The Finds: A Contextual Study* (Oxford: Clarendon, 2007).

9. Oakes, *Reading Romans in Pompeii*, 15–16, 22–26.

10. Oakes, *Reading Romans in Pompeii*, 47–56; Wallace-Hadrill, *Houses and Society*, 57–79.

11. For discussion of what constitutes elite housing, see Oakes, *Reading Romans in Pompeii*, 51, 53.

12. Oakes, *Reading Romans in Pompeii*, 20–32; Ling and Ling, *Insula of the Menander*, 2:140–45, 262–65.

of jewelry: a gold necklace, a pair of gold and pearl earrings, two gold earrings, and two gold rings. Two bodies of people who died in the eruption were found. One had twenty-six silver coins and forty-eight bronze ones. The other, younger person had twenty-six bronze coins. Upstairs there were a further fourteen silver and ten bronze coins. A number of further decorative items of moderate value were also discovered.[13]

One clue to the likely key economic relationships of the householder of I.10.7 is from blocked doorways (see house plan), which show that, at an earlier period, the house had been linked with the very large elite House of the Menander (I.10.4). A further clue to the potential power relationship involved with that link is that, about thirty years before the eruption, a small workshop and living space (I.10.6) was cut out of Houses I.10.4 and I.10.7.[14] That took out a fairly insignificant corner of the House of the Menander but a very prominent part of the House of the Cabinetmaker. The new workshop looks likely to have been a dependency of the House of the Menander. All this adds up to a likelihood that the cabinetmaking householder rented I.10.7 from the owner of the House of the Menander. This is not a surprise. In the first century the great majority

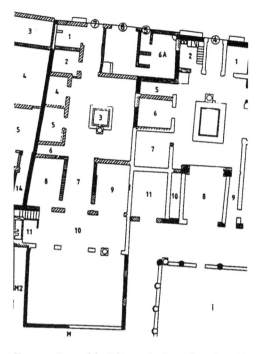

Figure 1.1. *House of the Cabinetmaker (I.10.7) floor plan, with I.10.6 and part of I.10.4 (the House of the Menander) to the right. Differing shading relates to building phases, indicating location of prior connections between atrium of I.10.7 and Rooms 5 and 6 of I.10.4. Source: Roger Ling,* The Insula of the Menander at Pompeii, vol. 1: The Structures *(Oxford: Clarendon, 1997), detail from fig. 26 (drawn by S. Gibson, J. S. Gregory, R. J. Ling, D. Murdoch, with thanks to Roger Ling for permission to reproduce the plan).*

13. Oakes, *Reading Romans in Pompeii*, 18–32, drawing on Allison, *Insula of the Menander*, vol. 3, nos. 1034–1584.

14. Oakes, *Reading Romans in Pompeii*, 8, citing Ling, *Insula of the Menander*, 1:148.

of property was owned by the elite. Extremely few craftworkers would have owned their workshops.

The cabinetmaker's renting of his house linked him to the owner of I.10.4 in a relationship of economic dependency. The relationship probably had something of a patron-client nature to it, albeit maybe in informal terms. As Bruce Malina writes, across the first-century Mediterranean world, the relationship between landlord and tenant often took on the character of favor-giving dependency via events such as deferring payments in times of hardship and the conversion of some rental payments to loans.[15] The relationship also meant that the cabinetmaker probably sought commissions for work via a network related to the owner of the House of the Menander. In return, the cabinetmaker might, for instance, paint up supportive election slogans if his patron ran for office, a pattern studied in depth by Henrik Mouritsen.[16]

Craftworkers would also have relationships with suppliers, in this case particularly for furniture-quality wood and material for inlays, and with a range of customers. One feature of I.10.7 is a bench just outside the front door. In other contexts, such benches are often viewed as being placed for the sake of clients of a householder.[17] For instance, benches on either side of the entrance to I.10.4 would tend to be seen that way. This raises the possibility that the cabinetmaker might himself act like a patron to clients. This sounds strange. Certainly, the cabinetmaker is unlikely to have been formally a *patronus*. However, he did rent more space than 70 percent of Pompeian householders, and some others beyond his household are quite likely to have had some long-term dependency on his favor. One instance to consider is the poorer households within the house church. There could be a two-way effect in which clients of the cabinetmaker are likely to join the house church, an event that then reinforces the patronal link. One particular type of patronage that the cabinetmaker would be likely to exercise is that of acting as a broker,

15. Bruce J. Malina, *The Social World of Jesus and the Gospels* (London: Routledge, 1996), 143–44. For broader discussion of patronage and of scholarly discussions on it, see Eric C. Stewart, "Social Stratification and Patronage in Ancient Mediterranean Societies," in *Understanding the Social World of the New Testament*, ed. Dietmar Neufeld and Richard E. DeMaris (London: Routledge, 2010), 156–66.

16. Henrik Mouritsen, *Elections, Magistrates, and Municipal Élite: Studies in Pompeian Epigraphy*, Analecta Romana Instituti Danici Supplement 15 (Rome: "L'Erma" di Bretschneider, 1988), discussed in Peter Oakes, "Urban Structure and Patronage: Christ Followers in Corinth," in *Understanding the Social World of the New Testament*, ed. Dietmar Neufeld and Richard E. DeMaris (London: Routledge, 2010), 178–93.

17. Olga Elia, "Pompei: Relazione sullo scavo dell'Insula X della Regio I," *Notizie degli scavi* 12 (1934): 264–344 at 278.

requesting favors of his patron (the householder of I.10.4) on behalf of people without a direct connection to him.[18] One more type of link that craftworkers frequently had was in an association/club. That would give social links with others in the same trade, including periodic banquets and, often, contribution to a fund to pay for burial.[19]

Some householders were women, but the great majority of householders with sufficient resources to rent a fair-sized house were men. The cabinet-maker's wife broadly shares his social status, as viewed from beyond the household, but her status within the household was lower than his and, usually, she would have few financial resources. At wealthier levels of society, a wife's father could effectively place some constraints on the husband's ability to control the wife's resources[20] but this would generally not operate at the level of a cabinetmaker's wife. She would usually have very little opportunity to use significant amounts of money except on her husband's say-so. The wife would have a certain status within the household, with primary responsibility for domestic cultic activities, care of children, and management of domestic slaves (in a house too small to have a steward), although in this case there would probably be only one domestic slave, if any at all. The wife would not directly participate in the mechanisms of patronage or of a trade association. However, in a modest-sized craftworking family the distribution of tasks and of outside contacts would be more subject to cooperation and to variation of roles than would happen further up the economic scale.

Children in a craftworking family would work from quite a young age. There could, however, be elementary schooling.[21] Children, like wives, would not usually have independent access to financial resources. This would no

18. For discussion of brokerage see, e.g., Alicia Batten, "Brokerage: Jesus as Social Entrepeneur," in *Understanding the Social World of the New Testament*, ed. Dietmar Neufeld and Richard E. DeMaris (London: Routledge, 2010), 167–77; Zeba A. Crook, *Reconceptualising Conversion: Patronage, Loyalty, and Conversion in the Religions of the Ancient Mediterranean*, Beihefte zur Zeitschrift für die neutestamentliche Wissenschaft 130 (Berlin: de Gruyter, 2004).

19. Philip A. Harland, *Associations, Synagogues, and Congregations: Claiming a Place in Ancient Mediterranean Society* (Minneapolis: Fortress, 2003); Richard S. Ascough, *Paul's Macedonian Associations: The Social Context of Philippians and 1 Thessalonians*, WUNT 161 (Tübingen: Mohr Siebeck, 2003).

20. Peter Garnsey and Richard Saller, *The Roman Empire: Economy, Society, and Culture* (London: Duckworth, 1987), 130–31.

21. Marrieta Horster, "Primary Education," in *The Oxford Handbook of Social Relations in the Roman World*, ed. Michael Peachin (Oxford: Oxford University Press, 2011), 84–100 at 87.

doubt differ in practice for grown-up children who were still at home. However, even for them, the father still officially controlled everything.

It is surprising to us that even quite small craftworking households often had slaves, mainly to participate in the craftwork. This is contrary to our expectation that any workers from beyond the family would be employed, rather than owned. A key dynamic in this pattern is that few of the slaves would have been bought (as adults). They would more frequently have been acquired directly or indirectly through abandonment (exposure) of infants. Raising a slave child cost money but produced both work and a saleable asset. Slaves could (like, in fact, other family members) by custom acquire money that the householder was expected to let them keep and use, the slave's *peculium*, although technically it remained the property of the family head. The most well-known use of *peculium* was for the slave to eventually purchase freedom, in cases where that was possible.[22]

The cabinetmaker's household as a whole was no doubt frequently in a financially precarious situation, a circumstance endemic among the great majority of the first-century non-elite. Adverse occurrences could easily blow the household disastrously off course. The ten members of the household were dependent on the economic resources controlled by the householder—the economic resources of this small craftworking enterprise. These resources needed to be nurtured and used carefully in a precarious economic environment.

Group 2: Other Householders and Their Households

In our model, other householders and their households form the bulk of the house church, half of the forty group members (a quarter of the group members are the host's household; categories 3–6 add up to the remaining quarter). As discussed above, all these householders rent smaller spaces than the house-church host and, while some of these households are entirely in the house church, other households are a mixture of church members and nonmembers.

The household head is still most likely to be male but is increasingly likely to be female as we go further down the scale of economic viability: for instance, households headed by widows are particularly likely to be facing financial hardship. Given the links of contact and friendship, the household are fairly likely to be engaged in similar work to that of the cabinetmaker: Richard

22. A. F. Rodger, "Peculium," in *Oxford Classical Dictionary*, 3rd ed., ed. S. Hornblower and A. Spawforth (Oxford: Oxford University Press, 1996), 1130.

Ascough pushes this scenario furthest, seeing the Thessalonian Christians as an association of leatherworkers who have taken on worship of Christ.[23] As argued above, some of these other households may have some economic dependency on the host householder. Links of dependency operate at all levels of society. In particular, the house-church host may be a broker giving indirect access to resources controlled by his patron. Some households joining a house church might gain some kinds of access that they had not had previously. Having said that, some householders other than the host would no doubt also have had other networks of dependence, on patrons and others, that did not run via the cabinetmaker.

Everything written above about the economic precariousness of a craft-worker household applies more so to these households, craftworker or otherwise, further down the economic scale. The poorer the household, the more exploitative any patronage toward them was likely to be. At the lower end of the range, the households would be perennially in financial difficulty. Another factor that complicates matters for some of the households is that not everyone in the household is part of the house church. The householder is financially responsible for everyone but, in these mixed households, some people in the household are not party to any decisions and commitments—including financially risky ones—that the church members may make.

Groups 3–5: Members of Households with Non-Christian Heads

Our model has about a fifth of the house-church members from households with non-Christian heads, that is, about eight people. This represents the various New Testament texts that discuss the implications of being in this situation (e.g., 1 Cor 7:13–16; 1 Pet 2:18–3:6). The eight could, for instance, be made up of four people from one household, the head of which is not a Christian, along with four other members of different households: people who have joined the Christian group through contact with a friend or through hearing preaching. The precise numbers are not important, but the situation is one that we need to consider.

The economic considerations above mainly apply (but see an exception below). As the heading of the subsection signals, groups 3–5 of our model could be taken as a single category. They are household members and, as such, share, to varying degrees, the economic ups and downs of the household as a whole. However, that observation also shows one value of distinguishing groups 3–5. Members of the biological or adoptive family of a householder

23. Ascough, *Paul's Macedonian Associations*.

(group 3) would share the household's ups to an extent that slaves and other dependents (groups 4 and 5) generally would not. There was also a reason for distinguishing groups 3–5 in the analytical development of the model. Members of a householder's family (in an English sense, rather than the Latin *familia*, which means something more like "household") shared, to a significant extent, the status of the householder. The four in the model were, roughly speaking, drawn from a random sample of Pompeians. Since the cabinetmaker has a larger house plan size than 70 percent of other householders, conversely 30 percent have larger houses than he does. This means that, in a random sample of four Pompeian householders, we would expect one, or possibly two, to have larger houses than the cabinetmaker. Similarly, in a random sample of four Pompeian members of householders' families, we would expect one, or possibly two, to be from families with higher incomes than that of the cabinetmaker (assuming that biological and adoptive family size is constant across the economic spectrum, which Egyptian census evidence shows to be not unreasonable).[24] The point of all this is that our model has one of the forty house-church members being from a family wealthier than that of the cabinetmaker. That person's family might well not be in the economically relatively precarious position occupied by the other thirty-nine people in the model. (New Testament texts such as Rom 16:23 suggest that there were also wealthier householders in some Christian groups. That would produce another model that would be interesting and valuable to analyze. However, this chapter will stay with the craftworker house church, as a model likely to be representative of more Christian groups.)

The particular complication for groups 3–5 is that they do not technically—and to a significant extent practically—have control over any economic resources. This has three direct effects. The first is that they are likely to be sharply limited in any financial contributions that they can make to the activities of the Christian group (e.g., meals) or to the support of other people, either within or beyond the group. Moreover, any money that they can give is likely to be at a disproportionate cost to themselves, since it will be from a rather limited reserve from which they may be permitted to spend. This would be starkest for slaves. If their owner allowed them to contribute to the Christian group from their *peculium*, every denarius that the slave donated could well be an extra period added to the expected period of servitude before they could gain their freedom by paying most of their *peculium* back to their owner.

---

24. Roger S. Bagnall and Bruce W. Frier, *The Demography of Roman Egypt* (Cambridge: Cambridge University Press, 1994), 68, table 3.3.

This example also indicates the second effect, which is that, in many cases, the group member would need their householder's permission in order to give money or goods to the house church. Of course, this is also part of a wider issue that the group members are likely to need their householder's consent to participate in Christian meetings. Since the householder does not share the group member's Christian allegiance or views, these issues of permission could be seriously problematic. In particular, the householder would have little motivation to permit the loss of some of the household's financial resource—and hence security in a perilous economic world—to this alien religious group.

The third effect is that the group members are economically dependent on their householders. Actions contrary to the householder's wishes could leave a group member cut off from economic support. A householder could oppose their actions either because of viewing the Christian groups as disreputable for one reason or another or, more simply, because the group member's time and energy spent with the Christians took away time from their economically important activities in the household. A further reason for likely householder concern about participation in the house church is that it sets up an alternative allegiance (in Greek terms, an alternative structure of *pistis*: "trust" and "loyalty").[25] A householder would probably be worried by a household member owing some allegiance to a group hosted by the head of another household. A householder may well also be worried by allegiance to Christ, who was not a figure in the household's regular pattern of allegiances given to benefactors such as patrons and deities, including the imperial family.

Group 6: Homeless Group Members

There was no mathematical basis for settling on two as a number of homeless people in our model house church. The homeless leave little archeological or indeed textual evidence: certainly not enough to quantify them in the pattern of society in Pompeii or elsewhere. However, we know they were there. We also have little reason to exclude them from the house-church model, especially given the rhetoric of various New Testament texts (e.g., Luke 14).

People unable to afford even the lowest rentals, or who were excluded from settled housing for other reasons, existed on the most marginal and unreliable of economic resources and were vulnerable in a wide range of other ways too. Everything we have said above about precariousness applies to them in

---

25. For discussion of *pistis* as a way of life, see Peter Oakes, "*Pistis* as Relational Way of Life in Galatians," *JSNT* 40 (2018): 255–75.

extreme measure, made even sharper by these people's lack of access to the support networks of a household or of embedding in social structures of a neighborhood or of relatively settled social relations.

How Members of the Model Craftworker House Church Relate to the Roman Empire

New Testament texts that relate to the Roman Empire in some way have many types of textual driver and are written for many different situations. A story about Jesus's encounter with a centurion (Matt 8:5–13) may be driven by comparison between responses of Jews and gentiles to the Christian message. A lurid depiction of Rome's downfall may be evoking motifs from a scriptural pattern of God's dealings with wicked cities (Rev 17–18).[26] The situation in heavily colonial Roman Philippi lends a particular force to Paul's description of his situation "in the Praetorium" (Phil 1:13).[27] The reading of various gospel passages to do with Roman institutions and characters will be affected by how the writing of each book relates to the events around the 70 CE fall of Jerusalem.

Factors such as these make inevitable some variation between Rome-related texts in various New Testament books. As footnoted above, I myself have written about some of these variations. However, our aim here is to consider how much variation in New Testament rhetoric is explicable just from the set of situations of people in our general model craftworker house church. Although it would be interesting to construct further models of Christian groups in, say, Philippi or post-70 Galilee, our current question is how much can be accounted for just by the socioeconomic situations of early non-elite house churches in general, rather than in particular places. As before, we will work though the groups of our model in turn.

Group 1: The Host Craftworker Household

The cabinetmaker's patron (whether formally or informally) is probably the owner of the House of the Menander (I.10.4). When the cabinetmaker visits

26. Peter Oakes, "Revelation 17.1–19.10: A Prophetic Vision of the Destruction of Rome." in *The Future of Rome: Roman, Greek, Jewish, and Christian Perspectives*, ed. Jonathan Price and Katell Berthelot (Cambridge: Cambridge University Press, 2020).

27. Peter Oakes, *Philippians: From People to Letter*, SNTSMS 110 (Cambridge: Cambridge University Press, 2001), 65–66.

his patron and waits in the atrium, he sees what may be evidence of his patron's loyalty to Rome. It is not evidence of explicit engagement with the political order of the day: there is no portrait of the emperor or anything similar. What there is is extensive depiction of the fall of Troy, a key event in Rome's ideology: the point of origin of the family that founded the city and an important element of Roman identity. However, the cycle of Troy pictures here is also part of the house's extensive collection of Greek mythological and cultural art, focused for the archeologists in the named portrait of the poet and playwright Menander. The collection expresses the owner's taste and rootedness in culture. Also in the atrium is a very prominent *lararium*, a shrine to the Lares and other household deities. Further back in the house is a shrine with small busts of deities or ancestors.[28] The cabinetmaker's patron is part of a chain of *pietas*, pious honoring of benefactors, going up through society to the gods and back through time, again ultimately to the gods. The cabinetmaker's house too, unsurprisingly, has a *lararium*, albeit more modest than in I.10.4.

Oddly, the closest piece of text directly honoring the emperor is one door further on. If the cabinetmaker visited the bar at I.10.2–3 and entered via the house door (I.10.3) rather than through the wide bar entrance (I.10.2), he would find in the entrance corridor a *lararium* that carried the words *Lares Augustos* (*CIL* 4.8282), which probably links this domestic shrine to the cult of the imperial family in some way.[29] The cult of the *Lares Augusti* was distributed around various areas of Rome and of other towns.[30] Perhaps a group responsible for the cult in this part of Pompeii met in a room in the bar. The cabinetmaker, and indeed all the members of the house church, would encounter imperial-cult temples in the town's main forum but would be unlikely to be directly involved in any activities at those temples. People of all socioeconomic levels would be likely to attend events in the amphitheater sponsored in connection with imperial-cult festivals such as the emperor's birthday. However, attendance there probably did not involve very active participation in cult activities.

28. For discussion see Ling, *Insula of the Menander*, 1:61.

29. Contra William van Andringa, *Quotidien des dieux et des hommes: La vie religieuse dans les cités du Vésuve à l'époque romaine* (Rome: École française de Rome: 2009), 247, who argues that the adjective *augustos* could just as well mean "revered" in a general sense. Steven E. Ostrow cites a range of evidence relating to *Lares Augusti* at Puteoli, including an example of *Lares Augustos*; see "The Topography of Puteoli and Baiae on the Eight Glass Flasks," *Studi di Storia Antica* 3 (1979): 77–140 at 94, citing *CIL* 10.1482.

30. For discussion of the cult, see Mary Beard, John North, and Simon Price, *Religions of Rome*, vol. 1: *A History* (Cambridge: Cambridge University Press, 1998), 185–86, 355.

The cabinetmaker's more substantive link to the town's imperial cult and to Roman government comes, again, via his patron in the House of the Menander. The owner of I.10.4 was at least a member of the decuriate, the ruling council of Pompeii. Given the size of his house he may also have had a role at Rome too, but we will focus here on his local civic role, which would be typical for the kind of patrons that house-church hosts were more likely to have. Under the leadership of *duumviri* and other officials, the decuriate both ran the town and acted as brokers for the town's access to favors from Rome. The decurions acted as patrons to the town, in particular by acting as brokers giving access to higher patrons in the Roman Senate or, ultimately, the emperor. This pattern is particularly clear in a Roman colony such as Pompeii, as it would be in Roman colonies with known early Christian communities, such as Corinth, Philippi, and Pisidian Antioch. However, inscriptions from cities and towns across the Mediterranean world show this pattern also in operation in places that had other forms of local government, such as Thessalonica and Ephesus: local dignitaries are regularly praised for gaining access to imperial benefits for a city. The emperors too are praised for such benefits in civic inscriptions.[31]

The key point from all this is that a Christian with a house large enough to host a house church was likely to be only one step of (formal or informal) patron-client linkage from a figure whose status as a town councilor would have been linked, personally or through actions of the councilors as a group, to seeking and celebrating imperial favors. The patronage of this figure would have been a central factor in the economic well-being of the cabinetmaker and, consequently, in that of the Christian group.

It is unclear the extent to which the cabinetmaker would have attributed to Rome the operation of law in Pompeii. The local magistrates governed areas that he would have regularly encountered, such as operation of markets: for instance, controlling weights and measures. The cabinetmaker will have known that most taxation, which will have had direct or indirect impacts on his business, was set in Rome. He probably had little experience of coercion by magistrates or of interaction with soldiers. If he was ever involved in a court case he would probably have sought the support of his patron to facilitate that (1 Cor 6 implies that a number of church members there actually had the resources for direct access to the courts).

31. For instance, *CIL* 2.1423, "Letter of Vespasian to the Town Councillors of Sabora." See commentary by Caroline Barron (5 Aug 2017) at judaism-and-rome.org/letter-vespasian -town-councillors-sabora-cil-ii-1423, accessed 22 Oct. 2019.

The cabinetmaker's wife and other members of the household would be linked into imperial issues through the same mechanisms as the cabinetmaker, but at one remove. They will have been very aware of the cabinetmaker's dependence on his landlord/patron and of the patron's civic involvement, but they would not generally have engaged directly with the patron. If the cabinetmaker was sufficiently well off, sons might have had enough education to reach the point of some absorption of Roman ideology through reading of standard texts.[32]

Slaves in the household would probably, to an extent, see the empire as the structure that had created slavery as they knew it. As noted above, slaves in a small craftworking household were more likely to have been acquired as infants than to have been bought in a slave market, expensively and without having prior knowledge of the appropriate craft skills. This means that the cabinetmaker's slaves were very unlikely to have been prisoners of war. However, the slaves of I.10.7 no doubt talked with others and must soon have encountered some slaves brought in by the empire from its fringes. Inherently, we would expect slaves not to have felt any loyalty to the empire or the emperor. However, slaves too were part of the dynamics of loyalty and dependence within the household, which involved connection to people who would certainly have had such loyalties. We also find that freed slaves frequently turn up epigraphically as *Augustales*, members of an order devoted to the imperial cult.[33] Such postfreedom activities presumably indicate that many, while still enslaved, followed their owners in revering the imperial family.

Group 2: Other Householders and Their Households

As we go further down the economic scale, householders are less and less likely to have had direct links to someone of decurial rank, such as the owner of the House of the Menander. They may occasionally have sought the cabinetmaker's help to gain some favor from his patron, but this would not have built an enduring link of concern between those householders and the owner of I.10.4, although it would no doubt build some sense of social debt and loyalty. In any case, if the cabinetmaker was economically important for the householders, his concerns would be significant for them too. If he was supportive of his patron's activities in relation to the empire, the other householders presumably would be too.

32. Horster, "Primary Education," 86.
33. Beard, North, and Price, *Religions of Rome*, 1:357.

Poverty in some of the households would tend to make their interactions with the civic authorities more problematic. Regulations, taxes, legal actions, coercion by magistrates, were all likely to be more frequently onerous than for better-off households. However, imperial festivals, with free shows and occasionally other benefits, would be proportionately more significant.

Groups 3–5: Members of Households with Non-Christian Heads

There is about a one-in-five chance that the one person in our model from a family wealthier than the cabinetmaker was a member of a decurial family. If that was the case, they were in a family, the head of which would have been directly involved in civic imperial-cult ceremonies, may have sponsored imperial festival events, and is likely to have participated in civic petitioning of the emperor. A member of such a family would clearly have been expected to have a strong loyalty to these structures and events. If this house-church member was not part of a decurial family, they would be in a similar position to members of the cabinetmaker's family, with the householder in a client-type relationship with a member of the elite. Since this house-church member's family is wealthier than the cabinetmaker, their head would be likely to be in a closer client-patron relationship than the cabinetmaker was.

The other members of groups 3–5 are in similar positions to other household members in the model, except that their householders would not have Christian views that might lead to skepticism about imperial-cultic claims. The slaves in group 5 could come from households of any economic level, and since the elite owned a substantial proportion of the town's slaves, slaves in group 5 are quite likely to come from an elite household. If their owner is wealthy they are likely to have been either bought in a slave market or born and raised in their owner's house. In the former case, they could have been captured in war, so could have views strongly antagonistic to Rome. In the latter case, they could, on the one hand, have imbibed the views of their elite household quite fully or, on the other hand, conceivably have known of familial links to slaves captured in war, on which see above.

Group 6: Homeless Group Members

Homeless people would usually have experienced a considerable amount of coercion from civic magistrates. Not being an officially located part of the town system, they would frequently be found not to be fitting in with it. We might expect that that would give them a dim view of the empire that was expressed in the judicial system. That might be the case. On the other hand, free imperial festivities probably had an even more prominent place in their view than it did among other poor members of the house church.

HOUSE CHURCHES AND ECONOMIC NEW TESTAMENT TEXTS

The full range of New Testament teaching on economic issues makes sense within the context of the economic situations in the model house church, as sketched above. The most radical end of the range is exemplified by Luke 14:33, quoted at the start of this chapter. The context is a set of calls to count the cost of discipleship:

> Large crowds were gathering to him [Jesus] and, turning, he said to them, "If someone comes to me and does not hate his own father and mother and wife and children and brothers and sisters, and even his own life, he cannot be my disciple. Whoever does not carry his own cross and come after me, cannot be my disciple." (Luke 14:25–26)

Jesus then offers two parables about counting costs and odds before embarking on building and warfare. He then ends the passage:

> "So, like this, anyone of you who does not give up all his own possessions cannot be my disciple." (Luke 14:33)

The parts of this threefold radical call to discipleship belong together. The economic part should not be separated from the others.

In relating it to the model house church we should begin with the most radical part, the call to carry one's own cross, which fits together with the call to hate one's own life. The house-church members would not hear the instruction to carry a cross as a call for a literal, Ezekiel-type long-term acting out of a prophetic sign of walking around town with a cross. All the types of people in the house church would no doubt hear this call as a demand that loyalty to Christ had to go so far as to be prepared to die, and even to undergo the most shameful death. Crucifixion was a judicial death so the Christians would probably hear it as primarily relating to death at the hands of the authorities. Theissen argues that the safety of wandering charismatic preachers was particularly tenuous.[34] However, the danger of judicial death would undoubtedly have been heard by Luke's audience as relating potentially to all Christians, including members of settled house churches. In fact, the cases that would be most likely to be known to Luke's hearers were the deaths in Rome in 64 CE under Nero. These were deaths of members of house churches in the city— maybe even some of the people named, just a few years previously, in the greetings of Rom 16. Although Nero's victims were killed in ways different to Jesus, the most well-known deaths were in a manner fairly close to crucifixion.[35] In any case, Luke's audience would apply the cross-carrying to more than that specific punishment, probably broadening it to include any kind of death resulting from Christian commitment. Wandering charismatics were certainly at such risk, but so were the economically endangered members of non-elite house churches, a much more extensive group of Christians of the period.

Moving to the first call in the passage, it is a call to hate close family members and one's own life. This would indeed fit well with the actions of Christians who abandoned families to become wandering preachers.[36] However, it would also fit well with the house-church situation. It would fit particularly well with the situation of groups 3–5 of our model and of households in group 2 that were split between Christian and non-Christian. In fact, there is a sense in which it would fit their situation better than that of the wandering preachers. Just as the carrying of one's cross is envisaged as a continuous action, Christians in split households would generally be continuously disregarding the views of other family members and, where the householder was a Christian and family members not, could also be seen as acting against their interests through time and resources devoted to the Christian group and through endangering the welfare of the household by joining such a marginal group. This point actually applies even to the cabinetmaker and to other heads of entirely Christian households. In various ways, their actions endanger the welfare of their household, showing a degree of disregard for the safety and well-being of the household members, for the sake of allegiance to Christ and the well-being of the Christian group.

This brings us to the final element of the call, the giving up of all one's possessions. It clearly fits well the lifestyle of a wandering mendicant preacher. However, Luke's audience would hear it as the same kind of rhetoric as the calls to hate family and one's life and to carry one's cross. These are very serious but

---

34. Theissen, *Sociology of Early Palestinian Christianity*, 14.
35. Tacitus, *Annals* 15.44.
36. Theissen, *Sociology of Early Palestinian Christianity*, 11–12.

nonliteral calls expressing the dislocations and risks inherent in allegiance to Christ. The third call does the same for economic sacrifice and risk. This works very well within the economically precarious life of the non-elite members of the house church. First-century craftworking life was nowhere near economically stable enough for it to be safe to take on risky and financially demanding commitments. It looks at first sight very odd that Luke 14:25–33 does not build toward the risk to life: carrying the cross. Instead, the punchline is economic. This fits the house-church context well. Although there could be some measure of danger of death as a Christian, the most pressing day-to-day cost of following Christ was likely to be expressed in economic risks and sacrifices: the slaves who risked their owner's favor and their *peculium*; the householders who risked the household's finances by giving to the poor or who risked vital patronage links or important contacts with people in their trade; the Christian members of non-Christian households, risking the relationships on which they were economically dependent.

Another type of New Testament economic rhetoric at the radical end of the spectrum was the rhetoric of economic reversal: blessings on the poor, woe to the rich. Once more this is expressed particularly clearly in Luke (6:20, 24). Again, this could fit fairly well with the ideology of itinerant charismatics, promising them end-time reward for their impoverished lifestyle now.[37] However, this rhetoric is more at home in the lives of members of the non-elite house churches. For wandering charismatic preachers, their poverty is a secondary matter. They have also taken on poverty voluntarily and for the sake of itineracy. In contrast, most of the members of our model house church are inescapably poor, always have been, and have taken on further economic risk in adopting allegiance to Christ. Slightly less poor members of the group are also likely to have exacerbated their financial precariousness as an inherent result of their Christian commitment.

There has always been a tendency for ascetic religious practitioners, such as monks, to co-opt for themselves the rhetoric of poverty in sacred texts. But this has always been a misleading distraction. The real poor are the homeless and those in inadequate housing with inadequate incomes. In our model, just over half of the house-church members are either in the very smallest housing or are enslaved or are homeless.[38] An eschatological hope of reversal of the economic situation would be very important to these people and, indeed, to

---

37. Theissen, *Sociology of Early Palestinian Christianity*, 13.
38. Oakes, *Reading Romans in Pompeii*, table 3.5.

most of the other house-church members, who were just slightly better off than this.

For the cabinetmaker, the rhetoric of economic reversal would have been more two edged. He probably still saw himself as on the poor side of the polarized rich/poor divide seen in Jesus's preaching, according to Luke. However, the cabinetmaker will have been constantly aware of being wealthier than others in the house church. On the other hand, he probably felt some solidarity with the rest of the predominantly poor Christian group, so would be encouraged by their enthusiasm for Jesus's teaching on this. Then again, there was the matter of the cabinetmaker's patron in the House of the Menander. The patron was undoubtedly rich so, according to Jesus, was facing a fall. How the cabinetmaker felt about that would depend on his attitude to his patron. Few ancient relationships carried an assumption of necessary affection, even marriage, so much less a patronal relationship. Both types of relationship demanded loyalty, *pistis, fides,* but loyal actions were not necessarily matched by emotion. If his patron wanted him to proclaim his loyalty loudly and publicly, in a political rally, he would do it. But he still might not have been disappointed by the idea of the patron's poor prospects in the world to come. Of course, there could be affection. The cabinetmaker could regret Jesus's woe to the rich, as it applied to the owner of I.10.4. This would be part of the sense in which the cabinetmaker existed somewhat between two worlds: only able to host the house church because he operated with access to resources that others in the group did not have.

Our model also provides interesting sets of analytical questions for New Testament texts that seem particularly at home in the world of the house church. The start of this chapter quoted 1 Cor 11:34, where Paul, rather surprisingly, rounds off his discussion about problems at the Lord's Supper in Corinth by offering the very unradical sounding advice: "If someone is hungry, let them eat at home." How would this sound to the various types of people in our model house church? One group to whom the instruction might sound strange is the host's household. Their home is where the Lord's Supper is taking place. However, they would presumably apply it to the other house-church members, rather than themselves. If the house-church host family takes the lead in providing food for the communal meal, they would probably be pleased that Paul's instruction would limit overeating by other Christians coming to the house. The scenario described by Paul in 11:21–22 would be particularly distressing to the hosts. They have (maybe with others) provided food for everyone to share, but some have eaten excessively, leaving others without. The Lord's Supper was provision of food (of some amount) for all, but not all were receiving it. Another way in which this must have irked the hosts, if they were the main providers, was that they were giving up economic resources to make the meal; others in the group also had economic resources for eating but they were drawing on the host's resources beyond what was expected. Some group members were not even in households with a Christian head. In that case, when those members overate at the Christian meal, it effectively saved the non-Christian household money, at the expense of the Christian host household. Homeless people in the house church would initially be disconcerted by Paul's instruction in 11:34. However, the phrasing of 11:21–22 makes it sound likely that the poorest in the house church are the ones most frequently going without. They would then be pleased if people who had no particular need of the food at the Lord's Supper showed more restraint through having eaten first at home.

HOUSE CHURCHES AND EMPIRE-RELATED NEW TESTAMENT TEXTS

> Therefore God highly exalted him and granted him the name that is above every name so that, at the name of Jesus, every knee should bend, of heavenly beings, and of earthly beings, and of those beneath the earth, and every tongue should acknowledge that Jesus Christ is Lord, to the glory of God the father. (Phil 2:9–11)

> And they exchanged the glory of the imperishable God for the likeness of an image of a perishable human. (Rom 1:23)

Drawing on a key idea of one of my mentors, Simon Price, I have argued previously that Paul remaps the universe.[39] This is true of the New Testament writers and texts in general. For first-century Jews, the remapping is subtle, giving Jesus a more developed place, near the center of the universe, than is envisaged in other texts about Jewish messianic figures. For first-century gentiles, like most or all of our Pompeian model house-church members, the change is stark. Prior to taking on Christian beliefs they saw, at or near the center of the universe, various gods, depending on the member's particular background,

---

39. Peter Oakes, "Re-mapping the Universe: Paul and the Emperor in 1 Thessalonians and Philippians," *JSNT* 27 (2005): 301–22, included as chap. 7 in the present volume; cf. S. R. F. Price, *Rituals and Power: The Roman Imperial Cult in Asia Minor* (Cambridge: Cambridge University Press, 1984), 235, 238–39, 247–48.

relationships, and ideas. The Roman imperial family would have tended to be very close to the central place. Various other deities were influential in more localized spots in the world: household and crossroads *Lares* for instance. All the New Testament writers sweep this away, putting Israel's God at the center, with Jesus in very close proximity or even at the center with God.

This clearly causes difficulties about the imperial cult. This was probably not directly a very pressing issue for most house-church members in the first century:[40] it becomes more crucial in the subsequent two centuries. There will have been the issue of whether to attend imperial festival games or to accept any associated handouts. However, such handouts were generally heavily skewed toward wealthy, prominent citizens, reaching the non-elite to only a small degree, if at all.[41] Attendance at games was probably a topic discussed back and forth in house churches, but without it having much freight. Matters would be much more significant if any people in the house church were members of groups responsible for aspects of imperial cult. Most such groups recruited from economic levels of society beyond the house church. However, some might have been involved in the local cult of the *Lares Augusti*, evidenced in the bar four doors along from the cabinetmaker's house. A serious choice about continued participation would need to be made. Withdrawal could lead to trouble, or at least to the breaking of socially or economically important relationships.

The people in our model with the closest enduring links to the imperial cult are the cabinetmaker and, if from an elite household, the wealthier member of a family with a non-Christian head. In each case they are dependent on someone who is active in civic imperial cult and, more generally, in engagement with the imperial authorities. In neither case would the church member be likely to be directly involved in civic imperial-cult ceremonies. The participants in such ceremonies were generally the elite household heads or sometimes children whose father had bought them a civic role.[42] However, the patron or elite family head would undoubtedly react unfavorably to a client or family member who rejected the imperial cult in some perceptible way. The cabinetmaker was unlikely to have visibly done this. The elite family member might have been more caught out about it, if the family extended their imperial-cult par-

40. Contra Bruce W. Winter, *Divine Honours for the Caesars: The First Christians' Responses* (Grand Rapids: Eerdmans, 2015).

41. Katharine M. D. Dinbabin and William J. Slater, "Roman Dining," in *Oxford Handbook of Social Relations in the Roman World*, ed. Michael Peachin (Oxford: Oxford University Press, 2011), 438–66 (esp. 452–55).

42. For instance, Alleia, priestess of Venus and Ceres, daughter of Alleius Nigidius at Pompeii, *Ephemeris Epigraphica* 8.315 (Berolini: Apud Georgium Reimerum, 1899).

ticipation into the domestic sphere, with offerings to the emperor's genius.[43] However, we do not know what Christians tended to do, at this period, about participation in domestic cult in non-Christian households.

Romans 13:1–7 is a call to conformist behavior toward authorities (cf. 1 Pet 2:13–17). Since the letter is sent to Rome and since the instruction includes taxes (Rom 13:6), the imperial authorities are certainly among those in view. The authority "is God's servant" (13:4) so the Christians should obey on the grounds of conscience, rather than just from fear (13:5). Oscar Cullmann is right that this subordinates Rome to God, decentering it.[44] However, that does not appear to be Paul's point here. He is legitimating civic obedience. It is, of course, strange that he portrays the authorities as praising the good person and punishing the bad (13:3–4): has he forgotten what happened to Jesus? He must also know of other injustices carried out by Rome and other authorities. This disconnect could lead us to suspect a hidden transcript here, with a covert message of resistance of some kind. However, Paul does appear to be talking in straightforwardly positive terms in 13:1–7.

This makes sense in the house-church context. Their remapped universe removed the emperor from his place of divinity. It also prophesied the future supplanting of all earthly authority by Christ and God. However, here and now, the Christians can accept the empire and live within its authority structures obediently and quietly. Paul's attitude and teaching in 13:1–7 make good sense if his horizon of view is the daily life of house churches. He legitimates their approach to empire and reinforces it with a theology, of governments serving God, that has a pedigree going back to Babylon (and, as in that case, is not incompatible with expectation of their ultimate overthrow).

This conformist approach is reinforced by New Testament calls to honor the emperor (1 Tim 2:2; 1 Pet 2:17). This is a Jewish approach to expressing *pietas* toward the emperor without participating in idolatrous activity.[45] The cabinetmaker and others can say that the Christians pray for the emperor's welfare. In the days before Christian belief gained a prominent negative profile among the elite, this could even be seen as positive by people such as the

---

43. John Scheid, "Genius," in *Oxford Classical Dictionary*, 3rd ed., ed. S. Hornblower and A. Spawforth (Oxford: Oxford University Press, 1996), 630.

44. Oscar Cullmann, *Christ and Time: The Primitive Christian Conception of Time and History*, trans. Floyd V. Filson (London: SCM, 1950), 191–210.

45. James S. McLaren, "Jews and the Imperial Cult: From Augustus to Domitian," *JSNT* 27 (2005): 257–78 (esp. 271–73), but note his discussion of the complexities of the evidence and issues.

cabinetmaker's patron: a bringing of the force of a new god in support of the emperor. These texts sit neatly in a house-church context.

Jesus's enigmatic response to the question about taxes, "Repay to Caesar the things of Caesar, and the things of God to God" (Mark 12:17 and parallels), has provoked a wide range of readings. A prominent "hidden transcript" reading is that of N. T. Wright, for whom Jesus is alluding to the words of the dying Mattathias in 1 Maccabees, calling his sons to "repay the repayment to the gentiles and give attention to the command of the law" (2:68).[46] In that reading Jesus's reply becomes something like a call to arms. However, whether or not an original saying of Jesus carried that message in the context of early first-century Jerusalem, Mark's Greco-Roman house-church audience are much more likely to have seen the saying as guidance in, and legitimation of, their way of life. They paid taxes. They lived a quiet public life. Their communal life as a group might be somewhat radical. Their cosmology and eschatology certainly was. But the continuation of these was enabled by conformist behavior toward authorities.

Could these people also listen to the stories of the overthrow of the beasts from the sea and from the land and of "the great city that has kingship over the kings of the earth" (Rev 17:18)? The rhetoric is more vivid and symbolic, but it still chimes with the Lukan rhetoric of economic reversal, which itself can encompass the image of Dives in the flames, calling out to Abraham (Luke 16:24). The people in our model house church are mainly poor or enslaved. Stories promising the overthrow of the rich and the powerful, songs about the God who "pulled down the mighty from their seats and exalted the humble" (Luke 1:52), would be meat and drink to them. Their lives indeed followed a hidden transcript, as in the examples of speech and behavior that led to James Scott's formulation of his ideas.[47] The house-church members behaved quietly and positively toward outsiders, no doubt including actually wishing many of them well. However, they did so while hearing and repeating ideas about the overthrow of the current world order, ideas that will have been present even while speaking respectfully to patrons, slave owners, and a range of wealthy people. However, to say that there was a disconnect between everyday positive expression and negative apocalyptic expectation in the Christians' interaction with outsiders does not necessarily imply seeing that disconnect in New Testament texts themselves in the form of hidden transcript. Viewed in a house-church context, the range of New Testament texts can be seen as

---

46. N. T. Wright, *Jesus and the Victory of God* (London: SPCK, 1996), 502–7.
47. Scott, *Domination and the Arts of Resistance.*

straightforwardly communicating the range of empire-related instructions and ideas appropriate to house-church life, from the life of obedience to authorities to the songs of the fall of Rome.

STRUCTURAL ISSUES AND CONCLUSION

The conclusion of this chapter is that the general structural situation of first-century Christian groups provides a satisfactory explanation for the range of New Testament texts on economic or empire-related issues: there is relatively little need to appeal to theories of texts being written in relation to divergent community types (Theissen), or texts containing hidden transcripts (Scott), or simply of texts in radical disagreement with each other on these issues (Wengst). There are two particular limits to this conclusion.

First, the chapter has not demonstrated that the house-church context actually generated the diversity among the texts. That would need stronger theories of early Christian groups as community generators of ideas and texts, as is found in twentieth-century form criticism or, with more specific relevance, for instance in the work of Dennis Smith, Matthias Klinghardt, and others, who see early Christian meal gatherings as the originators of much early Christian practice and thought.[48] Instead, this chapter argues that the first-century house-church setting provides a set of rationales for the existence of the range of New Testament texts. All parts of the range address issues that are pertinent, and often pressing, for the house churches. The second limit to the conclusion is that there are indeed various differences between New Testament texts that need to be accounted for in ways other than with reference to situations in the house churches in general. There are also texts that address issues in hidden ways, especially in the coding in apocalyptic texts and in riddle texts such as parables and, probably, Jesus's God-and-Caesar answer, notwithstanding our argument above that it makes sense as legitimation of house-church life. However, texts that look more straightforward can in general be read straightforwardly, in view (paradoxically) of the complexities of house-church situations.

---

48. Dennis E. Smith, *From Symposium to Eucharist: The Banquet in the Early Christian World* (Minneapolis: Fortress, 2003); Matthias Klinghardt, *Gemeinschaftsmahl und Mahlgemeinschaft: Soziologie und Liturgie frühchristlicher Mahlfeiern*, Texte und Arbeiten zum neutestamentlichen Zeitalter 13 (Tübingen: Francke, 1996); Dennis E. Smith and Hal Taussig, eds., *Meals in the Early Christian World: Social Formation, Experimentation, and Conflict at the Table* (New York: Palgrave Macmillan, 2012).

The basic structural characterization of first-century house churches, underpinning the above conclusion, is that they were usually economically precarious small groups, bound into the social structures of the Roman Empire by tight ties of economic dependency. Most of the group members were poor. Some were enslaved. Participation in the Christian group produced extra economic risk for most of its members. This combination of characteristics provides a reasonable rationale for the range, between radical and conformist, seen in New Testament texts on economic and empire-related issues.

Why have we gone beyond this general characterization into the specifics of the craftworker house-church model and, even beyond that, into the specifics of the particular Pompeian domestic situation that was used in its derivation? One answer is that the craftworker house-church model is a tool capable of broader use than this chapter, and, even within the field of this chapter, it raises issues beyond the specific argument. For instance, we have essentially asked how the rhetoric of rich and poor relates to the situation of the model house church as an aggregate of its members, concluding that it generally fits well with the way the group would probably relate to society around it. We could turn this around and ask how this rhetoric would be received in terms of intragroup dynamics. How would various types of people in the model hear its applicability to differentials of relative wealth and power within the group? This chapter is an exercise of putting a broader analytical tool to work in tackling a particular question.

A second, more fundamental answer is that historical progress can be made only through some degree of specificity. Without specifics, we are left only with generalities. As an academic ideal, we would have developed our Pompeian model craftworker house church on the basis of detailed study of a dozen craftworker houses. Also, having developed that model we would have set it alongside several other likely house-church models (for instance, the predominantly slave household church, as probably signaled in Rom 16:10–11, and the larger gathering indicated in 16:23), themselves developed from several instances of buildings and their contents, ideally in several locations. Such would be valuable, and I hope some of it is tackled at some point. However, it has not yet been done. We have our model and the specifics behind it. In any case, in this chapter (and elsewhere), too broad a plethora of details, drawn from too many instances, would replace the sharpness of a single narrative with either a collection of statistics or with a compilation of points from disparate narratives that might be misleading if stitched together. Such problems do to a degree affect this chapter too, but being closer to a single narrative helps keep them in check.

The kind of specific detail that our model provides to our argument is that at least nine of the forty house-church members have direct economic ties to people beyond the house church: the host householder, dependent on his elite patron (in a formal or informal sense), and the eight members whose householder (and, in two cases, owner) is not a Christian. The precise numbers are, of course, unimportant. What is important is the way in which constructing the model pushes us into considering the specifics of what the types and degree of economic dependency of various first-century Christians were likely to be, and how the dependencies of various people in the group would interact with each other. The kind of detail that our use of the House of the Cabinetmaker provides is that a house large enough to host a house church of a few dozen is larger than well over half the other housing in a town such as Pompeii. This, in turn, probably puts its tenant in a close relationship with a member of the town elite. The cabinetmaker's house is 30 percent of the way down the list of house sizes in Pompeii. So, if the elite occupy 5 percent of the houses, there are 25 percent of houses, and hence 25 percent of householders, between members of the elite and the cabinetmaker. That, in turn, means that if the elite had clients drawn from the householder pool between them and the cabinetmaker, each member of the elite would have five clients (25 percent/5 percent), if each client was unique to one member of the elite. The upshot of this is that the host of a non-elite house church would be of a social level likely to involve him in some sort of clientage to a member of the elite (whether the relationship was of a formal Roman type or something less codified), hence binding the house-church host into loyalty to someone closely involved with civic, empire-related issues. We also have specific evidence about the relationship between the House of the Cabinetmaker and the House of the Menander in blocked-up doors and the pattern of building work. We also have exact knowledge of many items that were part of the cabinetmaker's economic resources. We also know that the bar, four doors from his house, made reference to the *Lares Augusti*. Specific detail is vital for the construction of coherent and illuminating sets of circumstances, even if the questions under study and the conclusions are broad.

So, the members of first-century non-elite house churches, as typified by the model craftworker house church, faced economic risks in joining the group, which made the Lukan Jesus's calls for absolute economic sacrifice very pertinent. The group members also identified with the Lukan rhetoric of reversal between rich and poor. They also valued the New Testament texts that related directly to the life of house churches, and they continued to participate in the regular economic life of the Roman Empire rather than, except in a few cases, abandoning all to pursue itinerant ministry. Similarly, the house-church members bought into the vision of the universe that saw Israel's God and Christ at the center and destined to supplant every earthly authority, in particular, Rome. Yet the house-church members continued in their participation in the social system governed by the empire and vital to their economic interests.

Light and shade. Radical and conformist. The range of New Testament texts on economic and empire-related issues finds homes in the non-elite house churches of the first century. The various complexities of their precarious situation make them natural recipients of the complex range of New Testament rhetoric.

2 | Nine Types of Church in Nine Types of Space in the Insula of the Menander

"but . . . standing far off"

—Luke 18:13

"the assembly in their house"

—Romans 16:5

"while they were reclining and eating"

—Mark 14:18

"You, kindly sit here. . . . You, stand there or sit at my feet."

—James 2:3

Jerome Murphy-O'Connor argues for a scenario in which the divisions described in 1 Cor 11:17–34 relate to a split between the householder with his friends, eating in the *triclinium*, and the rest of the house church eating in the atrium. David Horrell counters by suggesting that Christians were meeting in an upstairs room (as happens in Acts 20:8). Robert Jewett also focuses on multistory buildings, arguing that the recipients of Paul's letter to Rome would have met in rooms in apartment blocks. Dennis Smith and Matthias Klinghardt (followed by the Society of Biblical Literature Seminar on Meals in the Greco-Roman World) see the key to the development of early Christianity as lying in the practice of eating together in dining rooms. Edward Adams and David Balch argue for the use of rented dining spaces in places such as taverns. Philip Harland and others argue more specifically for the Christian groups being like associations and meeting in their kinds of dining space. In *Reading Romans in Pompeii*, I argue for Christians meeting in craftworker workshops/dwellings. And in *The Earliest Christian Meeting Places*, Adams sets out the evidence relating to a wide range of options for spaces in which early Christians met.[1] What difference do the various types of space make? What issues are at stake in the scholars' suggestions? How can we compare the options?

Both Daniel Schowalter and Annette Weissenrieder argue for the relative insignificance of archeological evidence of types of potential meeting space for early Christian groups. In Schowalter's case, his key concern is that imaginative reconstruction, often made on the basis of insubstantial or irrelevant archeological evidence, easily transforms into confidence that one knows what early Christian meetings were like.[2] Weissenrieder's argument is that significant space is constructed by actions, rather than by the prior nature of the space, a point that comes into focus in arguing that the topic of "sitting" in the Christian meeting in 1 Cor 14:30 is more usefully dealt with by consideration of the action, sitting, than by thinking about the archeological possibilities for the space in which the sitting takes place.[3] To the skepticism of these two scholars (each of whom has considerable interests in both spatiality and ar-

1. Jerome Murphy-O'Connor, *St. Paul's Corinth: Texts and Archaeology*, 3rd ed., Good News Studies 6 (Collegeville, MN: Liturgical Press, 2002), 156; David G. Horrell, "Domestic Space and Christian Meetings at Corinth: Imagining New Contexts and the Buildings East of the Theatre," *NTS* 50 (2004): 349–69 at 361–68; Robert Jewett, *Romans: A Commentary*, Hermeneia (Minneapolis: Fortress, 2007), 64–65; Dennis E. Smith, *From Symposium to Eucharist: The Banquet in the Early Christian World* (Minneapolis: Fortress, 2003); Matthias Klinghardt, *Gemeinschaftsmahl und Mahlgemeinschaft: Soziologie und Liturgie frühchristlicher Mahlfeiern*, Texte und Arbeiten zum neutestamentlichen Zeitalter 13 (Tübingen: Francke, 1996); Dennis E. Smith and Hal Taussig, eds., *Meals in the Early Christian World: Social Formation, Experimentation, and Conflict at the Table* (New York: Palgrave Macmillan, 2012) (key work presented to the SBL seminar); Edward Adams, "Placing the Corinthian Common Meal," in *Text, Image, and Christians in the Graeco-Roman World*, ed. A. C. Niang and C. Osiek (Eugene, OR: Pickwick, 2012), 22–37; David L. Balch, "The Church Sitting in a Garden (1 Cor. 14:30; Rom. 16:23; Mark 6:39–40; 8:6; John 6:3, 10; Acts 1:15; 2:1–2)," in *Contested Spaces: Houses and Temples in Roman Antiquity and the New Testament*, ed. D. L. Balch and A. Weissenrieder, WUNT 285 (Tübingen: Mohr Siebeck, 2012), 201–35 at 232; Philip A. Harland, *Associations, Synagogues, and Congregations: Claiming a Place in Ancient Mediterranean Society* (Minneapolis: Fortress, 2003), esp. chaps. 7–8; Peter Oakes, *Reading Romans in Pompeii: Paul's Letter at Ground Level* (London: SPCK; Minneapolis: Fortress, 2009); Edward Adams, *The Earliest Christian Meeting Places: Almost Exclusively Houses?* Library of New Testament Studies 450 (London: Bloomsbury T&T Clark, 2013).

2. Daniel Schowalter, "Seeking Shelter in Roman Corinth: Archaeology and the Placement of Paul's Communities," in *Corinth in Context: Comparative Studies on Religion and Society*, ed. Steven Friesen, Daniel Schowalter, and James Walters (Leiden: Brill, 2010), 327–41.

3. Annette Weissenrieder, "Contested Spaces in 1 Corinthians 11:17–33 and 14:30: Sitting or Reclining in Ancient Houses, in Associations, and in the Space of *Ekklēsia*," in *Contested Spaces: Houses and Temples in Roman Antiquity and the New Testament*, ed. D. L. Balch and A. Weissenrieder, WUNT 285 (Tübingen: Mohr Siebeck, 2012), 59–107.

cheology), we could add the silent majority of scholars who see archeology as making only a marginal contribution to study of early Christian texts and of the groups evidenced in them.

The present chapter makes a comparison by looking for instances of the types of potential meeting space suggested by scholars of early Christianity—in one particular Pompeian block in which I have had a long-standing interest. The process of reexamining the block also turned up some further potential meeting spaces. Archeological evidence from the various instances of spaces will be used to consider the effects that the use of such a space would have on the nature and perception of a Christian group that met there. The aim will be to compile a list of issues that the spaces raise for the suggestion that early Christians held meetings in such a place. This should help toward an agenda for comparison across suggested types of meeting space. In doing these, it also acts as an argument for the significance of such archeological study.

Space and Approach to God

In the parable of the Pharisee and the tax collector, the first way in which Jesus characterizes the tax collector is that he was "standing far off." The tax collector's choice of location indicates the nature of his approach to God. However, to talk about the tax collector's "approach to God" is to present a spatial paradox. What the tax collector does not do is to approach God physically, if God is viewed as inhabiting the holy of holies in the temple at Jerusalem, where this parable is set. Yet, paradoxically, the tax collector's act of "standing far off" is presented by Jesus as a key to the tax collector's successful, real approach to God.

The same paradox is present in the situation of Christians (and, in fact, Jews) in Luke's day. From the earliest days of the Jesus movement, the Christians who did not live in Jerusalem sought to approach God without physically going to a temple. They did not see God as inhabiting any of the temples in cities around the Mediterranean, where their fellow citizens approached various gods. Nor did they generally see approaching God as involving traveling to Jerusalem, to the temple there. By the time when Luke was writing, the Jerusalem temple had probably been destroyed. Neither Christians nor Jews could seek to approach God there. For Jews, this led to the massive reorganizations of thought and practice that moved toward classical rabbinic Judaism.

Christians already "approached God" without that approach involving physically going to a temple. However, Christians did physically do something.

They met together. Some Christians in Rome habitually held an assembly in the house of Prisca and Aquila (Rom 16:5). This involved a group and a particular space. But it was an ordinary space, used at other times for other purposes. People's perception of a group that is meeting in a particular space is affected by the nature of the space. The actual nature of the group is also affected by the space (most obviously, in terms of size of space and group). Aspects of the early Christians' approach to God will have been affected by the varying nature of the spaces in which they met.

The tax collector's "standing far off" is not just a matter of not moving toward the holy of holies. It also carries a social signal. More broadly, a person's positioning in space is both influenced by social and cultural factors and generates social and cultural effects. The meetings of early Christian groups are cases of positioning of people in space. The group meeting is located in a space. The people in the group are distributed within the space. The disposition of the Christians in a particular type of space relates to social and cultural influences and effects.

Let us move toward specifics. How does meeting space relate to the nature and activities of a group that meets there? Because their groups used a range of spaces that had been designed for other purposes, designed for use by other kinds of groups, the question is particularly important for study of very early Christians. Space in the first century was heavily loaded in terms of location, architecture, decoration, and furnishings, all being strongly related to social and cultural structures. Anyone who used a first-century space was locating themselves in some way in relation to those structures. When a group, such as an early Christian church, met in an existing space, this produced all sorts of interactions between the social and cultural structures encoded in the space, and the norms of the formation and behavior of the Christian group.

Space and Resistance to the Significance of Archeological Evidence of Spaces

Consideration of spatial issues in the humanities has been a major factor for the last quarter of a century, especially looking back to Edward Soja's prominent advocacy of the approach. Ray Laurence is a leading figure in the application of spatial theory to study of Pompeii. A number of scholars of early Christianity, such as Laura Nasrallah, have also done work from this perspective.[4]

4. Edward W. Soja, *Postmodern Geographies: The Reassertion of Space in Critical Social*

However, there are many scholars who take no account of spatial issues in their study of early Christianity. There are also some who, while being interested in spatiality, question the possibility of learning about the historical nature of group meetings from study of the archeological remains of spaces. Thinking of the case of Corinth, Daniel Schowalter expresses great wariness about the possibility of placing Christian groups, even imaginatively, into spaces reconstructed by means of archeology of the site.[5] Partly, his objections are practical: the remains at Corinth are relatively scanty and complex to interpret. Pompeii clearly has the advantage here (although see below). He is also objecting that, in general, the difficulties of interpretation make any such use of archeology too problematic to be of significant value. This chapter will need to consider how far that is true. This objection is made in a more pointed way by Davina Lopez and Todd Penner. They argue that ancient spaces, however private they might appear, were "ideologically oriented." Their construction was "embedded in public social order."[6] According to Lopez and Penner, this prevents us from thinking that we can assume an association between various spaces and activities or social relationships. We will have to bear their cautions in mind as we tackle the subject, but I hope to show that, despite the undoubted obstacles, significant social inferences can be drawn from archeological evidence of spaces.

Annette Weissenrieder raises a more radical objection. She writes that most scholars agree with Jorunn Økland when she claims that for Paul "the material place where the ἐκκλησία gathers is rather irrelevant."[7] Økland argues that Paul sees the "ritual space" of the ἐκκλησία as being distinct from domestic space, even though it occurs in the same physical location.[8] However, Økland does not see the physical space as objectively having no significance. Drawing on the theoretical work of David Harvey, she argues: "There is already a material text there: the house-building, the artifacts and smells of the home represent

---

Theory (London: Verso, 1989); Ray Laurence, *Roman Pompeii: Space and Society*, 2nd ed. (London: Routledge, 2010); Laura S. Nasrallah, "Spatial Perspectives: Space and Archaeology in Roman Philippi," in *Studying Paul's Letters: Contemporary Perspectives and Methods*, ed. J. Marchal (Minneapolis: Fortress, 2012), 53–74.

5. Schowalter, "Seeking Shelter in Roman Corinth," 334–35.

6. Davina C. Lopez and Todd Penner, "'Houses Made with Hands': The Triumph of the Private in New Testament Scholarship," in *Text, Image, and Christians in the Graeco-Roman World*, ed. A. C. Niang and C. Osiek (Eugene, OR: Pickwick, 2012), 89–118 at 98–99.

7. Jorunn Økland, *Women in Their Place: Paul and the Corinthian Discourse of Gender and Sanctuary Space*, JSNTSup 269 (London: T&T Clark, 2004), 142; see Weissenrieder, "Contested Spaces," 86.

8. Økland, *Women in Their Place*, 137–43.

constraints and limitations on which alternative representations of space can actually be set."[9] We can go further and argue that any event in a particular space is an interaction with the perceived social and cultural characteristics of the space.

Weissenrieder herself argues that the space of a Christian meeting is constructed by the act of sitting together, in the manner of active listeners in a Greek political assembly or court, and by the Eucharist. She sees the act of sitting as more significant than the choice of space in which to sit.[10] Weissenrieder, in fact, uses a theoretical starting point that could be seen as leading on to a further field of study beyond her conclusions. She draws on the idea that space, as a socially significant element, is constructed by actions.[11] However, this means that a particular space is constructed by a history of actions, beginning from the mode of construction, via various known uses, to the moment of the particular use under consideration. As a result of this, sitting in the banqueting hall of the House of the Menander is a socially and culturally different action from sitting in the small bar in the next-door building. If, as Weissenrieder argues, the act of sitting signals a link to the Greek political ἐκκλησία, the nature of this Christian ἐκκλησία is affected by the perceived nature of previous actions in the space that is used. As noted above, when an early Christian group met in an existing space, this produced interactions between the social and cultural structures encoded in the space, and the nature and perception of the Christian group.[12]

---

9. Økland, *Women in Their Place*, 143, cf. 79, citing David Harvey, *The Condition of Postmodernity: An Enquiry into the Origins of Cultural Change* (Oxford: Blackwell, 1989), 211–25.

10. Weissenrieder, "Contested Spaces," 86–88, 103. Weissenrieder does allow for the value of archeological and art historical studies, as long as they are linked to textual study.

11. Weissenrieder, "Contested Spaces," 63, drawing on the theoretical work of Pierre Bourdieu, *Zur Soziologie der symbolishen Formen*, 2nd ed. (Frankfurt: Suhrkamp, 1983), and, more broadly, Ernst Cassirer, *Philosophie der symbolischen Formen*, vol. 3: *Phänomenologie der Erkenntnis*, ed. J. Clemens, Gesammelte Werke 13 (Darmstadt: WBG, 2002).

12. A further, perennial problem with the present type of project is the variation in terminology in use among scholars. For instance, this chapter uses the term "house" to denote a dwelling unit with at least some space on the ground floor. "House church" will be used to denote a group of Christians who meet in space that is at least partly domestic. For an alternative approach, see Adams, *Earliest Christian Meeting Places*, 201–2.

THE INSULA OF THE MENANDER AND ISSUES IN USING POMPEIAN EVIDENCE

The Insula of the Menander offers an outstanding combination of preservation and documentation of evidence of spaces and their contents. The block was excavated at one of the high points of Pompeian archeological technique and reporting, in the 1920s and early 1930s. It was very soon documented in unusually full publications by Amadeo Maiuri on the House of the Menander, Olga Elia on other units in the block, and Matteo Della Corte on the graffiti and other textual evidence.[13] In the late 1970s a team from Manchester and Southampton began carrying out a major project resurveying the block. They conducted various forms of analysis (such as investigating the history of the building techniques of each wall in the block) from which they drew conclusions about the pattern of development of the block from its initial construction, sometime very roughly around 200 BCE, through to its destruction in the eruption of 79 CE. The results are being published in a series of volumes that began in 1997 with a book on the block's structures by Roger Ling, who led the project. A second volume, by Roger and Lesley Ling, covers the frescoes and mosaics. A third is a substantial further piece of research by Penelope Allison, who found and analyzed the stored finds from each room in the block. A fourth, by Kenneth Painter, covers the silver dinner service and related pieces recovered from one of the cellars in the House of the Menander.[14] A further volume on the graffiti and other texts from the block is in preparation.

Andrew Wallace-Hadrill's seminal work, *Houses and Society in Pompeii and Herculaneum*, surveys the distribution (in various spaces) of types of socioeconomic and cultural markers, such as the provision of a traditional atrium

13. Amadeo Maiuri, *La Casa del Menandro e il suo tesoro di argenteria* (Rome: La Libreria dello Stato, 1933); Olga Elia, "Pompei: Relazione sullo scavo dell'Insula X della Regio I," *Notizie degli scavi* 12 (1934): 264-344; Matteo Della Corte, "Epigrafi della via fra le isole VI e X della Reg. I," *Notizie degli scavi* (1929): 455-76; Matteo Della Corte, "Pompei: Iscrizioni dell' isola X della Regione I," *Notizie degli scavi* (1933): 277-331. See also *CIL* vol. 4.3.I, which Della Corte edited.

14. Roger Ling, *The Insula of the Menander at Pompeii*, vol. 1: *The Structures* (Oxford: Clarendon, 1997); Roger Ling and Lesley Ling, *The Insula of the Menander at Pompeii*, vol. 2: *The Decorations* (Oxford: Clarendon, 2005); Penelope M. Allison, *The Insula of the Menander at Pompeii*, vol. 3: *The Finds: A Contextual Study* (Oxford: Clarendon, 2007); see also Penelope M. Allison, *Pompeian Households: An Analysis of the Material Culture*, Monograph 42 (Los Angeles: Cotsen Institute of Archaeology at UCLA, 2004); Kenneth S. Painter, *The Insula of the Menander at Pompeii*, vol. 4: *The Silver Treasure* (Oxford: Clarendon, 2001).

and the installation of mosaics. In that work, he gives considerable attention to the Insula of the Menander. Art historian John Clarke uses the House of the Menander as a key case study in his approach of elucidating the way in which "the Romans tended to think of each space in a house in terms of the ritual or activity that the space housed." Carolyn Osiek and David Balch use the peristyle courtyard and the dining spaces in that house to exemplify a type of potential meeting space for the early Christians. In *Reading Romans in Pompeii*, I discuss the structures, decoration, and loose finds in several dwellings in the block, using them to build a socioeconomic model of the composition of a craftworker-hosted house church, then raising issues about interpreting Paul's letter to the Romans in relation to the model and to various social types of people within it.[15]

The Insula of the Menander lies in what archeologists call Region One of Pompeii, numbered as Region I Block 10 (cited as I.10). It is situated several blocks east of the Forum and one street back from the major thoroughfare of the so-called Via dell'Abbondanza. The block is a fairly unified overall structure but consists of a number of individual houses, apartments, and other types of space, all butted up against each other. Pompeian archeologists call it an *insula*, meaning an area of buildings surrounded by streets. This use of the term should not be confused with its more common application to something more like an apartment block or with more technical ancient usage.[16]

The Insula of the Menander is named after the House of the Menander, which dominates the block. By the time of the eruption it took up well over half the block and had five entrances (so when it is referred to fully by number it is I.10.4, 14–17, with the numbers after the second point referring to the entrances). The House of the Menander is so titled because there is a named picture of the poet and playwright Menander painted in one of a row of alcoves in the main peristyle garden of the house (see fig. 2.1 for the layout of the *insula*). There are seven dwelling units along the north side of the block:

15. Andrew Wallace-Hadrill, *Houses and Society in Pompeii and Herculaneum* (Princeton: Princeton University Press, 1994), 243 (containing a list of full references); John R. Clarke, *The Houses of Roman Italy, 100 BC–AD 250: Ritual, Space, and Decoration* (Berkeley: University of California Press, 1991), 1, 170–93 (for the House of the Menander); Carolyn Osiek and David L. Balch, *Families in the New Testament World: Households and House Churches* (Louisville: Westminster John Knox, 1997), 202; Oakes, *Reading Romans in Pompeii*.

16. Andrew Wallace-Hadrill, "*Domus* and *Insulae* in Rome: Families and Housefuls," in *Early Christian Families in Context: An Interdisciplinary Dialogue*, ed. David L. Balch and Carolyn Osiek (Grand Rapids: Eerdmans, 2003), 3–18 at 9.

Nine Types of Church in Nine Types of Space in the Insula of the Menander

- House 1
- Bar/House 2–3
- House of the Menander
- Apartment 5 (up a set of stairs leading from the street entrance)
- Workshop 6
- House/Workshop 7, House of the Cabinetmaker (usually called the *Casa del Fabbro,* "House of the Craftworker")
- House/Workshop 8

On the west side there are a one-room shop (I.10.9) and the *Casa degli Amanti* (House of the Lovers), named after a wall inscription. The south side has only the entrance to Shop 12. The east of the block has Bar 13, entrances 14–17 of the House of the Menander, and finally House 18. In this chapter we will consider

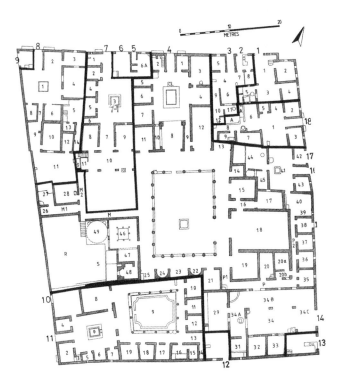

Figure 2.1. *The Insula of the Menander. Source: Roger Ling,* The Insula of the Menander at Pompeii, vol. 1: The Structures *(Oxford: Clarendon, 1997), fig. 24 (drawn by S. Gibson, J. S. Gregory, R. J. Ling, D. Murdoch, with thanks to Roger Ling for permission to reproduce the plan).*

some spaces within House 1, Bar/House 2–3, the House of the Menander, Workshop 6, and House/Workshop 7.

Apart from the problems in principle (discussed above), use of evidence from Pompeii raises some particular difficulties in practice, despite its copiousness compared to other sites. These difficulties also force me to make some decisions on how to proceed. The two characteristic Pompeian difficulties are that (a) much has been removed or damaged (or destroyed) since 79 CE and (b) what remains is evidence at the point of eruption of a massive volcano. Jumping straight to the specifics of this chapter: the Insula of the Menander, like other blocks in Pompeii, was not in normal use at the time when the site was covered by the eruption. The situation of the dwellings that we will focus on is broadly as follows:

- The loose finds (i.e., items excavated that were not part of the structure) in House 1 suggest that it had been occupied recently but not on the day of the eruption.
- Bar/House 2–3 was probably occupied (although no bodies were found) but not in normal use as a bar at the time of the eruption.
- The House of the Menander was certainly occupied but was undergoing extensive repairs from earlier seismic activity and contained only a limited number of the normal furnishings of such an extensive house.
- Workshop 6 was occupied, although the inhabitants left before the workshop was covered, so they presumably took items with them.
- The House of the Cabinetmaker was certainly occupied, with food being cooked the day of the disaster. However, for quite some period, the use of the house had been somewhat at odds with elements of the decoration of some of the rooms.

It would clearly be pointless to conduct our investigation as a study of what Christian groups would have been like if they generally met in the immediate run-up to a volcanic eruption. It would also mean missing out on the broader value of the extraordinarily extensive social and cultural evidence that the eruption caused to be preserved. We need to find a middle way between, on the one hand, the naïve assumption that Pompeii preserves a normally working town and, on the other, an excess skepticism that leads to discarding of evidence that has a richness not found elsewhere.

The approach of this chapter will be as follows:

- House 1 (see fig. 2.2) will be considered as if it were an occupied house.
- Bar/House 2–3 will be considered as if it were a working bar. However, the loose finds will clearly offer only very limited help in understanding how the bar would have functioned.
- The House of the Menander will be considered as if it were an elite house in normal use. The loose finds are of somewhat more help here than for Bar/House 2–3 because they are of high quality. However, many pieces needed for normal functioning are missing (e.g., most couches), so the spread of loose finds cannot directly guide us over normal use. Various scholars have argued that the owner of the House of the Menander was of senatorial level.[17] This chapter will consider it generally simply as an instance of a large elite house (although see the comment on Osiek and Balch's use of the house, below).
- Workshop 6 will be treated as such.

Figure 2.2. *View of north side of Insula of the Menander. House 1 is closest.*

17. For instance, Matteo Della Corte, *Case ed abitanti di Pompei*, 3rd ed. (Naples: Faustino Fiorentino, 1965), 293–95. But see doubts expressed in discussion in Ling, *Insula of the Menander*, vol. 1. However, Ling does take the house as being of at least about duoviral social level (senior local magistrate).

- The House of the Cabinetmaker will be treated as a workshop and dwelling.

For each chosen space, my approach is to seek to maximize usable evidence by drawing what is possible from the structure, location, and decoration, then combining that with evidence from loose finds, where it makes reasonable sense to do so. The objective is to think about each space in terms of some sort of realistic use to which it was put over a period of time, even though that time was, in some cases, not in the immediate run-up to the eruption.

We now turn to a series of nine possible models of Christian meeting that relate in some way to types of space of which the Insula of the Menander offers concrete instances. We will seek to draw conclusions about a list of possible parameters of relationship between a space and the nature of an early Christian group habitually using such a space.

Model 1: Murphy-O'Connor's Polarized Church in Triclinium and Atrium/ Peristyle (I.10.4 Room 11 + Peristyle)

Everyone begins with Murphy-O'Connor when discussing the relationship between early Christian meetings and space. He was a scholar so immersed in archeology that it feels natural that he was struck by the exegetical idea that the "divisions" (σχίσματα) reported by Paul as occurring at meals in 1 Cor

Figure 2.3. Triclinium *11 in the House of the Menander.*

11:17–34 could stem from the difference between the limited, luxurious space of a *triclinium* dining room and the less furnished space of an atrium. Once he set the capacity of a *triclinium* alongside his expectation of a typical Christian meeting size of forty, it was clear that most members would not be able to get into the dining room. Murphy-O'Connor combined this observation with expectations about the behavior of an elite house owner.[18] The result was a very neat and satisfying account of the divisions of 1 Cor 11.

In the elite House of the Menander, Rooms 11, 12, and 18 were probably dining rooms. The absence of couches *in situ* leaves some room for uncertainty. However, Room 11 in particular has the classic decorative layout of a *triclinium* (see fig. 2.3). There are high quality frescoes around the walls, and the floor mosaic is strongly centered on a fairly small, detailed panel, which would be visible in the space between the three dining couches. The villa at Anaploga (which Murphy-O'Connor drew on) had its *triclinium* (if that is what it is)[19] opening off an atrium. In the House of the Menander, Room 11 opened off the peristyle. Dining Room 12 originally opened off the atrium. However, by the last phase of the life of the house, that door had been sealed and the dining room opened off the peristyle, giving a view of the garden and taking access to the space out of the semipublic area that was the atrium. One room that is adjacent to the atrium and may have functioned as a *triclinium* at some point is Room 3. However, by the time of the eruption it had had a more mundane use for some time, as evidenced by the construction of a hearth against the south wall.

The essence of Murphy-O'Connor's model is that the church was spread across two types of space that were socially differentiated. Some reclined on couches in the high-status *triclinium*. Others sat, or reclined on the ground, in a space, which, in terms of use for eating, marked people as of lower status. In the House of the Menander, Murphy-O'Connor's model would probably best fit use of a space such as Room 11, combined with use of space in the peristyle.

Murphy-O'Connor's church is socioeconomically polarized. There is a binary division between the elite host's social near-equals, who are in Room 11, and the other three-quarters of the church of forty. The holding of the meals in the elite house, with the participation of the householder, implies that Murphy-O'Connor's host acts to a significant extent as a patron of the church. However,

---

18. Murphy-O'Connor, *St. Paul's Corinth*, 156.

19. For discussion of the development of usage of the room, see Horrell, "Domestic Space and Christian Meetings at Corinth," 353–56.

this is in some tension with the behavior implied by the way in which the meals are eaten. Smith points out that the ideology of what he calls "banquets" (i.e., significant meals held as a group) includes ideas of equality.[20] Although this was worked out in a framework that inevitably involved status differentiation (such as varied ranking of places around the dining couches),[21] it would appear unlikely to extend to something as gross as the host reclining with some friends while other supposed friends were excluded from the room. As well as Smith's appeal to "banquet ideology," basic features of early Christian rhetoric and practice would look likely to have precluded, even in problematic groups at Corinth, the kind of drastic distinction that Murphy-O'Connor proposes in suggesting simultaneous use of two types of space, where the distinction between the types of space is strongly socially marked.

Among further implications of the model of church implied by Murphy-O'Connor's proposal about use of space are that economic resources and education are probably strongly concentrated among the small elite within the church. This could stand in tension with various elements of Paul's rhetoric about the Spirit's distribution of gifts (1 Cor 12, etc.). However, Murphy-O'Connor could reasonably respond that such elitism is precisely what is attested in the situation that provokes Paul to write 1 Corinthians.[22]

Model 2: Osiek and Balch's Very Large Church Sitting and Reclining in Peristyle Garden and Another Garden and Banqueting Hall (a Post-Amphitheater-Crowd-Type Church) (I.10.4 Garden R + Peristyle Garden + Room 18)

Carolyn Osiek and David Balch use the peristyle (with its garden), Garden R, and Room 18 (see fig. 2.4) in a calculation: "The House of the Menander (I.10.4/14–17) is 1,800 square meters including two gardens (c. 150, 115 sq. m.) with a dining hall of 93.8 square meters. . . . Calculating a half square meter per

---

20. Smith, *From Symposium to Eucharist*, 11–12; see also Dennis E. Smith, "The House Church as Social Environment," in *Text, Image, and Christians in the Graeco-Roman World*, ed. A. C. Niang and C. Osiek (Eugene, OR: Pickwick, 2012), 3–21.

21. Dennis E. Smith, "The Greco-Roman Banquet as a Social Institution," in *Meals in the Early Christian World: Social Formation, Experimentation, and Conflict at the Table*, ed. Dennis E. Smith and Hal Taussig (New York: Palgrave Macmillan, 2012), 23–33 at 28–29.

22. Andrew D. Clarke, *Secular and Christian Leadership in Corinth: A Sociohistorical and Exegetical Study of 1 Corinthians 1–6*, Ancient Judaism and Early Christianity 18 (Leiden: Brill, 1993).

Figure 2.4. *Peristyle and garden in the House of the Menander.*

person and another half for statues, and so on, 360 people could be served."[23] This follows their similar calculation that the House of the Citharist could accommodate a meeting of 1,135 people. The point they are making is that scholars have been wrong to think that being a house church inherently puts an upper limit of thirty to fifty on the size of the group.[24]

They demonstrate their point very effectively, albeit by allowing a rather tight amount of space per person and by using calculations that are specifically based in meeting in houses that are so grand as to imply that the householder is of very high elite level. For a church to have such a patron at this stage would seem unlikely. However, Osiek and Balch circumvent this problem by observing that garden spaces of this size occur in association with quite a wide range of sizes of house.[25] Balch has returned to this topic more systematically in "The Church Sitting in a Garden."[26]

In the peristyle garden of the House of the Menander, people would be

23. Osiek and Balch, *Families in the New Testament World*, 202.
24. Osiek and Balch, *Families in the New Testament World*, 202.
25. Osiek and Balch, *Families in the New Testament World*, 202.
26. Balch, "Church Sitting in a Garden."

able to sit on the balustrade or recline on the ground. Balch's article draws on Wilhelmina Jashemski's work to offer a calculation for the numbers who could recline in groups on the ground.[27] Applied to the peristyle garden here, they suggest about 110 people reclining to eat.[28] Garden R might be more problematic, in that it could have been planted with crops. This would seriously reduce the usability of the space for meals. The same would be true of quite a few of the gardens that are attached to more modest houses. Balch also notes the provision of commercial outdoor catering facilities for groups of spectators who have come from shows at the amphitheater.[29] Experience of this type of setting could have formed a precedent for early Christian organization of outdoor meals.

The very large Banqueting Hall 18 is a feature of the high elite nature of the House of the Menander, so may not be very relevant for thinking about early Christian meetings. However, it is the kind of space that, in other settings, could act as a place for meeting of an association. As Philip Harland and others have argued, this could well be a sphere of practice on which the early Christians effectively drew in developing their own meal practices.[30]

Model 3: Dennis Smith's Heavily Patronized Church Reclining in a Triclinium (or in More Than One) (I.10.4 Room 11, etc.)

Dennis Smith dismisses the approaches of Osiek and Balch and of Murphy-O'Connor, who see the early Christians meeting in spaces such as an atrium or peristyle. Smith is convinced that early Christian meetings were meals eaten in dining rooms, conducted in the mode of a Greek banquet: reclining (with possibly a few sitting) to eat food followed by a *symposium*, a drinking party at which conversation, songs, and other activities that made up church life would take place; the pattern is bread then wine.[31] Matthias Klinghardt is also an advocate of this type of approach to understanding early Christian meals.[32]

27. Balch, "Church Sitting in a Garden," 227; see also Wilhelmina F. Jashemski, *The Gardens of Pompeii: Herculaneum and the Villas Destroyed by Vesuvius*, 2 vols. (New Rochelle: Caratzas, 1979–93), 2:83.

28. Size of space in square meters times 9/12.5.

29. Balch, "Church Sitting in a Garden," 227.

30. Philip A. Harland, *Associations, Synagogues, and Congregations: Claiming a Place in Ancient Mediterranean Society* (Minneapolis: Fortress, 2003), esp. chaps. 7–8.

31. Smith, *From Symposium to Eucharist*, 14–18, 178; Smith, "Greco-Roman Banquet as a Social Institution," 23–25; Smith, "House Church as Social Environment," 11–12.

32. Klinghardt, *Gemeinschaftsmahl und Mahlgemeinschaft*, 1986.

On the question of numbers, Klinghardt argues that, if there were too many for the seven to seventeen that might fit into a dining room, the norm in the communal meal tradition would be to bring a second dining room into use if it was available.[33] Smith argues that if the group grew too big for the dining room, "we should assume that another house church would be organized."[34] In either case, the larger number would result in two meetings taking place. In the House of the Menander, if we were looking for several dining rooms, Rooms 11, 12, and maybe 18 could come into consideration.

A key implication of Smith's approach is that the church is very strongly under the patronage of the host. For instance, Smith sees the host as issuing invitations to the group members to attend a meal.[35] The church meeting in the host's dining room could be seen as taking on the appearance of a group of the host's clients, meeting as an expression of his (or, occasionally, her) patronal generosity. This would be markedly at odds with the rhetoric of New Testament texts. Clients honor their patron. The Christians' honoring is focused much more strongly on Christ and God than would be expressed in Greco-Roman banquets by the offering of libations.[36] In the meals in the Gospels and the meetings in the Epistles, there is very little focus on the human host. This would be strange if that was basic to the social structure of the churches.

The posture is also an issue. A curiosity of the New Testament accounts is that in the Gospels people recline at meals (e.g., Matt 9:10; Mark 6:39; 14:18; John 12:2), whereas in the Epistles people sit in meetings (1 Cor 14:30; Jas 2:3).[37] Should we envisage some meetings being meal based and some not, or should we envisage some meals at which people generally sit, rather than reclining?[38] Either would be at odds with Smith's view. He allows for a limited use of sitting but he sees the characteristic posture as reclining.[39]

One problem of seeing a Christian group as meeting solely in a *triclinium* such as Room 11 is that it would be difficult, in practical terms, to run and de-

33. Matthias Klinghardt, "A Typology of the Communal Meal," in *Meals in the Early Christian World: Social Formation, Experimentation, and Conflict at the Table*, ed. Dennis E. Smith and Hal Taussig (New York: Palgrave Macmillan, 2012), 9–22 at 14.

34. Smith, "House Church as Social Environment," 11.

35. Smith, "House Church as Social Environment," 14–15.

36. For libations and other token sacrifices to the gods during meals, see Klinghardt, "Typology of the Communal Meal," 11–12.

37. The Greek terms used do not absolutely exclude reclining, but they would much more frequently be used of sitting.

38. For an extended discussion of this issue, see Weissenrieder, "Contested Spaces," esp. 88, 105.

39. Smith, "Greco-Roman Banquet as a Social Institution," 24.

velop groups by use of spaces with a small, fixed upper limit. Groups generally do not function well if they exactly fit their space. The number of people who turn up at a meeting would tend to vary, which would cause problems of accommodation. As noted above, Smith's response would be that early Christian hosts followed normal banquet practice by using invitations to ensure correct numbers at the meal. However, the idea of Christian meetings being gatherings by individual invitation, rather than offering a broader welcome, sits very awkwardly with a wide range of New Testament rhetoric and with the path of development of Christian meetings when they become more heavily documented in Late Antiquity. A further problem with the use of small fixed spaces is that church growth would have been a constant matter of splitting and reorganizing groups. This is a difficult process, involving separations that are often painful and lead to practical difficulties in terms of availability of skills and resources.

Having said all this, the view espoused by Smith and others does have the advantages that, in their model, the early Christians eat in spaces where people were known to eat and that the *symposium* setting did produce a range of texts that often relate in interesting ways to aspects of the development of early Christianity.

Model 4: A Church in a Small House (I.10.1)

So far, we have been looking at spaces in the House of the Menander. The spaces have mainly just been evocative of broad issues that could equally be illustrated from other large houses, especially given the absence of furnishings of the rooms in question. However, we now turn to House 1, which presents a picture much less familiar to scholars of early Christianity.

Scholars have tended to polarize the possibilities for early Christian meeting places, seeing them as meeting either in houses (generally thought of as elite dwellings) or in other types of space such as apartments (generally seen as places where the non-elite lived). A sharp example of this is Robert Jewett's approach in his commentary on Romans, where his "tenement churches" are patronless, egalitarian assemblies and seen in contrast to house churches dependent on elite patrons.[40] In Rome, there is something partly to be said for this. The cost of land there meant that to rent a house as such would generally be extremely costly. On the other hand, apartment blocks actually contained very many elite dwellings as well as those of the less well off. However, beyond

---

40. Jewett, *Romans*, 64–65. We will return to Jewett's idea about patronless groups below.

Figure 2.5. House 1, Rooms 1 and 3.

Rome, there were certainly non-elite houses in every place. A church in a house does not need to mean a church in an elite house.

Figure 2.5 is indicative of the standard of House 1. The house has a reasonable amount of space. There are four downstairs rooms, some further spaces upstairs, and a courtyard with a kitchen bench and latrine. The ground floor plan area adds up to about ninety square meters. The wall decoration is professional but not very elaborate or expensive. Penelope Allison noted fifty-two finds or groups of finds. There are vases, jugs, and dishes, including some nice *terra sigillata* ware. There are lamps, beads, a bronze mirror, a strigil, a pestle and mortar, the odd loom weight, stylus, and forceps. Most substantially there is a terracotta herm, probably of Persephone, that was placed in a niche in the kitchen courtyard (see fig. 2.6).[41]

A pile of lime in Room 3 indicates that the house was undergoing some repairs at the time of the eruption. Various nails and other metal and bone fittings that were found attest to wooden objects. However, there is no clear set of dining furniture. Room 3, or possibly 2 or 4, could have been used for dining, although none was large enough for a normal *triclinium* layout. If a meal was held in Room 3, at about fourteen square meters (150 square feet), then, employing a

41. Allison, *Pompeian Households*, 41–47.

Figure 2.6. House 1, Courtyard 5 with kitchen bench and niches.

calculation like the second type used by Balch,[42] about ten people could be accommodated. If most of Room 1 was brought in as well, we could double that.

This meeting, of up to about twenty people, would be hosted by the householder of a house of ninety square meters. If we place him (or possibly her) onto a scale of sizes of property in Pompeii,[43] he is renting more space than about 30 percent of other householders there. If we take this householder to be the wealthiest person in the group, then the group is drawn from roughly the 30 percent lowest-income householders' immediate families (spouses, children, and other close relatives), together with people who do not fall into that category (slaves, other dependents, and the homeless), who probably constituted up to 50 percent of the population.[44] A further feature of the type of Christian group that could have met in House 1 is that a substantial percentage of the group would have been members of the household of that house.

While looking at House 1, there is an incidental feature that is of interest. One

42. See n. 27.

43. For the scale and its construction, see Oakes, *Reading Romans in Pompeii*, 48–55. The scale is derived from the survey in Wallace-Hadrill, *Houses and Society*, esp. 67–79.

44. Oakes, *Reading Romans in Pompeii*, 59–60.

question about Christian groups in houses is how they would handle domestic cult shrines, particularly *lararia*. Would they have put them out of use somehow, and what would have been the social consequences of that? In House 1 we happen to have an instance of a *lararium* fresco that was put out of commission during remodeling of the house. It was on the inside wall near the entrance and was covered up during construction of a staircase. This shows that such action could be taken, although presumably that went along with replacement of the *lararium* and some kind of ritual around the moving of the household gods.

Model 5: A Church in a Bar (I.10.2–3)

Next door to House 1 is a bar, entered through Doorway 2, which merges with a house, which has a further Doorway 3. As a place for a church to meet, a bar has several advantages. It is accessible to the public. It is generally equipped for dining and could supply food. A bar would also frequently have spaces that could be rented by a private party such as a church meeting. Edward Adams suggests such a possibility for a Christian group meeting in Corinth. He notes that an exegetical advantage of this kind of option is that when Paul, in 1 Cor 11:22, 34, asks about, then recommends, eating at home, that could

Figure 2.7. *Bar/House 2–3, viewed from inside. The bar counter (partly destroyed) is visible near the doorway on the right side.*

more straightforwardly apply to every one of Paul's hearers if they met, not in the house of a member, but in a rented space that was no one's home.[45] David Balch also discusses the possibility of a Christian group using eating space in a bar, possibly in a garden area.[46]

Although Bar/House 2–3 (see fig. 2.7) was probably inhabited (there are fairly extensive, quite good quality finds from upstairs rooms), the shortage of finds in the bar and the condition of the serving facilities suggest that it was not in commercial use at the time of the eruption. However, graffiti indicate aspects of usage when it was functioning. On the walls of the bar are what look like scores relating to games or money (*CIL* 4.8239, 8251, etc.). There are also graffiti referring to women, particularly *Capella Bacchis* (*CIL* 4.8238)[47] and *Prima domina* (*CIL* 4.8241), with whom a graffito price is often linked (*CIL* 4.8248).[48] On the wall outside the bar is a graffiti "slanging match" between Successus and Severus, two rivals for the affections of a bar serving girl called Iris (*CIL* 4.8258, 8259).[49] Also on the wall is the name Primigenia (*CIL* 4.8274). This name turns up elsewhere in a graffito recommending a prostitute in the nearby town of Nuceria (*CIL* 4.8356). In the entrance corridor to House 3, there is a graffito, *Felix aeris as IV, Florus X* (*CIL* 4.7339). This too has often been connected with prostitution. Van Andringa has challenged this, arguing instead that they were donations related to the *lararium* in the corridor.[50] However, that would seem a rather unlikely subject for such graffiti. As indicated, the entrance corridor also contains a *lararium* niche and picture, next to which is a graffito reading *Lares Augustos* (*CIL* 4.8282).

We will set aside the issue of what size of group could fit into this particular bar. Our interest is in its nature as a bar and the activities that are represented as taking place there, especially those that were at odds with early Christian moral teaching. The graffiti in Bar/House 2–3 reinforce the picture in a range of Roman texts of bars as places of prostitution.[51] As Nigel Kay argues, the reference to Bacchus in the name of one of the women probably alludes to

45. Adams, "Placing the Corinthian Common Meal."
46. Balch, "Church Sitting in a Garden," 232.
47. See n. 52.
48. John DeFelice, "Inns and Taverns," in *The World of Pompeii*, ed. J. J. Dobbins and P. W. Foss (London: Routledge, 2007), 474–86 at 482.
49. For the text and a translation, see Oakes, *Reading Romans in Pompeii*, 33.
50. William van Andringa, *Quotidien des dieux et des hommes: La vie religieuse dans les cités du Vésuve à l'époque romaine* (Rome: École française de Rome: 2009), 247.
51. For range of evidence and discussion see Laurence, *Roman Pompeii*, 92–101.

the sale of wine in the bar.[52] Ray Laurence categorizes this establishment as a *popina* and argues that that carries the likelihood of a reputation for drunkenness and rowdy behavior: "These drinking establishments were not places for respectable people even to set foot in."[53] John DeFelice takes issue with Laurence about the extent to which bars in Pompeii were connected with disreputable activities. However, even he cites Bar/House 2–3 as one of the places where prostitution was happening.[54]

How would all this affect the likelihood of Christians holding meetings in such a bar, for instance by hiring a dining space there? If a church did meet there, how would the location affect the nature of that church?

Roman rhetoric about bars suggests that meeting in such a location would restrict participation by women who viewed themselves as respectable. Such women are a prominent feature of various accounts relating to early church groups (e.g., Acts 17:4). If a place was deemed unsuitable for them to attend meetings, it could, for instance, sharply affect the economic viability of the group. Use of certain types of meeting space could have economic consequences. It could also, no doubt, possibly result in them not being used at all.

However, in terms of early Christian rhetoric about activities in bars, especially drinking and prostitution, we could possibly make the same distinction that we observed above in relation to reclining or sitting. The Gospels repeatedly speak of reclining. The Epistles feature more sitting and standing. Similarly, the rhetoric in the Epistles against prostitution and heavy drinking is strongly put (e.g., 1 Cor 6:12–20; Gal 5:19–21). In contrast, the Gospels repeatedly note Jesus's associating with "sinners" (e.g., Luke 15:2), and he commends prostitutes for their response to the message (Matt 21:31; probably Luke

---

52. Nigel M. Kay, *Epigrams from the Anthologia Latina: Text, Translation, and Commentary* (London: Bloomsbury, 2013), 195. In an earlier work (*Reading Romans in Pompeii*, 36), I took *Capella Bacchis* as equivalent to *capella Bacchi* ("chapel of Bacchus"), a joke about the nature of the establishment. I now realize that this is not lexically feasible. The similarity to *Anthologia Latina* 115 (126R) does offer some conceptual support. There, a library converted into a tavern is jokingly called a temple of Bacchus. However, the term *capella* (or *cappella*), meaning "chapel," occurs in Latin only much later than the first century. Gillian Mackie discusses the strange derivation of the term, from the name of a particular relic, the *capella Martini*, the cloak of Martin of Tours (ca. 316–97). It was transferred from the object itself to the tentlike structure in which it was displayed, then into much wider use; see G. V. Mackie, *Early Christian Chapels in the West: Decoration, Function, and Patronage* (Toronto: University of Toronto Press, 2003), 4.

53. Laurence, *Roman Pompeii*, map 5.4 and p. 93.

54. DeFelice, "Inns and Taverns," 479–82.

7:50). He also is reputed to be a drinker (Matt 11:19). Although the rhetoric of the Epistles fits awkwardly with meetings in bars, the rhetoric of the Gospels could be seen as somewhat conducive to it. If such meetings did take place, the church would presumably receive some of the same accusations of disreputability that were leveled at Jesus.

Model 6: A Very Small Church in the Stoneworkers' Workshop (I.10.6)

We now come to two settings that were discussed at length in *Reading Romans in Pompeii*, so will be handled more briefly here. Workshop 6 is a simple shop structure with a wide entrance. There is one room attached at the side. An unusually full set of dining utensils suggests that the workshop was inhabited at the time of the eruption. Many of the loose finds relate to trade in small decorative stone items. There are good washing facilities in the workshop but no evidence of sculpture taking place. This would appear consonant with something like salvage, cleaning, and resale of garden stonework. The workshop was cut out, in the middle of the first century CE, from the House of the Menander and the House of the Cabinetmaker, which itself had once been connected to the House of the Menander. This suggests that Workshop 6 was a dependency of the House of the Menander—a small business run by a couple of slaves or freed slaves from the house.[55]

If a church met here it would be small. The side living room is about ten square meters, so could accommodate about eight people. Picking up Smith's point about meeting in dining space: this space was indeed used for dining. This is where the plates and bowls were, and the only other space was the workshop. The side room was presumably not a space for banquets as such, although the inhabitants would presumably have reclined on cushions or mattresses to eat. There were no remains relating to chairs, so the only furniture must have been organic matter such as straw-filled mattresses. This small church would probably be socially very homogeneous and would have very limited financial resources.

---

55. For discussion of the above, see Oakes, *Reading Romans in Pompeii*, 1–11.

Figure 2.8. House 7, view of asymmetric atrium from entrance corridor.

Model 7: Oakes's Craftworker-Hosted Church in the House of the Cabinetmaker Garden and Portico and Back Rooms (Jewett's Patronless Church?) (I.10.7)

House 7 is quite a spacious dwelling (see fig. 2.8). Its floor plan is 310 square meters (including the garden) and there are upstairs rooms above all the enclosed downstairs ones. However, in its final phase, much of the space was given over to storage and work. The unusual asymmetric atrium was lined with cupboards filled with a wide range of domestic and work-related artifacts. In the back portico the excavators found a four-wheeled cart. That area, the garden behind, and a room (8) that was expensively decorated as if for use for sleeping or dining contained a wide array of tools, mostly for woodworking, and a range of bone pieces of types used in furniture making. This was an active base of operations for a household of craftworkers or possibly traders. Key evidence that it was a single household rather than a collection of apartments is that there was a single large collection of tableware, which fell down from an upstairs room as a result of the eruption. A substantial collection of surgical instruments also came down from upstairs. The kitchen was probably in use for cooking on the day of the eruption. Two bodies were found in the one expensively decorated downstairs room (9) that had not been turned over to commercial activity. That room would have been suitable to be a *triclinium*. However, at the time of the eruption it contained just one couch.[56]

In *Reading Romans in Pompeii*, I argued that this was a type of craftworker house that would function well as a base for a substantial craftworker-hosted house church such as that of Prisca and Aquila, mentioned in Rom 16:5. The householder of I.10.7 controlled more space than about 70 percent of other householders in Pompeii. On the other hand, he (or possibly she) had a house that was less than a third the size of the smallest houses that one would tend to think of as elite. It is also extremely unlikely that the householder owned the property, a key characteristic of the elite. The loose finds from the house support this picture. They include items quite a way beyond the basics of subsistence but very far from the assemblage that we would expect from an elite house.[57] Having taken the elite out of the equation, we might think that this leaves us with the type of patronless, inherently egalitarian group that Robert Jewett argues as forming the "tenement churches" of Rome in Paul's day.[58] However, a house church, or a tenement church, began from a household. This immediately provides a group that is inherently hierarchical. Adding further partial households, generally of lower income than the host, would build further hierarchy and something like patronage, even if the usual formal vocabulary of that would not tend to be used (as indeed it rather rarely was in patronal relationships in general). I argued for the following as a model of the type of house church that would be likely to meet in a space such as House 7. The model is a hypothetical group of forty people made up of the following:[59]

1. A craftworker whose house is about three hundred square meters, his wife, children, a few (male) craftworking slaves, a (female) domestic slave, a dependent relative.

2. Several other householders (mainly, but not necessarily all, male) with smaller houses, some (but not all) of their spouses, children, slaves, and other dependents. Their houses are within a range from just under three hundred square meters to about twenty square meters.

---

56. For discussion, see Oakes, *Reading Romans in Pompeii*, 15–33. In that book, because the great majority of the craftworking finds suggest something like furniture making, I called I.10.7 the House of the Cabinetmaker.

57. Oakes, *Reading Romans in Pompeii*, 15–33.

58. Jewett, *Romans*, 64–65.

59. See Oakes, *Reading Romans in Pompeii*, table 3.6.

3. A few members of families where the householder is not part of the house church.
4. A couple of slaves whose owners are not part of the house church.
5. A couple of free or freed dependents of people who are not part of the house church.
6. A couple of homeless people.

Model 8: A Slave-Led Church in the Stable Yard (or in the Staff Dining Room) (I.10.14 Space 34 [or above Rooms 20, 20a, 20b])

Romans 16:10–11 sends greetings to members of the households of Aristobulus and Narcissus, without greeting the householders themselves. This probably indicates that there are Christian groups within two large households. Given the typical makeup of large households in Rome, that probably means that most, or all, of the members of these two household churches are slaves.[60] Where would such groups gather?

The House of the Menander exhibits a sharp differentiation between the areas containing the highly decorated rooms and the other areas, which contain a kitchen, latrines, a stable yard, and various other service-related spaces. These service areas are tucked away down narrow Corridors M and P. The best decorated of the rooms in these zones is on the upper floor, above Rooms 20, 20a, and 20b. The room is about thirty square meters, lit by a large window, and decorated, fairly simply, in the Fourth Style. Roger Ling suggests that being the best of the spaces in the service area could mean that it was the dining room for those who worked in the house.[61] If Ling's suggestion is correct, this would appear to be a very appropriate place for Christian meetings. It would be equipped for dining and usefully separated both from the dirt of work and from the areas in use by the householder.

One constraint is that there would need to be sufficient members of the household involved in the meetings to enable the Christians to have use of the space. This would make the church a large body of the household, following different cultic practice from that of the householder. Since, in the case of Christianity, this came with a controversial range of ideas and probably the avoidance of acknowledgement of other cults, we could imagine the house-

60. See, for instance, James D. G. Dunn, *Romans 9–16*, Word Biblical Commentary 38B (Grand Rapids: Zondervan, 1988), 895.
61. Ling, *Insula of the Menander*, 1:120.

Figure 2.9. House of the Menander, stable yard (34).

holder being rather suspicious. Unlike the situations where the householder was a member, this kind of situation would appear rather unstable. In fact, the householder would probably need to act as patron in any case, even though not a member. Patrons of cultic groups, for instance in the case of associations, need not share the practices of the members. However, the case of a household church would seem difficult to fit into this.

One implication of the above is that this model of house church does not avoid patronage altogether. It does not avoid hierarchy either. Even if all the members were slaves, there would be a strongly marked hierarchy in a large household.

Ling's staff dining room suggestion makes sense of the archeology. However, it does feel as though there could be too much of the ideas of modern philanthropic employment practice in it. Most of our evidence about treatment of Roman slaves suggests that they would not, as a whole group, tend to have special facilities provided. That is not to say that some senior slaves and freed slaves would not have better facilities than other slaves. A decorated dining room could fit into such a scenario. However, in that case, it would not be so likely as a potential meeting place for a Christian group that drew from the full range of slaves. A more open option would be a lower grade but accessible space such as the stable yard (see fig. 2.9). A church in this space

Figure 2.10. House of the Menander, Atrium 41 of the Steward's House.

would still need to include most members of the household and would need to gain the patronage of the owner. The meetings would, however, be in a dirtier environment, less convenient for eating.

Model 9: A Retainer-Led Church in the Steward's House (I.10.16)

Finally, a variant on the above. A household church could meet under the supervision of a senior household member. In the House of the Menander a body was found in Room 43 with a ring commonly viewed as a steward's seal ring.[62] The Steward's House (Rooms 41–45) offers a range of spaces (see fig. 2.10). It offers some privacy and facilities for cooking and eating. A household church here would not need to include almost all the household members because the space would be under the steward's control, rather than being a core facility used by all, such as the stable yard. This house church would

62. Maiuri, *La Casa del Menandro*, 20. Ling, *Insula of the Menander*, 1:144, discusses the evidence and concludes that he "was clearly a trusted member of the family" but that it cannot be proved that he was a steward. My argument in this chapter does not depend on House I.10.16 being that of a steward as such. The key point is that the dwelling unit appears to be in use by someone of retainer class.

probably still need to be under the householder's patronage. However, it could appear a safer structure, both because of its supervision by someone directly accountable to, and trusted by, the householder and because it need not be as large a group. The group would effectively have a double patronage, both by the householder and by the steward who acted as host. The steward would effectively be acting as broker for the group to have access to a secure social location in the household.

The key aspect of the relationship between space and the type of church in this case is that this space is controlled by a particular type of person. If we were to generalize from the situation of the steward, we could describe him as a "retainer." This is a term used by Gerhard Lenski to describe a class of people who are closely associated with the elite but are not themselves part of the elite. It includes a range of people such as priests and minor officials. These people are literate, have a range of other skills, and have access to the elite and to resources owned by them.[63] Various scholars have seen early churches as being typically retainer led, especially in the case of scribal/legal groups often seen as responsible for production of the Gospels, particularly that of Matthew. For instance, Charles Talbert writes: "Matthew's community was composed mostly of the nonelite. The author(s) of the First Gospel belonged to the retainer class (scribes), as did the community's leaders."[64]

Consideration of the implications of a church meeting in the Steward's House in the House of the Menander offers a further way into thinking about characteristics that a retainer-led church could have.

Conclusion: The Effects of Space

The earliest Christians did not build churches. They met in spaces that also had other purposes. The scholars listed in the first paragraph of this chapter were led to their various suggestions for early Christian meeting places by various signals in early Christian texts. Murphy-O'Connor, Smith, and Klinghardt were primarily driven by early Christian references to eating. Jewett, Horrell, and I were primarily driven by textual and historical argument that Christian

63. Gerhard Lenski, *Power and Privilege: A Theory of Social Stratification* (New York: McGraw-Hill, 1966), 82.
64. Charles H. Talbert, *Matthew*, Paideia Commentaries on the New Testament (Grand Rapids: Baker Academic, 2010), 5. Discussion has often centered on the saying in Matt 13:52 about the scribe who is trained for the kingdom of heaven.

house-church hosts were mainly non-elite. This led to consideration of what spaces non-elite hosts could use. Jewett elaborated his idea through consideration of housing in Rome. Horrell looked at the Corinthian archeological evidence available to him, for spaces capable of use for meetings. I looked at loose finds from Pompeii that linked particular spaces with craftworkers. Balch, Adams, and Harland looked for dining spaces available for groups to use beyond the home. In Harland's case, this is part of an argument relating early Christian groups to associations. Adams documents the overall range of textual evidence that points to early Christians meeting in several types of space. The present chapter uses evidence from one block of houses to argue that the various spatial suggestions make a difference.

This chapter uses reflection on a concrete example in order to construct a list of issues that the nature of various spaces raises for the nature of an early Christian group that held meetings in such a space. Differences between the possible spaces can be seen to correspond to a range of types of difference in the nature of the group, seen in terms of the following:

- internal relationships and hierarchies
- patronage
- socioeconomic profile
- economic resources
- degree of homogeneity
- group size
- eating practices
- comparability to "banqueting"
- modes of group growth
- group reputation
- potential perceived threat to household
- class location of church leadership

It is striking how wide ranging a list this is despite the patchiness in the evidence adduced for the various spaces under consideration. More could be said even on these particular spaces in the Insula of the Menander. Beyond this, considerably more could be drawn in from broader consideration of types of space elsewhere in Pompeii and Herculaneum.

Despite originating in the study of spaces specifically in Pompeii, the above list of issues relating space to meetings clearly has extensive relevance elsewhere. The virtue of the Pompeian material has been that coordination between the types of archeological evidence allows breakthrough links to be made—for instance, between graffiti and space, or between the social identity of a specific inhabitant and space, as in the case of the steward.

That final example, the church in the House of the Steward, particularly exemplifies the move in scholarship that this chapter seeks to make. The idea that first-century Christian groups were often likely to be led by people of retainer class has been extensively discussed. However, the resources used to do so have generally been literary. This chapter argues that this and other debates about the nature of early Christian groups can usefully bring into consideration space and archeological evidence relating to space. The world of early Christianity is not merely textual, it is also spatial. The deployment of groups in space has crucial relationships to the nature of those groups. The surviving evidence of the nature of first-century spaces can usefully be brought much more extensively into the field of study of the early Christians.

PART II

Economics

3 | Methodological Issues in Using Economic Evidence in Interpretation of Early Christian Texts

Economics and Early Christian Texts

When the Good Samaritan left money with the innkeeper for the care of an injured traveler, how long would this have covered the cost of keeping him? Was it enough to make the innkeeper look after him with particular care? In his book *Jesus and the Peasants*, Douglas Oakman explores "The Buying Power of Two Denarii (Luke 10:35)."[1] Was the Samaritan making a substantial sacrifice, or was it loose change? Understanding the sum of money is a small but significant element in interpreting the type of impact that the story was expected to have.

Elsewhere in the book, Oakman sets up one of the sharpest issues in the interpretation of early Christian texts. What is happening when the acts and sayings of a Galilean peasant (or something close to that) are expressed in written form by members of an urban, literate class?[2] When Luke's Jesus says, "Blessed are you who are poor" (Luke 6:20), should we think of this in the peasant economic context of Galilee, or the Greco-Roman urban context of Luke, or the shadowy world of the scribal transmitters of Luke's sources? In the Gospels, we have a poor teacher and his followers being described by the somewhat wealthier kinds of people who could write.

The use of economics in the study of early Christian texts ranges between these two limits, from elucidation of texts that directly refer to some aspect of the first-century economic system through to use of theories in which the

---

1. Douglas Oakman, *Jesus and the Peasants*, Matrix: The Bible in Mediterranean Context 4 (Eugene, OR: Cascade, 2008), 40–45.

2. Oakman, *Jesus and the Peasants*, 3. He characterizes Jesus as a "crucified, illiterate peasant."

economic situation of writers, readers, or characters in the texts is related to class interests that are seen as shaping every aspect of the text.

Within this very broad and highly contested field, the aims of this chapter are quite limited. It seeks to do three things. First, it seeks to bring a little extra clarity to work in this area by differentiating fairly sharply three possible relationships between economics and interpretation. Many people, when faced with a book that uses economics in textual interpretation, will tend to mix the three possibilities together, resulting in confusion and, sometimes, an undue nervousness in using anything that relates to economics. Second, the chapter draws on my own encounters with archeological material, textual material, and comparative material to make a few comments about how each of these sources can be used as economic evidence and about some difficulties that stand in the way of doing so. Third, the chapter returns to questions of economic stratification on which I have written briefly before and suggests that a way forward lies in focusing on single economic variables that produce models that, although they only partially reflect social structure, can do so in a way designed to be useful for interpretation of early Christian texts.

This means that this chapter is not contributing to the ongoing post-Finley debate about the nature of the ancient economy, or lack of one. For work on that, see, for example, Peter Bang, Mamoru Ikeguchi, and Harmut Ziche's book *Ancient Economies, Modern Methodologies*.[3] Neither is this chapter about social class per se. For some of the complications on that, one can still profitably read Richard Rohrbaugh's 1984 article.[4] We will have to talk about some class issues because class forms the basis of one of the possible relationships between economics and interpretation. However, when we consider stratification in the final section of this chapter, our concerns will be specifically economic. The question on which we will focus is that of the extent to which various possible models of society map the distribution of economic resources among various groups in ways that are fruitful for interpretation of early Christian texts. We will not be considering whether any of the models provides a viable concept of class.

Having made these disclaimers, we cannot avoid one theoretical issue at the outset. There is a temptation for modern interpreters to see economics as a

3. Peter F. Bang, Mamoru Ikeguchi, and Harmut Ziche, *Ancient Economies, Modern Methodologies: Archaeology, Comparative History, Models, and Institutions* (Bari: Edipuglia, 2006).

4. Richard Rohrbaugh, "Methodological Considerations in the Debate over the Social Class Status of Early Christians," *Journal of the American Academy of Religion* 52 (1984): 519–46.

free-standing aspect of a society. Economists tend to analyze issues of resource distribution as a system dependent on specifically economic variables such as supply and demand. They tend to avoid getting too far into analysis of other issues, such as politics and religion. (This compartmentalization has actually become rather difficult to maintain: many economists increasingly do interact with all sorts of disciplines, including some, such as meteorology, that would have seemed very surprising not long ago.) In studying the first few centuries of the Christian movement, any attempt to isolate economics from other social factors such as politics would be doomed. As Karl Polanyi argues, all ancient economies were "embedded economies."[5] Financial decisions in such economies were rarely taken for financial reasons alone. For example, the nature of patron-client relationships ensured constant distortion of what we might expect to be market interaction. Distribution of resources was dependent much more on power relationships than on the market.

With this in mind, what counts as economic evidence? When, as an undergraduate, I took a course on economics, I remember the lecturer defining it as "the study of the allocation of scarce resources." In one major current textbook, Michael Parkin defines it as "the social science that studies the *choices* that individuals, businesses, governments, and entire societies make as they cope with *scarcity* and the *incentives* that influence those choices."[6] Air is not scarce, so it is generally free. Breathing is not usually an economic issue. Wine is not free. Its production and distribution require land, water, transport, storage, and labor, all of which are scarce resources. (We will return to wine production in a little more detail later as a good example of the range of types of economic evidence available). At a couple of points, Parkin's definition sounds a little awkward for an ancient context. The focus on choice is problematic in a society where most economic activities are governed more by custom or compulsion. I suppose it works fairly reasonably as long as one remembers that the choices lie with the powerful elite. The stress on incentives might be useful, but only if it is realized that, for most people, they were generally of an "offer you can't refuse" type. There was not the kind of varying levels of inducement that a modern market system might include.

Avoiding this kind of definition entirely, Ekkehard and Wolfgang Stege-

---

5. Karl Polanyi et al., *Trade and Market in the Early Empires* (Chicago: Regnery, 1971), 250. For a useful summary and application to New Testament studies, see Halvor Moxnes, *The Economy of the Kingdom: Social Conflict and Economic Relations in Luke's Gospel* (Philadelphia: Fortress, 1988), 28–32.

6. Michael Parkin, *Economics*, 7th ed. (Boston: Addison Wesley, 2005), 2 (emphasis original).

mann prefer to base their study of economics in the early Christian movement on a definition of economy by cultural anthropologist Marvin Harris as "the sum of all actions that are responsible for the provisioning of a society with goods and services."[7] Although this can clearly fit scenarios in a wide range of cultures, I would rather not use it for first-century society. Much activity that we should describe as economic is not centered on provisioning anyone. I prefer the first definition that I offered, "the study of the allocation of scarce resources." Despite being rooted in study of modern economics, this definition can work for ancient embedded economies as well. It does not presuppose whether the resources are allocated by a market or by diktat from the powerful. As well as money, it can cover issues such as labor, including slave labor. It also allows an interface with class issues, because all theories of class have some relation to resource allocation. In line with this definition, we will take economic evidence as being evidence of the patterns of allocation, the processes of allocation, the initiators or recipients of allocation (or intermediaries in the process), and the scarce resources being allocated.

All these categories of evidence could be significant in, for example, a full contextual interpretation of 1 Thess 4:11. There Paul urges his hearers, "Work with your hands." In first-century Thessalonica, which socioeconomic groups "worked with their hands"? Should we infer that all the letter's recipients were among those groups? If not, what would it have meant to give this exhortation to someone from a socioeconomic group that did not usually work with their hands? Had some Thessalonian Christians stopped working? If so, what would be the economic implications? Were first-century craftworking families likely to have savings to live off for a few months? Was there a banking system that extended to the non-elite? Were they likely to own possessions that they could sell and live off for a time? Might some in the church have started supporting others so that they did not need to work? If so, was this a patronage structure? Was Paul's exhortation aimed at preventing laziness, or debt, or patronage? A full range of economic evidence could usefully be put to work.

---

7. Ekkehard W. Stegemann and Wolfgang Stegemann, *The Jesus Movement: A Social History of Its First Century*, trans. O. C. Dean Jr. (Minneapolis: Fortress, 1999), 16, citing a 1989 German translation of what is now Marvin Harris and Orna Johnson, *Cultural Anthropology*, 5th ed. (Boston: Allyn & Bacon, 2000).

POSSIBLE RELATIONSHIPS BETWEEN ECONOMICS AND INTERPRETATION

We need to distinguish between three possible types of link between economics and interpretation. First, economics can provide an *overall analytical framework* for interpretation. Second, the *aim* of the interpretation of a text may be to gather economic evidence. Third, economic evidence may be a *resource* that is used in interpretation.

Using an Economic Analytical Framework for Interpretation

"The farmer and the cowman should be friends!" This song sums up the socioeconomic narrative that underlies the musical *Oklahoma*. Rodgers and Hammerstein present the founding of the state as resting on a reconciliation between the interests of cattle ranchers, who wanted wide-open spaces to run cattle, and of agriculturalists, who wanted the land divided into smaller units. The reconciliation rather favors the farmer: Curly the cowboy ends by giving up his saddle, horse, and gun to win the hand of the farmer's daughter.

In that musical, the economic issues are, fairly clearly, a fundamental structural element of the plot. However, many scholars use economics as their key framework for analysis, irrespective of whether the text seems overtly to deal with economic issues. For example, Itumeleng Mosala's reading of the story of Cain and Abel could be summarized as "the pastoralist and the agriculturalist cannot be friends—and God is on the side of the pastoralist!" Mosala (following quite a number of other scholars) locates the production of the story in the social struggle between groups that raised sheep and those that grew crops.[8] Douglas Oakman's analytical framework of considering the potentially competing interests of peasants, represented by Jesus's actual teaching, and scribal groups, responsible for producing that teaching in written form, goes as far as to see some of these scribes as conceivably being opponents of Jesus.[9]

Interpreters will have various reactions to the idea of using economics to provide the central analytical framework. It will be the prime method if the interpreter sees economic issues as inherently the fundamental ones, as in a Marxist view. Equally, if the aim of the particular piece of interpretation is

8. Itumeleng J. Mosala, *Biblical Hermeneutics and Black Theology in South Africa* (Grand Rapids: Eerdmans, 1989).

9. Oakman, *Jesus and the Peasants*, 303. In this he evokes the fictional Andreas from Gerd Theissen's *The Shadow of the Galilean: The Quest of the Historical Jesus in Narrative Form*, trans. J. Bowden (Minneapolis: Fortress, 1987).

to draw economic conclusions, such a framework may be suitable. However, some interpreters will worry about what they see as economic reductionism inherent in such a method. When the primary interpretative questions posed to a text are about whose economic interests it serves and how it serves them, then, inevitably, the primary results of the interpretation will be economic and political. Other aspects of the text may not be brought to light. More subtly, there is a risk that, when analyzing the interests of a writer, too much weight is put on class interests rather than individual interests. In the case of Paul, for example, it is probable that the effects of his particular individual combination of background and experiences are more frequently significant than are the effects stemming from his general socioeconomic level.

On the other hand, to some degree these systemic economic questions are inescapable. If we are interpreting Luke's Gospel, with Mary's announcement of the downfall of the mighty (Luke 1:52) and Jesus's announcement of his calling to preach good news to the poor (4:18), we must consider the socioeconomic location of Luke, his sources, and his expected audience. Moreover, the issue goes beyond the obviously economic passages, to reach even those dealing with apparently the most theological subjects such as sin, forgiveness, and prayer, in which ideas about indebtedness and petition to higher authorities are a vital part of the interpretative mix. What was the role of indebtedness in the lives of Galilean peasants or the Greco-Roman urban non-elite? What would forgiving a debt mean in such contexts? How might that affect its use as an expression relating to sin? Just as some methods may be described, from some viewpoints, as being economically reductionistic, many other methods are anti-economically reductionistic. On either side, the danger is of using a method that fails to bring to light significant aspects of the text.

Gathering of Economic Data as the Aim of Interpretation

A second possible relationship between economics and interpretation is that the aim of the interpretation is to use the text as a source for gathering economic evidence. This is a major feature of the People's History of Christianity project, which has resulted in the publication of a series of books under that title. In the introductory essay to volume one, Richard Horsley describes the aim of the project as being not interpretation of texts but recovery of history of ordinary people, evidence of whose lives can be gleaned from the texts.[10]

---

10. Richard A. Horsley, "Unearthing a People's History," in *Christian Origins*, ed. Richard A. Horsley, A People's History of Christianity 1 (Minneapolis: Fortress, 2005), 1–20 at 5.

The aim is history, especially socioeconomic history. Any interpretation is only a means to that end. This approach is of particular value in questioning past overreliance on the sweeping narrative schemes produced by writers such as Eusebius and Bede, which tend to focus on church leaders and secular rulers. The use of early Christian texts as a source of economic evidence is a crucial part of the task of correcting and filling out the picture produced by "grand narratives."

Drawing economic evidence from Christian texts is important in any historical study of the period. Many Roman social historians have been forced into the murky waters of interpretation of the book of Revelation when studying popular responses to the imperial cult. Revelation also includes economic evidence, such as a real or imagined (but still interesting) list of Rome's imports: "gold, silver, jewels and pearls, fine linen, purple, silk and scarlet, all kinds of scented wood, all articles of ivory, all articles of costly wood, bronze, iron, and marble, cinnamon, spice, incense, myrrh, frankincense, wine, olive oil, choice flour and wheat, cattle and sheep, horses and chariots, and bodies and souls of people" (Rev 18:12–13 NRSV, altered)

As long as the historian is careful enough to tackle issues such as the relationship between this text and Ezek 27, there are still interesting points to be gleaned from how this late-first- or early-second-century apocalyptic writer from the province of Asia chose to depict economic aspects of the envisaged downfall of Rome.

Early Christian texts are particularly valuable for social history because of the wide economic range of the movement's members. The only other ancient writings that reach as far down the economic scale are fairly brief, functional texts such as nonliterary papyri and graffiti. Only early Christian texts offer something such as 1 Thessalonians, a letter from an itinerant preacher to a group of people—maybe mainly craftworking families—whom he had persuaded just a few weeks earlier to abandon their traditional religious practices in favor of giving honor to a crucified Galilean preacher and healer. And this is not just a letter of greetings or recommendation as we might find among the papyri, but a substantial text, teaching how to live and how to face death: a substantial first-century text, written for a non-elite audience.

Using Economic Evidence as a Resource for Interpretation

The third possible relationship is where economic evidence is used to contribute to interpretation. The rest of this chapter is given to thinking about how this happens. The best place to begin this is by thinking about the nature of the evidence. We will look at various types of evidence and some opportunities and difficulties in using them.

The Nature of the Economic Evidence

Let us return to wine. To grow vines requires land ownership or tenancy. Vines need planting and tending. Grapes need harvesting and pressing. Wine needs fermenting, storage in amphoras, transport, marketing, and pouring into cups in bars and homes. There are also collateral economic effects, such as sale of food in bars and the need for someone to pay for damage caused by some of the people who drink the wine. There is *archeological* evidence of every stage of this story of wine production and distribution. There is also considerable *textual* evidence, which has been published fairly exhaustively by John Kloppenborg in his book *The Tenants in the Vineyard*.[11] A third category of evidence to help us understand ancient wine production would be *comparative* evidence drawn from studies of more recent communities that produced wine in traditional ways. We shall take each of these three forms of economic evidence in turn: archeological, textual, and comparative (although realizing that some types of evidence, such as inscriptions, fall into more than one category).

Archeological Evidence

The most productive first-century archeological site, Pompeii, yields a wide range of economically significant evidence. Scholars of early Christianity have tended to ignore it. This is mainly because no Christian texts originated there. It is probably also because access to usable data has been difficult. The first of these reasons is, I will argue, misguided. The second is very reasonable but the situation has been rapidly improving, to the point where there is now undoubtedly evidence that can be put to use.

At a macrolevel is the layout of the town. The distribution of housing and businesses, in terms of location and size, suggests various points about the economic organization of society there. Ray Laurence has done valuable work on the geographic patterns.[12] Andrew Wallace-Hadrill has surveyed the range

11. John S. Kloppenborg, *The Tenants in the Vineyard*, WUNT 195 (Tübingen: Mohr Siebeck, 2006), 355–586.
12. Ray Laurence, *Roman Pompeii: Space and Society*, 2nd ed. (London: Routledge, 2007).

of individual houses.[13] We will return to his work when thinking about economic stratification. Individual blocks also tell us interesting things about socioeconomic structure and development. Roger Ling is currently editing a series describing one block in detail, the Insula of the Menander.[14] For almost the first time, through the work of Ling, Penelope Allison, and others, we can see the coordination between various types of evidence in a well-preserved block of houses. For example, the loose finds in House 7 of the block suggest that the inhabitant was something like a cabinetmaker, who maybe also did part-time surgery. The size of the house shows that such a person could afford about eleven or twelve fair-sized rooms. The wall decoration shows that he could also pay someone to come in and paint for him.[15] On an outside wall of the block, a set of graffiti shows that a weaver living nearby was probably literate to some degree. He appears to have read a piece of insulting graffiti about him and to have written a reply (albeit in Latin that is sometimes rather incomprehensible).[16] These kinds of evidence are useful contributions to considering the socioeconomic implications of the description of early Christians as typically being craftworking families. Some craftworkers had money for discretionary spending such as wall decoration—or support of itinerant missionaries. Among poorer craftworkers there could still be functional literacy to permit at least a basic engagement with written texts. There were sufficient social commonalities among Greco-Roman urban centers for this rich Pompeian evidence to be relevant to the debates, despite the town not being the source of Christian texts.[17] As well as the Insula of the Menander, there has been an economically interesting publication of some other Pompeian houses, especially with Joanne Berry's work on finds.[18] Some studies also use tech-

13. Andrew Wallace-Hadrill, *Houses and Society at Pompeii and Herculaneum* (Princeton: Princeton University Press, 1994).

14. Roger Ling, *The Insula of the Menander at Pompeii*, vol. 1: *The Structures* (Oxford: Clarendon, 1997); Roger Ling and Lesley Ling, *The Insula of the Menander at Pompeii*, vol. 2: *The Decorations* (Oxford: Clarendon, 2005); Penelope M. Allison, *The Insula of the Menander at Pompeii*, vol. 3: *The Finds: A Contextual Study* (Oxford: Clarendon, 2006).

15. Ling, *Insula of the Menander*, 1:152–63; Ling and Ling, *Insula of the Menander*, 2:140–47; Allison, *Insula of the Menander*, 3:348–49.

16. M. Della Corte in *CIL* 4.3.I nos. 8258–59. For one possible translation, see N. Lewis and M. Reinhold, eds., *Roman Civilization: Selected Readings*, vol. 2: *The Empire*, 3rd ed. (New York: Columbia University Press, 1990), 277.

17. For a fuller discussion of the Pompeian evidence and its implications see my *Reading Romans in Pompeii: Paul's Letter at Ground Level* (London: SPCK; Minneapolis: Fortress, 2009).

18. For example, Joanne Berry, "Household Artefacts: Towards a Re-interpretation of

niques such as analysis of plant remains and skeletons to draw conclusions about diet and medical care.[19]

Although not as full as at Pompeii, there is economically significant archeological evidence from sites throughout the areas in which early Christian texts were written and read. At Philippi, the archeological evidence shows the substantial Hellenistic framework of the city and indicates its early economic base in gold mining and agriculture. We then see the sharp Roman remodeling of the town after colonization, especially in the Claudian and Antonine forum developments, which testify both to the city's (agricultural) prosperity and to the economic and political domination of the town by Roman colonists. There are also archeological indications of the continuing existence of a substantial, but economically subordinate, non-Roman population.[20] This provides a context for analysis of topics such as the suffering that Paul's letter to the Philippians describes as going on among the largely non-Roman Christians there.[21]

Corinth has been the most common focus of debates in New Testament scholarship on socioeconomic issues. David Horrell and Edward Adams's edited collection, *Christianity at Corinth*, reprints and discusses many of the classic studies.[22] Daniel Schowalter and Steven Friesen edited a useful interdisciplinary collection of work on the city.[23] The debate in which the links between archeology, economics, and interpretation have been most direct has been over whether the aedile Erastus, who donated a pavement to the city,[24] is Erastus, ὁ οἰκονόμος τῆς πόλεως ("the steward of the city"), from whom greetings are brought in Rom

Roman Domestic Space," in *Domestic Space in the Roman World: Pompeii and Beyond*, ed. Ray Laurence and Andrew Wallace-Hadrill, Journal of Roman Archaeology Supplement 22 (Portsmouth, RI: Journal of Roman Archaeology, 1997), 183–95.

19. For Pompeian plant remains, the classic study is Wilhelmina F. Jashemski, *The Gardens of Pompeii: Herculaneum and the Villas Destroyed by Vesuvius*, 2 vols. (New Rochelle: Caratzas, 1979, 1993). See also Jashemski and Frederick G. Meyer's edited collection, *The Natural History of Pompeii: A Systematic Survey* (Cambridge: Cambridge University Press, 2002). For skeletal evidence, the book by Estelle Lazer, *Resurrecting Pompeii* (London: Routledge, 2009), is of particular interest.

20. For the range of Philippian evidence, see especially Peter Pilhofer, *Philippi*, vol. 1: *Die erste christliche Gemeinde Europas* (Tübingen: Mohr, 1995).

21. Peter Oakes, *Philippians: From People to Letter*, SNTSMS 110 (Cambridge: Cambridge University Press, 2001).

22. David G. Horrell and Edward Adams, eds., *Christianity at Corinth: The Quest for the Pauline Church* (Louisville: Westminster John Knox, 2004).

23. Daniel Schowalter and Steven J. Friesen, eds., *Urban Religion in Roman Corinth: Interdisciplinary Approaches* (Cambridge: Harvard University Press, 2005).

24. Erastus appears in this section because of his link to a particular structure in Corinth, but he could just as well have appeared in the "textual evidence" section.

16:23.[25] A further interpretative debate fueled by archeology and economics centers on Corinthian eating practices (we return to this below).

Rome is another site that has, of course, received particular attention, most notably in Peter Lampe's monumental work, which draws eclectically on archeological and textual evidence to trace the socioeconomic development of early Christianity there.[26] There has also been considerable economic analysis of archeological remains from Galilee and Judea. Major studies include those by Sean Freyne, by Douglas Oakman and K. C. Hanson, and by Jonathan Reed.[27]

There are many obstacles to good use of archeological economic evidence. First, archeology is an entire discipline in its own right, with a range of theories and methods. Moreover, as Kevin Greene argues, its use in relation to economics is particularly likely to be best served by several methods.[28] Even the archeology of a single site can be a major subdiscipline. Use of Pompeian evidence, for example, requires careful attention to issues relating both to disrupted circumstances in the decades prior to the eruption and to removal of artifacts in the centuries afterward. Having basically understood the archeological reports on an artifact or site of interest, we then usually need to move on to study aspects of the social history of the period if we are to understand the economic significance of the evidence. Furthermore, to gather worthwhile economic evidence, we often need to use a survey of a sizeable set of data. This brings in the complication of more or less sophisticated mathematics. We can rarely jump from one archeological example to the interpretation of a particular point in a text.

All this constitutes a fascinating challenge for a specialist study. The process, archeology understood in relation to social history and interpretation

25. For arguments in favor see, e.g., Andrew D. Clarke, *Secular and Christian Leadership in Corinth: A Sociohistorical and Exegetical Study of 1 Corinthians 1-6,* Ancient Judaism and Early Christianity 18 (Leiden: Brill, 1993), 46-56. For those against see, e.g., Justin J. Meggitt, *Paul, Poverty, and Survival,* Studies of the New Testament and Its World (Edinburgh: T&T Clark, 1998), 135-41.

26. Peter Lampe, *From Paul to Valentinus: Christians at Rome in the First Two Centuries,* trans. M. Steinhauser, ed. M. D. Johnson (Minneapolis: Fortress; London: T&T Clark, 2003).

27. Sean Freyne, *Galilee from Alexander the Great to Hadrian, 323 BCE to 135 CE* (Wilmington, DE: Glazier, 1980); K. C. Hanson and Douglas E. Oakman, *Palestine in the Time of Jesus: Social Structures and Social Conflicts,* 2nd ed. (Minneapolis: Fortress, 2008); Jonathan Reed, *Archaeology and the Galilean Jesus* (Harrisburg, PA: Trinity, 2000).

28. Kevin Greene, "Archaeological Data and Economic Interpretation," in *Ancient Economies, Modern Methodologies: Archaeology, Comparative History, Models, and Institutions,* ed. Peter F. Bang, Mamoru Ikeguchi, and Hartmut Ziche (Bari: Edipuglia, 2006), 109-36.

of text, can be very fruitful. There is also one more stage in this process, one that takes us from the text to the archeology in the first place. This can vary from a simple observation (e.g., the New Testament name Erastus appearing at a certain place on the site at Corinth) to a complex theory. Oakman, for example, draws on a range of social-scientific theories that take him from the text to particular kinds of evidence and then inform the process by which he moves from the evidence back to textual interpretation.

Help is available in handling the interdisciplinary complexity. Many archeologists and ancient historians have put considerable effort into gathering and drawing together economic evidence. Kevin Greene has already been mentioned.[29] Both Richard Duncan-Jones and Peter Garnsey present material in ways that are particularly usable.[30] An important current way into the scholarship is the *Cambridge Economic History*, edited by Walter Scheidel, Ian Morris, and Richard Saller.[31] One of the most practical imperatives produced by the complexity that we have been looking at is the need for interdisciplinary interaction, both in seminars and one-to-one. A high-quality example of this is the volume on early Christian families edited by David Balch and Carolyn Osiek.[32]

Textual Evidence

Textual evidence comes from papyri, ostraca, inscriptions, graffiti, and literary texts, including early Christian ones. As with archeological evidence, textual evidence can be drawn on either by looking at specific cases in detail or, more frequently for economic issues, by surveying a range of instances of a type of evidence. A crucial area of evidence is the study of papyri of Egyptian census returns. The classic presentation is Roger Bagnall and Bruce Friers's *The Demography of Roman Egypt*,[33] which has been subject to critique by scholars

29. Kevin Greene *The Archaeology of the Roman Economy* (London: Batsford, 1986).

30. For example, R. Duncan-Jones, *The Economy of the Roman Empire: Quantitative Studies*, 2nd ed. (Cambridge: Cambridge University Press, 1982); Peter Garnsey, *Cities, Peasants, and Food in Classical Antiquity: Essays in Social and Economic History*, ed. Walter Scheidel (Cambridge: Cambridge University Press, 1998).

31. Walter Scheidel, Ian Morris, and Richard Saller, eds., *The Cambridge Economic History of the Greco-Roman World* (Cambridge: Cambridge University Press, 2007).

32. David Balch and Carolyn Osiek, eds., *Early Christian Families in Context: An Interdisciplinary Dialogue* (Grand Rapids: Eerdmans, 2003).

33. Roger S. Bagnall and Bruce W. Frier, *The Demography of Roman Egypt* (Cambridge: Cambridge University Press, 1994).

such as Tim Parkin and April Pudsey.[34] The surveys are the main source of frequently quoted results, such as the "average family size" of four. In fact, the results are more specific. In urban settings, the average family size is 4.04, and the average household size is 5.31. The corresponding figures for rural villages are 4.46 and 4.82.[35] For some Egyptian Christian texts, the production context is very close to that of the censuses. For other texts, the sharpest critical issue is how far the Egyptian evidence is specific to its locality and how far it is typical. As with the Pompeian evidence, the Egyptian censuses provide such unparalleled detail that, if used with caution, they are bound to be a factor in debates about households elsewhere in the empire. Another economically interesting example of evidence on papyri and ostraca is the collection of bills and receipts from the Roman fort of *Mons Claudianus* in Eastern Egypt.[36] Graffiti at Pompeii and Herculaneum also yield evidence for prices by advertising the cost of wine and prostitutes.[37]

Among inscriptions, those of associations are of particular socioeconomic interest. For example, the inscriptions listing the *cultores* of Sylvanus at Philippi include people from a range of social statuses, from Orinus *coloniae*, who was presumably a civic slave, to P. Hostilius Philadelphus, who appears both in the list of members and at the top of the inscription as the dedicant and so was probably of high status and wealth.[38] One effect of this and similar association inscriptions is to induce caution in arguing that early Christian communities were distinguished from Greco-Roman associations by the wide socioeconomic spread of church membership. The churches' socioeconomic patterns do indeed differ from those of associations, but the differences are subtler than was once thought.[39]

34. Tim G. Parkin, *Demography and Roman Society* (Baltimore: Johns Hopkins University Press, 1992); April Pudsey, *Sex, Statistics, and Soldiers: New Approaches to the Demography of Roman Egypt, 28 BC–259 AD* (Manchester: University of Manchester Press, 2007).

35. Bagnall and Frier, *Demography of Roman Egypt*, 68, table 3.3.

36. Published in reports by Jean Bingen, Adam Bülow-Jacobsen, and others. The texts are available in the Duke Databank of Documentary Papyri, accessible via the Perseus website: perseus.tufts.edu.

37. For a convenient collection, see the relevant sections of Jo-Ann Shelton, *As the Romans Did: A Sourcebook in Roman Social History*, 2nd ed. (Oxford: Oxford University Press, 1998).

38. Peter Pilhofer, *Philippi*, vol. 2: *Katalog der Inschriften von Philippi*, WUNT 119 (Tübingen: Mohr, 2000), 163–66.

39. As well as being experts on wine production, John Kloppenborg and his research team at Toronto have led the field in gathering and analyzing the evidence for associations; John S. Kloppenborg and Stephen G. Wilson, eds., *Voluntary Associations in the*

Another key group of inscriptions are funerary ones. A classic survey of these is Pertti Huttunen's study of social strata represented in epitaphs from Rome.[40] Funerary inscriptions can also yield evidence about trades and family relationships. As always, there are methodological complications. Valerie Hope, for example, has shown how representation of family relations is not simple documentation but includes projection of how the dedicant wished to be seen.[41]

Literary texts, and other texts that are substantial although not clearly literary (such as astronomical texts and many early Christian texts), yield both general and specific economic evidence. At a systemic level they give evidence of interests and aims of various groups who produce texts. If we are considering, say, someone of scribal class producing the Gospel of Matthew, or someone of Augustine's background producing *The City of God*, analysis of works by other writers of similar socioeconomic level should give some control to speculation about what the relevant interests are. In terms of more specific economic evidence, even elite texts can give good evidence of wider economic life. Seneca's description of apartment living and Pliny the Younger's comments on conditions in Bithynia are of considerable value. And not all Greco-Roman writers are wholly elite. Even some Roman writers who ended up close to imperial circles came from non-elite backgrounds. Horace's father was a freedman (albeit wealthy), and Horace occupied various status levels in his life. We need to exercise caution in drawing economic evidence from Greco-Roman writers. They often have an economically foreshortened view of society, lumping the poor together. There can also be questions of genre that make economic inference complex. The satirical form of Juvenal's works, in particular, is often problematically neglected by social historians who use

---

Graeco-Roman World (London: Routledge, 1996), followed by Richard S. Ascough, *Paul's Macedonian Associations: The Social Context of Philippians and 1 Thessalonians*, WUNT 161 (Tübingen: Mohr Siebeck, 2003); Philip A. Harland, *Associations, Synagogues, and Congregations: Claiming a Place in Ancient Mediterranean Society* (Minneapolis: Fortress, 2003); and Alicia Batten, "Brokerage: Jesus as Social Entrepreneur," in *Understanding the Social World of the New Testament*, ed. Dietmar Neufeld and Richard E. DeMaris (London: Routledge, 2010), 167–77.

40. Pertti Huttunen, *The Social Strata in the Imperial City of Rome: A Quantitative Study of the Social Representation in the Epitaphs Published in the Corpus Inscriptionum Latinarum VI* (Oulu, Finland: University of Oulu Press, 1974).

41. Valerie Hope, "A Roof over the Dead: Communal Tombs and Family Structure," in *Domestic Space in the Roman World: Pompeii and Beyond*, ed. Ray Laurence and Andrew Wallace-Hadrill, Journal of Roman Archaeology Supplement 22 (Portsmouth, RI: Journal of Roman Archaeology, 1997), 69–88.

him as a source. However, Greco-Roman writers remain a vast reservoir of material relating to socioeconomic realities.

Comparative Evidence

When C. R. Whittaker wanted possible figures for the proportion of Rome's population that were poor, he looked further afield. He writes, "One method of getting some idea of Rome's population is by a comparative view of what life looked like in better documented ages."[42] He draws on thirteenth-century Florence, where 70 percent of households had needs that exceeded incomes, and fifteenth- to eighteenth-century Norwich, Lyon, Toledo, and Rome. In these cities, fairly consistently, 4–8 percent could not earn a living, a further 20 percent were permanently in crisis, and 30–40 percent faced periodic crises.[43]

On a broader level, anthropologists such as Julian Pitt-Rivers and historians such as Peregrine Horden and Nicholas Purcell speak of a preindustrial Mediterranean cultural area, which has certain economic features, such as being an advanced agrarian economy with olive production, and some other features with economic implications, such as the common prioritizing of concerns of family honor above creation of conditions for open markets.[44] This conceptual framework made its greatest impact on early Christian studies through the Context Group for Biblical Research, especially Bruce Malina, whose textbook *The New Testament World: Insights from Cultural Anthropology* has run to several editions.[45]

To what extent should we draw economic evidence from contexts that differ geographically, temporally, or socially from the setting of the text that we are interpreting? How can we control the accuracy of use of such comparative evidence? This actually affects our archeological and textual evidence as well. To what extent is Pompeii relevant for Ephesus, or Seneca relevant for Thessalonian craftworkers? This issue affects all fields, not just economics, but,

---

42. C. R. Whittaker, "The Poor in the City of Rome," in *Land, City, and Trade in the Roman Empire*, ed. C. R. Whittaker, Variorum (Aldershot: Ashgate, 1993), 1–25 at 4.

43. Whittaker, "Poor in the City of Rome," 4.

44. Julian Pitt-Rivers, *The Fate of Shechem or the Politics of Sex: Essays in the Anthropology of the Mediterranean* (Cambridge: Cambridge University Press, 1977); Peregrine Horden and Nicholas Purcell, *The Corrupting Sea: A Study of Mediterranean History* (Oxford: Blackwell, 2000).

45. Bruce Malina, *The New Testament World: Insights from Cultural Anthropology*, 3rd ed. (Louisville: Westminster John Knox, 2001).

as in the Whittaker example, it has been a central methodological issue for economic questions. Let us look at some examples.

In 1 Cor 11, Paul criticizes the behavior of the Christians when they meet for communal meals. David Horrell has challenged Jerome Murphy-O'Connor on his use of the Anaploga villa at Corinth as a typical setting that illuminates the issues that could arise if wealthier and poorer people ate together in substantial numbers in a Roman house. Horrell argues that Murphy-O'Connor incorrectly dates the key dining room that he uses. Horrell also suggests a large upstairs hall in an area of housing east of the theater in Corinth as a more likely type of setting for such a meal.[46]

Both Murphy-O'Connor's and Horrell's studies are valuable for interpretation of 1 Cor 11. Murphy-O'Connor moves consideration of the issues into a concrete Greco-Roman context, making effective use of archeological evidence about the economic disparities in dining and the ways in which Roman architecture enshrined them. Horrell has corrected some errors in Murphy-O'Connor's work and has moved the debate forward by describing a type of space for dining that was likely to be more accessible to the Corinthian Christian community. However, a key methodological question is, How far should they be focusing on specifically Corinthian housing to provide the socioeconomic evidence for interpreting the text?

A reasonable first step in contextual study of 1 Cor 11 is to use Paul's letters to Corinth, and archeological and textual evidence about Corinth, to reflect on the probable social makeup of the Corinthian church. We can then think about types of housing the church's members were likely to live in, especially wealthier members, who were most likely to host meals. However, this second step could be done with reference to Greco-Roman housing as a whole, with a particular focus on well-preserved housing. Remains of housing at Corinth would come into this process as a guiding factor. For example, if they suggested a prevalence of apartment blocks, we might focus on examples of such blocks in Rome and Herculaneum. However, in general we should consider a substantial set of possible houses or apartments, a number of which could then be used in reconstructing possible scenarios for 1 Cor 11. Although exclusive use of mid-first-century Corinthian housing avoids some methodological difficulties, this advantage is outweighed by the fact that doing so excludes the

---

46. David G. Horrell, "Domestic Space and Christian Meetings at Corinth: Imagining New Contexts and the Buildings East of the Theatre," *NTS* 50 (2004): 349–69, responding to Jerome Murphy-O'Connor, *St. Paul's Corinth: Texts and Archaeology*, 3rd ed., Good News Studies 6 (Collegeville, MN: Liturgical Press, 1990).

vast majority of the best-preserved relevant evidence. Murphy-O'Connor does actually use some evidence from elsewhere, to show that the Anaploga villa is typical. However, I would suggest that, in principle, both he and Horrell have *overlocalized* the issue. I think this is especially so in Horrell's criticism of Murphy-O'Connor on the dating of the dining room. Since the aim of the exercise is imaginative interpretation by use of a typical setting, it is beside the point to worry about the structure of the rooms at particular dates, unless one could argue that the changes were ones that affected most dining rooms of a relevant type across Corinth as a whole.

Peter Lampe's work on Rome shows the value of localizing a study. Its strength comes from being a well-analyzed collection of evidence that is specifically related to early Christians at Rome. Even so, the analysis would have benefited from more use of comparative material to contextualize the evidence from Rome. For example, when he discusses whether "the external image" of the house churches might have involved comparison with associations, he could usefully have compared aspects of the Roman house churches with aspects of associations elsewhere in the empire.[47] Some of his arguments are also overlocalized in a social sense. A key element of his discussion of the economic level of the early Christians is consideration of which parts of the city of Rome the Christians lived in. As part of this, he looks at burial practices, taking the locations of early Christian catacombs and tracing back into Rome along main roads to find likely locations for Christians who used them.[48] However, by restricting his discussion to Christian evidence he has overlocalized it socially. He needs to consider evidence from other social groups. The method really requires study of all the early burial places, non-Christian as well as Christian. Only by thinking, for the population as a whole, about how burial locations related to where people lived can useful conclusions be drawn about how Christian burial places related to where Christians lived.

Do C. R. Whittaker and, even more so, Bruce Malina go too far in the other direction and underlocalize their studies of aspects of the first-century world? Sometimes this does happen. The significance of slavery in Roman society poses some sharp questions both for use of data from medieval Florence and for Malina's general models of preindustrial urban populations, which try to cover both slave-based and non–slave-based economies.[49] However, although Florence and Norwich are not Rome, there is clearly some analytical value

---

47. Lampe, *From Paul to Valentinus*, chap. 38.
48. Lampe, *From Paul to Valentinus*, 23–38.
49. Oakes, *Philippians*, 40–46, responding to Malina, *New Testament World*, 72–73 (1983 ed.).

in finding out what proportion of urban dwellers tend to be poor in such contexts. Similarly, many of Malina's main economic characteristics of the Mediterranean world, such as a peasant concept of limited good,[50] are clearly relevant to the early Christian period.

For interpreters, the ideal solution to the localization issue must be to keep in mind all levels from the most local to the most general. A practical way forward may be to work with three levels: preindustrial Mediterranean, Roman Empire, and immediately local to the text. For example, to reflect on possible socioeconomic ideas in a text from Rome about petitionary prayer, we might want to think in general about relationships involving dependency and petition in preindustrial Mediterranean societies; we might go on to think about the Roman patronage system; and we might end by thinking about how tenants in a first-century apartment block in Rome would go about trying to gain a favor from someone more powerful.[51]

Keeping these three levels in view seems a practical way of trying to maximize fruitful use of economic evidence. It also provides something of a control for occasions when ideas proposed at one of the levels may not fit well with those relating to one of the others. For example, to help interpret Paul's response to the Philippians' financial gift, we could bring in Seneca's essay *On Benefits*, which handles gift giving and proper responses. This is a useful "Roman Empire level" resource. However, we ought to control its use by analysis of the local socioeconomic situation in the Philippian church, which might limit the relevance of the formal patronage and friendship interchanges that Seneca discusses.

STRATIFICATION MODELS

A methodological issue that has pervasive effects on interpretation of early Christian texts in relation to economic matters is that of how to handle social stratification. No model of social structure can successfully be all things to all people. The question here is about what forms of social-structure modeling can handle economic issues in ways that are as helpful as possible for the interpretation of early Christian texts.

Many scholars of early Christianity make use of Geza Alföldy's classic di-

---

50. Malina, *New Testament World*, 81, 94 (2001 ed.).

51. For an actual study of prayer in relation to patronage, see Jerome Neyrey, *Render to God: New Testament Understandings of the Divine* (Minneapolis: Fortress, 2004), 21-25.

agram of first-century social stratification. His triangular diagram divides its upper part into seven horizontal bands, representing levels within the 1 percent of the population who form the elite. Below that, in the other 99 percent of the population, there is no differentiation in social level as such. However, there is differentiation, at the same social level, between urban and rural and between free-born, freed, and slave.[52] In systemic terms, Alföldy's structure represents a society in which a very small hierarchical elite rules a non-elite that is weakened as a class by division into mutually distrustful categories: urban-rural, free-slave. This is very much in line with Ernest Gellner's model of the "agro-literate state," in which the hierarchical elite rule "laterally insulated communities of agricultural producers."[53]

The chief difficulty in using Alföldy's structure if we are studying early Christian texts is that our interest is almost entirely in the non-elite and he has no differentiation of social level within the non-elite. If our interests are economic, then a further problem is that Alföldy's structure is based on the official Roman status levels, the *ordines*. Even though admission to various upper levels of the *ordines* was based on property qualifications, the *ordines* do not correspond directly to an economic structure. For example, many equestrians were richer than some senators. Alföldy tries to handle some of the anomalies in his system by inserting a small dotted triangle, straddling the elite and non-elite, to represent slaves and freedmen of the imperial household and rich freedmen in general. However, the essential basis of his structure is not economic.

Gerhard Lenski provides another model used by scholars of early Christianity. Whereas Alföldy's is a structure for Roman society, Lenski's is for advanced agrarian economies in general. One way in which the diagram of Lenski's model differs from that of Alföldy is that it rises to a tall narrow point, representing the small numbers of the elite and the wide range of their levels of wealth. Lenski also includes a class of retainers: people just below the socioeconomic level of the elite and dependent on them.[54] This affects studies

52. Geza Alföldy, *The Social History of Rome* (Totowa, NJ: Barnes & Noble, 1985), 146.

53. E. Gellner, *Nations and Nationalism*, 2nd ed. (Oxford: Blackwell, 2006), 9–10, fig. 1, discussed in Ian Morris, "The Early Polis as City and State," in *City and Country in the Ancient World*, ed. John Rich and Andrew Wallace-Hadrill (London: Routledge, 1991), 25–59 at 46–47 and fig. 6.

54. Gerhard Lenski, *Power and Privilege: A Theory of Social Stratification* (New York: McGraw-Hill, 1966), 82. For use in New Testament interpretation, see Dennis C. Duling, "Matthew as Marginal Scribe in an Advanced Agrarian Society," *Hervormde Teologiese Studies* 58 (2002): 520–75.

of early Christian texts because most scribal groups would often be regarded as part of the retainer class. This gives them a close relationship with the elite, which makes the status of texts rather ambiguous. Should they be regarded as non-elite productions if their writers, as a class, are inevitably quite closely identified with the interests of the elite? This must remain a sharp question, especially for texts such as Luke and Acts that are offered to a patron. On the other hand, for study of the socioeconomic makeup of the early churches, Lenski's model is rather too generalized. As with Alföldy, there is not enough differentiation among the non-elite, once our interests move to people below the retainer class.

The view of social structure in Justin Meggitt's *Paul, Poverty, and Survival* is rather like Alföldy's in that Meggitt does not see significant stratification among the non-elite. This is because he is seeking to correct Gerd Theissen and others by arguing that "the non-elite, over 99 percent of the empire's population, could expect little more from life than abject poverty."[55] He argues that all first-century Christians fell into this category, so Theissen is wrong to think that there were some elite among the Christians and that some tensions within churches were due to sharp differences of social level. There are many strengths in Meggitt's handling of an impressive range of economic evidence, and his book has acted as a focus for a great deal of discussion, which we will not revisit here. However, one methodological difficulty is frequently also a problem for other scholars who handle economic issues. It relates to the laws of probability. Meggitt constructs a long series of arguments about individuals mentioned in Pauline texts. The basic form of each argument is "although some scholars have said that such-and-such a piece of evidence shows that person X is affluent, that is not necessarily the case." He then concludes that none of the Christians in the Pauline churches were affluent. A problem with this is that, roughly speaking, he needs to multiply together the probabilities of each person not being affluent to get the probability that not a single one of them is affluent. This is bound to end up as a very low probability.[56] No one handling economic issues (or, ultimately, any issues) can avoid the fact that

55. Justin J. Meggitt, *Paul, Poverty, and Survival*, Studies of the New Testament and Its World (Edinburgh: T&T Clark, 1998), 50.
56. For example, if one out of every three long-distance travelers in the Roman Empire were affluent, it would be true to say that any given traveler was not necessarily affluent. However, if you had ten random travelers, the probability that none of them was affluent would be two-thirds times two-thirds times two-thirds . . . and so on, ten times. The result of that multiplication is less than one-fiftieth—i.e., there is more than a forty-nine in fifty chance that at least one of them is affluent.

their arguments need to be combined in accordance with the laws of prob-ability. In Meggitt's case this seriously weakens his argument. One further difficulty in Meggitt's book is over exactly what should be counted as affluence. We will return to this shortly.

Ekkehard and Wolfgang Stegemann somewhat combine Alföldy and Lenski. Their triangular diagram starts from the top with aristocracy and then retainers. They introduce differentiation of social level among the non-elite by dividing them into "relatively poor, relatively prosperous," "minimum existence," and "absolutely poor." They calculate minimum existence by use of calorific intake, converted into a minimum necessary wage or a minimum necessary size of farm.[57] This threefold division of the non-elite is a substantial step forward. Some information can be gleaned from early Christian texts about wage levels for the people depicted in them—most prominently in the case of day laborers in Jesus's parables. These can be related to the model. However, the differentiation among the non-elite is still fairly limited and there are questions about whether minimum existence is the best criterion for delineating poverty.

This takes us to Steven Friesen's influential 2004 article, "Poverty in Pauline Studies."[58] Friesen constructs what he calls a "poverty scale for the Roman Empire" (see below).[59]

Scale	Group	Percent	Makeup of Group
PS1	imperial elites	0.04%	includes a few retainers and local royalty
PS2	regional or provincial elites	1%	
PS3	municipal elites	1.76%	includes some merchants
PS4	moderate surplus resources	7%?	includes some merchants, some traders, some freed persons, some artisans (especially those employing others), and military veterans

57. Stegemann and Stegemann, *Jesus Movement*, 53–88, especially Social Pyramid I on p. 72.
58. Steven J. Friesen, "Poverty in Pauline Studies: Beyond the So-called New Consensus," *JSNT* 26 (2004): 323–61.
59. Adapted from Friesen, "Poverty in Pauline Studies," 337–47, esp. figs. 1 and 3.

PS5	stable near subsistence (with reasonable hope of remaining above minimum to sustain life)	22%?	includes many merchants and traders, regular wage earners, artisans, large shopowners, freed persons, and some farm families
PS6	at subsistence level (and often below minimum to sustain life)	40%	includes small farmers, laborers, artisans (especially employed), wage earners, most merchants/traders, and small shopowners
PS7	below subsistence level	28%	includes some farm families, unattached widows, orphans, beggars, disabled, unskilled day laborers, and prisoners

In my article responding to Friesen, my main concern was with what constituted a poverty scale and how to define poverty. I took current sociological work on poverty in places such as Britain and India and argued that it is best defined in terms of deprivation, that is, the economically enforced inability to participate in the normal activities of society. The onset of poverty comes quite a way above subsistence level. An effective poverty scale would measure the extent of a person's inability to participate in normal activities.[60] I also had questions about Friesen's figures. At the lower end, he is dependent on Whittaker, so there are the issues about use of evidence from medieval Florence. At the upper end, Friesen, like Alföldy, uses the *ordines*—senator, equestrian, and decurion—as his basic organizing framework. This can particularly be seen in his calculations (some of which use really hair-raising combinations of disparate types of scholarly study). If we are trying to produce an economic model of social structure, the criteria for stratification must be economic. Again, we cannot use the *ordines* as a shortcut to avoid economic analysis. A useful example of why this is so can be seen in John R. Clarke's work on the House of the Vettii at Pompeii. He sees the house as an instance of art among the non-elite.[61] This is reasonable if the *ordines* form the boundary of the elite. The Vettius brothers are freedmen and thus not part of the elite *ordines*.

60. Peter Oakes, "Constructing Poverty Scales for Graeco-Roman Society: A Response to Steven Friesen's 'Poverty in Pauline Studies,'" *JSNT* 26 (2004): 367–71.
61. John R. Clarke, *Art in the Lives of Ordinary Romans: Visual Representation and Non-elite Viewers in Italy, 100 BC–AD 315* (Berkeley: University of California Press, 2003), 98.

However, anyone who has seen their opulent house will know that, if we are using an economic social scale, Clarke's point is far from true. In economic terms, the Vettii are certainly to be numbered among the elite. Social historians and scholars of early Christianity have tended to blur these distinctions.

Given these difficulties, how can we make progress in creating models of economic stratification that are useful for study of early Christian texts? Probably the answer is to think practically. Our aim is not to produce a perfect economic model of society. We only need something that functions well for handling particular texts. We can work with selected, accessible economic indicators, without worrying that we are not depicting every aspect of society.

Each of the following could be a usable economic indicator and is accessible through archeological work: house size, quality of wall and floor decoration, quantity of loose finds of types relating to discretionary expenditure, frequency of access to expensive medical care as indicated in skeletal remains, degree of variety in diet as indicated by study of food remains, and estimated expense of funerary monument.

Each of these could yield an economic scale. Some scales would cover more aspects of society than others. Each scale could incorporate some description of elite/affluent and poor. For example, an economic scale based on variety of diet could, say, take elite households to be those whose diet included a number of high-value imported foods and could take households to be poor if their diet consisted almost exclusively of one or two low-cost staples. Such a diet-based economic scale would be unable to distinguish social structure within households. It would also cover only those households that dumped food remains in certain archeologically recoverable ways. On the other hand, an economic scale based on the medical condition of skeletal remains would work well at relating to individuals rather than just households. However, there would clearly also be all sorts of difficulties with this scale because of issues such as those relating to general standards of health in various groups.

In research for *Reading Romans in Pompeii*, I used control of urban space, measured by house-plan size, as the economic variable for construction of a social scale. Viable samples of this are obtainable at various sites. I used evidence from Andrew Wallace-Hadrill's survey of houses in Pompeii and Herculaneum[62] and followed him in dividing the house-plan sizes into bands of 100 square meters, giving the percentage of houses in each band. At one end of the scale, 34 percent of householders had houses of less than 100 square meters in ground-floor area, 22 percent had houses between 100 and 200 square meters,

---

62. Wallace-Hadrill, *Houses and Society*, appendix 1.

and so on. At the other end of the scale, 0.7 percent had houses between 800 and 1,000 square meters, and 5 percent had houses of more than 1,000 square meters (ranging up to 2,800 square meters).[63]

This produced a model that achieved the key functional objective of differentiating strongly between non-elite households in a first-century context, dividing them into ten economic bands (taking 1,000 square meters as the top; see below), with percentages for each. The model also offers an interesting economic definition of "elite." The percentage of houses in each 100 square meters band decreases fairly steadily until about 1,000 square meters. There is then a small bulge above that size. This suggests that a wealthy group are monopolizing more resources than you would expect in a random distribution of wealth. In that circumstance, I think we can talk about there being an economic elite in that society. My definition of an economic elite would be that they are a wealthy group that monopolizes an undue proportion of scarce resources, as represented in this case by house-plan size. Elite householders, in this model, are those with houses covering an area larger than about 1,000 square meters. The model is not so good at offering a definition of "poor." House-plan sizes go down fairly steadily until some minimum size units, which, in any case, tend to be shops, although typically with some accommodation. We might pick a certain small house size as marking a limit of poverty, but that would be a fairly arbitrary decision.

Many limitations of the model are clear. It represents only ground-floor area. If we were to factor in space upstairs, the strongest effect would be to increase average size at the bottom end of the scale because most inhabited one-room dwellings had a mezzanine upper floor. The model does not distinguish among types of space or location. A vegetable garden comes up looking like a fair-sized house. However, this still represents control of an amount of the rather limited urban space. The model does not represent ownership. Most householders were tenants. However, again, these householders were exercising control over space, whether they paid rent or a purchase price. Most significantly, the model represents only householders. This is a limited fraction of the population. A substantial further group would be members of the householders' immediate families. The rest of the population (maybe about half) would be living as dependents or slaves in other people's houses or

---

63. These are draft figures as of June 2008. The percentages are based on the average of Wallace-Hadrill's three samples, slightly adjusted to reflect different decisions on the inclusion of certain buildings.

would be homeless or living in marginal structures. Dependents varied widely in wealth. The model does not show up that aspect of social structure.

Given all its limitations, and given that it is based on Pompeii, how can this model of social structure be functionally worthwhile for interpreting early Christian texts? It is of value because the Pompeian evidence keys into the kind of economic evidence that many early Christian texts give about their writers, expected audience, or characters in narratives. For example, early Christian texts often give clues about people's occupations. In many instances, Pompeian house contents indicate the occupations of the house's inhabitants. Since we know the size of each house, we can then map some instances of various occupations onto the model of social structure based on house floor-plan size.

Having done this, the model, despite its limitations, begins making exegetically interesting points. Priscilla and Aquila (Acts 18:2; Rom 16:3; etc.) are well-traveled craftworkers who employed Paul in Corinth and hosted a house church. If we put them at a similar social level to the cabinetmaker of House 7 of the Insula of the Menander, that would give them, at Pompeii, a house of 310 square meters.[64] This would be a larger house than 70 percent of householders—a fair way up the scale of householder wealth, and even further up the scale than we would get if we included nonhouseholders. In this craftworker's house they would not have very large rooms, but they would have a garden, a small colonnade, and a couple of rear-facing dining rooms that, altogether, could probably host a meeting of a few dozen. They could, if they wanted, afford a couple of nice Greek mythological paintings on the wall, but they could not run to expensive decoration in every room. Overall, they would have about six times as much housing space as the average person among the bottom 34 percent of householders. Pompeii is not Rome or Ephesus, where we know of Priscilla and Aquila acting as house-church hosts. However, it is interesting, and potentially fruitful for interpretation, to think about the house and culture of a person of Priscilla and Aquila's kind of economic level, even one living at Pompeii.

---

64. Peter Lampe, *From Paul to Valentinus*, 187–95, would put Priscilla and Aquila at a lower economic level, in a workshop of about 27 square meters, with maybe a mezzanine sleeping area above. I agree with his skepticism about scholars who picture them as major entrepreneurs. However, he probably overcompresses the social range of ordinary craftworkers. Within that range, Priscilla and Aquila are likely to have been toward the upper end. For example, although, as he argues, the total cost of their journeys may not have been above about one thousand *sestertii*, this had to be paid out of their surplus, not their basic income. A craftworker at the poorer end of the scale would surely have had great difficulty in generating such a surplus.

Conclusion

I have argued that a number of methodological points should be borne in mind when handling economics and early Christian texts. First, it needs doing. As well as the texts that obviously raise economic questions, about tax collecting, and so on, there are economic issues inherent in many (some would say, all) other texts, either because the socioeconomic location of author, audience, or patron is significant for interpretation or because the theology of the text is expressed in ideas relating to everyday life and hence, often, to economics. Second, we need to distinguish clearly three possible relationships between economics and the text: economics as an analytical framework, gathering of economic evidence as the aim of interpretation, and economic evidence as a resource for interpretation. Third, we can use archeological, textual, and comparative sources for gathering economic evidence. Each has much to offer but has its own methodological challenges. Finally, many models of socioeconomic stratification have proven valuable, and will continue to do so, for interpretation of early Christian texts. However, there could be scope for further progress by use of models that focus on single economic indicators, chosen because they relate in potentially fruitful ways to texts under consideration.[65]

---

65. I would like to thank Dennis Duling and Douglas Oakman for their kind comments on a draft of this chapter.

4 | Economic Approaches: Scarce Resources and Interpretive Opportunities

The relevance of economics to the reading of Paul's letters goes far beyond discussing what he meant by instructing the Corinthians to gather money for his proposed collection for Jerusalem by putting aside, each week, "a sum of money in keeping with his[/her] income" (1 Cor 16:2 NIV) or "whatever extra you earn" (NRSV). Not that this is without great interest in itself. Did the members of the house assemblies have much surplus income? What about any slaves who were members—did they have income too? How was the money held? Did it go into a bank and earn interest? How was it to be transported to Jerusalem, given that it would all be coinage? Why was it needed there? Should we get the idea that the translators of NIV and NRSV were operating on differing assumptions about economics?!

In fact, our discussion is already opening up issues that have significant effects on the reading of all Paul's letters. To whom, in socioeconomic terms, is he writing? Are they typically wage earners? Do these assemblies include slaves or the very poor? On the other hand, are there members of the economic elite? Such questions about the socioeconomic makeup of the communities can have far-reaching consequences. In a particularly influential study, Gerd Theissen concludes that the Corinthian assemblies included members of the elite. He then argues that the social tensions between the rich and the rest of the community members lie behind many of the problems that Paul is trying to deal with in 1 Corinthians. For instance, in 1 Cor 8–10, Theissen argues, it was the social elite who had the attitudes and opportunities conducive to eating food offered to idols.[1] Andrew Clarke similarly sees the presence of the elite among the Corinthians as having led to problems because they continued

---

1. Gerd Theissen, *The Social Setting of Pauline Christianity: Essays on Corinth*, trans. John H. Schütz (Edinburgh: T&T Clark; Philadelphia: Fortress, 1982).

to behave as the elite did everywhere in the Greco-Roman world, competing with each other for honor and precedence.[2]

More broadly, from an economic point of view, what is Paul doing when he writes? He asks for money for his collection to take to Jerusalem. How important a part of his relationship with the assemblies was this? More generally, how did the finances of Paul's life and mission work? Were his letters largely written to his financial supporters? What is going on in the texts where he talks of refusing money from certain communities (e.g., 1 Cor 9)? Thinking structurally, how did Paul's socioeconomic position relate to that of his readers? Was he a member of the educated elite writing for the illiterate poor? Or did he, somehow, share the socioeconomic position of many of the assembly members?

Economics has long had an involvement with Pauline studies, from Adolf Deissmann's study of the social structures of the earliest groups, via the work of Edwin Judge and others,[3] through to a substantial amount of economics-related work, whose authors range across a wide theological spectrum from, for instance, the evangelical Bruce Winter to the radical Richard Horsley.[4] Two major projects highlight the current interest. The People's History of Christianity series switches its focus of interest deliberately away from the prominent, often wealthy, Christian leaders and Christian secular rulers, who dominate traditional church histories, to turn toward the ordinary members of Christian groups, who tended to be far from wealthy.[5] A lecture series at Saint Andrews University and the resulting book, *Engaging Economics*, edited by Bruce Longenecker and Kelly Liebengood, looks at economic issues in relation to a wide range of New Testament and other early Christian texts.[6]

2. Andrew D. Clarke, *Secular and Christian Leadership in Corinth: A Socio-Historical and Exegetical Study of 1 Corinthians 1–6*, Arbeiten zur Geschichte des antiken Judentums und des Urchristentums 18 (Leiden: Brill, 1993).

3. Adolf Deissmann, "Das Urchristentum und die unteren Schichten," in *Die Verhandlungen des neunzehnten Evangelisch-sozialen Kongresses*, ed. Wilhelm Schneemelcher (Göttingen: Vandenhoeck & Ruprecht, 1908), 8–28; Edwin A. Judge, *The Social Pattern of the Christian Groups in the First Century: Some Prolegomena to the Study of New Testament Ideas of Social Obligation* (London: Tyndale, 1960).

4. Bruce W. Winter, *Seek the Welfare of the City: Christians as Benefactors and Citizens*, First-Century Christians in the Graeco-Roman World (Carlisle: Paternoster; Grand Rapids: Eerdmans, 1994); Richard A. Horsley, *Covenant Economics: A Biblical Vision of Justice for All* (Louisville: Westminster John Knox, 2009).

5. Richard A. Horsley, ed., *Christian Origins*, A People's History of Christianity 1 (Minneapolis: Fortress, 2005).

6. Bruce W. Longenecker and Kelly D. Liebengood, eds., *Engaging Economics: New Testament Scenarios and Early Christian Reception* (Grand Rapids: Eerdmans, 2009).

Recent decades have particularly seen a very vigorous debate on the socio-economic level of the members of the Pauline assemblies. The renewed discussion on this long-standing issue was triggered by Justin Meggitt's 1998 book, *Paul, Poverty, and Survival*, in which he argued that all the Pauline community members were, broadly speaking, poor.[7] This was met by an exceptionally vigorous response in a review article by Dale Martin (alongside a less hostile one from Gerd Theissen).[8] In 2004 Steven Friesen supported Meggitt's view but articulated a range of economic levels among the poor by means of a poverty scale.[9] Bruce Longenecker has argued for the presence of a higher percentage than Friesen allowed of people some way above poverty.[10] I have also offered a model for the socioeconomic makeup of a Pauline house assembly, based on analysis of the range of housing in Pompeii.[11] These kinds of studies will continue to feed into discussion of whether we should be reading Paul's writings as letters to encourage mutual support within communities of the poor (as Meggitt would argue) or as letters that navigate their way through the complex issues raised by a wide social mix of people found in the early house assemblies (Theissen, Clarke).

QUESTIONS OF DEFINITION AND SCOPE

Scholars who write on Paul and economic issues come at the subject from a wide range of angles and often use terminology in differing ways. In this field it is always worth looking carefully at the definitions that are being used. Words like "rich" and "poor" are notoriously difficult to define. The term "economics" is itself the subject of competing definitions. Most readers will not need

7. Justin J. Meggitt, *Paul, Poverty, and Survival*, Studies of the New Testament and Its World (Edinburgh: T&T Clark, 1998).

8. Dale B. Martin, "Review Essay: Justin J. Meggitt, *Paul, Poverty, and Survival*," *JSNT* 84 (2001): 51–64; Gerd Theissen, "The Social Structure of Pauline Communities: Some Critical Remarks on J. J. Meggitt, *Paul, Poverty, and Survival*," *JSNT* 84 (2001): 65–84.

9. Steven J. Friesen, "Poverty in Pauline Studies: Beyond the So-called New Consensus," *JSNT* 26 (2004): 323–61, with responses from John Barclay and Peter Oakes.

10. Bruce W. Longenecker, "Exposing the Economic Middle: A Revised Economy Scale for the Study of Early Urban Christianity," *JSNT* 31 (2009): 243–78. See also Bruce W. Longenecker, *Remember the Poor: Paul, Poverty, and the Greco-Roman World* (Grand Rapids: Eerdmans, 2010), 36–59, 220–58.

11. Peter Oakes, *Reading Romans in Pompeii: Paul's Letter at Ground Level* (London: SPCK; Minneapolis: Fortress, 2009), 46–97.

to get too far into the technicalities of this, but it is worth looking at a few prominent options.

I think that a classic kind of definition of economics works well for the first-century world: "the study of the allocation of scarce resources."[12] The word "scarce" is being used here in a technical sense, to mean anything that is not a free, unlimited resource. Air is not generally a scarce resource, although it would be so on a spacecraft. However, for biblical research, this idea of scarcity will usually be assumed, so it is probably safe to simplify the definition to "the study of the allocation of resources."

This kind of definition is not actually popular among current economics textbooks. They tend to prefer something that more closely matches what modern economists spend their time doing. So for instance, a well-known current textbook by Michael Parkin gives a definition that focuses on "the *choices* that individuals, businesses . . . make."[13] I can see how that relates fairly well to the present day. However, it seems to me that it would sit awkwardly with first-century society because, in the first century, the exercise of choice was so restricted for so many that it seems unwise to make choice the key economic topic. Another kind of definition of economics is that of Marvin Harris, a cultural anthropologist. His definition focuses on "provisioning of a society with goods and services."[14] This is clearly related to the definition that I favor. However, Harris's phraseology seems to make the movement of resources sound too benignly purposeful to be ideal for the first century. The "allocation of resources" definition also has the advantage of fitting with the nature of ancient economies as "embedded economies."[15] This term refers to economies that are embedded in their context in such a way that financial factors are inseparable from many other factors such as family, patronal, or political ties. In the first century, resources were not allocated by a free market.

Economics, on the above definition, deals with questions such as: Who allocates resources? Who receives resources, and how much? By what processes are

12. This often-repeated formulation generally continues: "among unlimited and competing uses." It relates to ideas in Lionel Robbins's *Essay on the Nature and Significance of Economic Science* (London: Macmillan, 1932).

13. Michael Parkin, *Economics*, 7th ed. (Boston: Addison Wesley, 2005), 2.

14. Marvin Harris and Orna Johnson, *Cultural Anthropology*, 5th ed. (Boston: Allyn & Bacon, 2000), as cited (from an earlier edition) by Ekkehard W. Stegemann and Wolfgang Stegemann, *The Jesus Movement: A Social History of Its First Century,* trans. O. C. Dean Jr. (Minneapolis: Fortress, 1999), 16.

15. Karl Polanyi et al., *Trade and Market in the Early Empires* (Chicago: Regnery, 1971), 250.

resources allocated? More specifically, what material resources did the early assembly communities have? How did they interact with controllers of resources? How did assembly members allocate the resources that they did control?

I have discussed elsewhere issues in defining the terms "economic elite" ("rich" is a vague term) and "poor." For "economic elite" a viable definition would seem to be "a wealthy group that controls a larger share of scarce resources than would be expected in a random distribution."[16] Many suggestions have been made for defining "poverty." The most persuasive seem to be behavioral ones such as "economically enforced lack of socially perceived necessities."[17] In particular, this draws in a more appropriate, wider range of people than definitions that see only those at or below food subsistence as poor. That loses sight of the many other economic pressures on people in the first century.

Theoretical work on intersectionality has rightly stressed that a person's experience of life relates to a wide range of variables—gender, ethnicity, and so on—that interact in varying ways.[18] This means that a classic Marxist analysis, in which economic factors are substructure and all else is superstructure, is an oversimplification. However, insights on intersectionality do not do away with the fact that many identity variables, while important in their own right, are also important economic markers. For instance, if a first-century group was predominantly female they would, on average, tend to have less access to economic resources than would a predominantly male group of the same size. Gender is significant in its own right. However, it also needs considering from an economic viewpoint. Many other identity markers that are found in New Testament texts also have economic implications: the nature of a person's work, geographical location (e.g., urban/rural), ethnicity, religious practice, and status as slave, freed, or freeborn. The presence of all these in the New Testament texts, alongside more direct economic discourse about collections, wealth, and poverty, and also alongside structural factors such as the socioeconomic location of authors and audiences, invites us to engage in economic analysis of the texts.

16. Oakes, *Reading Romans in Pompeii*, 53–55, exemplifies this definition in relation to house sizes.

17. Peter Oakes, "Constructing Poverty Scales for Graeco-Roman Society: A Response to Steven Friesen's 'Poverty in Pauline Studies,'" *JSNT* 26 (2004): 367–71 at 369, adapted from Joanna Mack and Stewart Lansley, *Poor Britain* (London: Allen & Unwin, 1985), 39.

18. See Elisabeth Schüssler Fiorenza's helpful introduction to the subject in Laura Nasrallah and Elisabeth Schüssler Fiorenza, eds., *Prejudice and Christian Beginnings: Investigating Race, Gender, and Ethnicity* (Minneapolis: Fortress, 2009), 5–18.

THREE TYPES OF ECONOMIC APPROACH

Confusion easily arises between different ways in which economics can be involved in an approach to a text. Three types of approach can be distinguished. Economics can provide the *analytical framework* for interpretation, it can provide the *aim* of interpretation, or it can provide *resources* for interpretation.

In the first approach, *economics provides the analytical framework for interpretation.* This approach is based on assessing the socioeconomic location of the writer, likely readers, and other significant figures in the context. The text is then interpreted by analyzing which socioeconomic groups' interests are promoted by the text and how this is done.

Frequently, such studies will focus on the interests of scribal groups since, inevitably, the producers of texts are very often, in some sense, scribes. This could be seen as true of Paul but most work so far has focused on the Gospels, maybe especially in studies of Q.[19] Gerhard Lenski offered an analysis of ancient social structure in which people such as scribes were part of a "retainer" group.[20] Retainers are a socioeconomic group that, in terms of wealth, tends to sit between the elite and most of the non-elite. Although not elite themselves, retainers are closely dependent on the elite and may, to an extent, identify with elite interests. As well as scribes, priests would, in many societies, be classic instances of retainers (although Roman society was often an exception to this because many priestly roles were held by the elite).

To take a simple example of this approach: a religious text that greatly multiplied and complicated the religious laws that the hearer was expected to keep could be seen as serving the interests of the scribal class by increasing the number of occasions on which their services would be needed to explain the ramifications, and rule on the implications, of the complex legal system. The interpreter might seek to understand ways in which the elements of the text enmeshed the hearers in ever-increasing complexity, induced them to value careful compliance with the system, and encouraged recourse to scribal advice.

The word "class" slipped into the last paragraph, and, indeed, this kind of use of economics in interpretation would, above all, be typical of a Marxist class-based analysis.[21] However, the issues go beyond purely Marxist ones. As

19. For example, Douglas Oakman, *Jesus and the Peasants*, Matrix: The Bible in Mediterranean Context 4 (Eugene, OR: Cascade, 2008), 298–307.

20. Gerhard Lenski, *Power and Privilege: A Theory of Social Stratification* (New York: McGraw-Hill, 1966), 82.

21. See, e.g., Fernando Belo, *A Materialist Reading of the Gospel of Mark* (Maryknoll, NY: Orbis, 1981).

Theissen has shown, the Synoptic Gospels can be analyzed as texts representing the interests of wandering charismatic preachers—a socioeconomic group indeed, but not one that would easily fit into a Marxist scheme.[22]

The response of many to this approach will be skepticism as to its value. However, at some level, these questions must be considered. When Luke writes about Mary singing that God "has brought down the mighty from their seats and has exalted the humble and meek" (Luke 1:52), we surely have to ask whose interests are being served by Luke citing this in his tractate for the "most honored Theophilus."

In the second approach, *economics is the aim of interpretation*: the interpreter reads the text in order to discover economic information about the community members or the first-century world more broadly. Friesen's article does this.[23] He studies Paul's letters, looking for clues to the economic situation of the named characters and groups. The conclusions of the article are economic descriptions. This approach is also characteristic of the People's History of Christianity series. Understanding the socioeconomic circumstances of the Christian groups who are addressed or referred to in the texts is a key aim of the series. The analysis of the texts serves this end.

Anyone attempting this approach needs to be aware that there is an extra complexity to the task beyond the already-difficult problem of trying to find economic clues in the texts. The extra complication is that the interpreter may well need to consider the issues of the first approach alongside the second one. The interests that shape the production of the text will tend to prevent it being a repository of economic clues that can be interpreted in a straightforward way. The text's representation of the economic circumstances of the community members is itself part of the rhetoric of the text. For instance, when Paul, as part of a request for contributions to the collection, tells the Corinthians that the Macedonian assembly members gave "out of their extreme poverty" (2 Cor 8:2), the interpreter needs to consider how this description functions as part of the rhetoric of the passage.[24] Irrespective of the extent to which the interpreter buys into the value of analyzing economic interests, as the

22. Gerd Theissen, *Sociology of Early Palestinian Christianity*, trans. J. Bowden (Philadelphia: Fortress, 1978).

23. Friesen, "Poverty in Pauline Studies."

24. Wayne A. Meeks, *The First Urban Christians: The Social World of the Apostle Paul*, 2nd ed. (New Haven: Yale University Press, 2003), 66, although I think that this verse does actually give good evidence of poverty among the Macedonian assemblies; see Peter Oakes, *Philippians: From People to Letter*, SNTSMS 110 (Cambridge: Cambridge University Press, 2001), 69.

first approach does, the interpreter must still consider how the text functions rhetorically in a variety of ways that may make it less than straightforward to derive economic evidence from it.

In the third approach, *economics provides resources for interpretation*. At the detailed end this relates to understanding the sums of money involved in Jesus's parables. At the broader end is interpretative work such as that of Meggitt, who uses his picture of first-century socioeconomic structure and of the Pauline communities within it to argue that various texts in Paul's letters represent a strategy of mutual economic support among the poor.[25]

Economic evidence that can be drawn on for interpretation can be in various forms: archeological, textual, and comparative.[26] Archeological evidence includes loose finds such as coinage—particularly interesting when found near a body in a particular domestic setting, as in some cases of people trapped by the eruption of Vesuvius.[27] There are also large-scale fixed finds such as housing and associated wall decoration.[28] Textual evidence includes non-elite, nonliterary texts such as ostraca (pieces of pottery reused as writing surfaces), most papyri, and graffiti—for instance the list of wine prices on the wall of a bar in Herculaneum or ostraca carrying lists of goods delivered to the Roman fort of *Mons Claudianus* in Egypt. Other texts are elite, literary works. Again, the rhetoric of these texts needs careful interpretation, but they carry a fair amount of economic evidence, even about non-elite life.[29] Comparative evidence draws on social situations more recent than the first century that operate within patterns that have some comparability to first-century conditions. For instance, the yields of olives from trees farmed in a traditional manner are unlikely to have changed radically over the centuries.

Bringing economic evidence to bear on interpretation of a New Testament text can range from being fairly straightforward to very complex. We have a good idea of what the laborers' wages in the parable of Matthew could have

---

25. Meggitt, *Paul, Poverty, and Survival*, 155–78.

26. Peter Oakes, "Methodological Issues in Using Economic Evidence in Interpretation of Early Christian Texts," in *Engaging Economics: New Testament Scenarios and Early Christian Reception*, ed. Bruce W. Longenecker and Kelly D. Liebengood (Grand Rapids: Eerdmans, 2009), 9–34, included as chap. 3 in the present volume.

27. For example, Penelope M. Allison, *The Insula of the Menander at Pompeii*, vol. 3: *The Finds: A Contextual Study* (Oxford: Clarendon, 2007), nos. 1241–46.

28. For a systematic survey of one location, see Roger Ling and Lesley Ling, *The Insula of the Menander at Pompeii*, vol. 2: *The Decorations* (Oxford: Clarendon, 2005).

29. For instance in the satirical works of Martial and Juvenal.

bought for them.[30] On the other hand, Meggitt's task is, in principle, complex: to deploy his socioeconomic profile of the Pauline assemblies in such a way as to understand the way in which quite a range of texts interact with that profile. A further level of challenge arises when we seek to use economic evidence as a resource for interpretation of New Testament texts that do not relate directly to financial issues. For instance, how does poverty relate to eschatology? Does Paul expect his hearers to be longing for a change in the world, or are they in economic circumstances that encourage them to be quite happy with matters as they are?

We will now turn to a passage that I have much engaged with, Rom 12.[31] How does this text look if studied using each of our three types of economic approach?

Within an Economic Analytical Framework:
An Itinerant Missionary Writes to a Potential Support Base

A basic element of this approach is that Paul is not, in principle, considered as a unique individual. He is considered as representing a socioeconomic group whose interests he is assumed to be promoting when he writes. The one sense in which this approach sees Paul as an individual is that, while promoting the value of his socioeconomic group, he is also seen as promoting his own interests over against other members of that group. Putting this in concrete terms: Paul is seen not as a distinct personality but as representing the interests of itinerant missionaries and as competing with other itinerant missionaries.

In line with this type of reading, Paul can be seen as seeking to perform three functions in the chapter: first, promoting the value of itinerant missionaries and practical support for them; second, strengthening the potential support base, that is, the assembly groups at Rome; third, encouraging the groups to have allegiance to him.

Much of the evidence for the first and third points belongs together. Looking at the text, in the first instance, in relation to itinerant missionaries as a group, we can see the whole chapter as carrying the implicit message: You assembly members at Rome need guidance from outside—there are important things about the life of this community that you haven't figured out for yourself. This is, of course, true of all the teaching sections of Paul's letters,

---

30. See, for instance, the calculation in Stegemann and Stegemann, *Jesus Movement*, 81–85.

31. Oakes, *Reading Romans in Pompeii*, chap. 4.

but it is important nonetheless. It is particularly clear in a passage such as Rom 12, in which the external writer is giving advice about the mechanics of how the groups at Rome should organize their internal affairs. It is also true notwithstanding Paul's disclaimer in 15:14–15. That text values the Roman assembly members' knowledge and insight, but it does not stop Paul thinking that they need his advice. Structurally, the New Testament letters represent a pattern of settled assembly groups in various towns, being resourced by a network of traveling teachers who visit them and write to them. A structural aspect of the rhetoric of the letters is that it reinforces dependence on the network of teachers.

More specifically, the way in which the opening of Rom 12 sits in the letter shows the itinerant missionary as the one with the insight (and education) to ground his practical instructions in a complex and compelling theological framework (Rom 1–11). This is a level of skill that is not likely to be available to a local house assembly. Paul reinforces this more specifically with a reference to the missionary calling of the itinerant teacher: "through the gift that I have been given," which enables him to "say to each one among you" (12:3). In 12:4–5 Paul uses the first-person plural to talk about the body of Christ and ministries within it. As well as a rhetoric of solidarity, this switch to "we" tends maybe to draw attention to the element of experience that the itinerant missionary brings: "we" have seen what happens in house assemblies all over the place. The itinerant missionary brings a breadth of experience that less-traveled community members lack. Among further specialist skills that Paul demonstrates in the chapter is knowledge of the Bible and of how to interpret it for their situation (12:19–20). Most house assemblies would presumably not even possess a copy of the Septuagint. The itinerant missionary could know many key texts and would have a hermeneutical system for applying them to the present time.

Romans 12:13 probably presents the early Jesus movement as being more than local. Here, and explicitly in 15:25–28, there are seen to be financial links between assembly communities in different places. Paul's "one body in Christ" statement in 12:5 probably also includes some sense of translocal unity. A movement with translocal links, such as the early Jesus movement, needs people who move around, in order for the links to function. The translocal aspect of the early Jesus movement therefore validates the role of itinerants. More specifically, Paul, as an itinerant, acts as the person organizing financial support between these groups. Their financial-support network depends on itinerant missionaries.

The second exhortation in 12:13 is about "pursuing hospitality." One can understand why the NRSV chose to render the Greek as "extend hospitality to strangers." The translators presumably wanted to avoid the impression that Paul was referring to members of a house assembly feeding each other. However, their introduction of the term "strangers" may miss a key application of the verse. It is likely to have related, among other things, to the prominent early practice of assembly communities welcoming and economically supporting itinerant missionaries. Paul effectively asks for such hospitality in 15:24 (cf. Phlm 22). Although itinerant missionaries might be strangers in the sense of being outsiders visiting a house assembly, they must generally have arrived as people of whom the house church already had some knowledge and who often carried letters of recommendation, as Phoebe does in the text of Rom 16:1–2.

This reading interprets Rom 12 in two further ways. The teaching of the chapter is seen as strengthening the group of recipients. It does so in terms of their organization (12:6–8), their cohesion (12:3–5, 9–10, 15–16), and their interactions with outsiders (12:14, 17–21). Economically, this can be seen as enhancing the stability of the potential support base for the itinerant missionary. A stronger group can offer fuller support. Finally, as indicated above, all the evidence in Rom 12 about Paul promoting the role of the itinerant missionary can also be read as Paul encouraging the group to have allegiance to him. Although they have not previously benefited from his ministry (except indirectly through people such as Prisca and Aquila), he has a particular gift from God that enables him to speak to each one of them (12:3). Paul makes this point at length in 15:15–19. Now he wants to come to them and have their support while he is with them and in his proposed mission to Spain.

As an Economic Source Text:
Contributing to a Socioeconomic Profiling of Early Groups

In this approach the text is being read with the aim of discovering economic data. There are two kinds of data that we could look for. First, we could look for evidence of existing economic circumstances among the hearers to whom Paul thinks he is writing. If Paul knows the situation of the Roman house assemblies, the text could give evidence about that. If Paul knows little about them, we would need to view the text as more generally indicating the circumstances of house assemblies that he had encountered. Second, we could look for evidence of the types of socioeconomic relationships that Paul wanted his hearers to adopt. These relationships are unlikely to be purely aspirational. They are more likely to represent practices that, at least to an extent, are already in place in some assembly groups that Paul considers to be running well.

The first economic evidence that Rom 12 provides is a general indication of the sort of numbers in early groups. Group size is a basic factor in estimating the total amount of economic resources available to a group. The first indication of number is the word "many" in 12:5: "we who are many are one body in Christ." Although the "we" in that sentence suggests that Paul could be thinking of all who are "in Christ" everywhere, the list of ministries that follows suggests that he also has the local "in Christ" group in mind in his discussion of "members" and "the body." In that case, there would be "many" in an assembly community. Clearly, "many" is not a fixed number, but it at least implies several, probably going beyond a single family. This point is supported by the list of "gifts" that Paul sees as providing forms of service in the house assemblies (12:6–8). The degree of elaboration in these, and the types of gifts—leading, teaching, and so on—imply that the groups are reasonably large: say, twenty and upward.

Economically, a key significance of group size is that the group, collectively, controls economic resources that are an order of magnitude (that is, more than ten times) greater than the resources that most of the individuals control. This provides the group with increased ability to withstand financial shocks. It also opens up possibilities for actions that most individuals could not undertake, such as providing money to external groups such as the recipients of Paul's collection.

As well as numbers, the system of gifts and ministries in 12:6–8 implies certain socioeconomic structures. It may imply a structure in which some people dedicate part of their time to house-assembly activities rather than work that brings in money. Life for most of the first-century non-elite was economically so constrained that virtually all available time will normally have been used, when possible, for craftwork and so on. Even meeting together regularly will have been financially difficult for some. The taking on of any roles that required time beyond the meetings must usually have meant some other person or people effectively contributing to their support, even if that was only in releasing them from expectation of work, rather than paying them as such, although we do know of financial support of leaders being an issue in other letters (Gal 6:6).

The list of gifts in Rom 12:6–8 includes "sharing," which is done "with generosity." James Dunn argues that the association of "cheerfulness" with "showing mercy" implies that that too is likely to be an economic issue.[32] These gifts

32. James D. G. Dunn, *Romans 9–16*, Word Biblical Commentary 38B (Grand Rapids: Zondervan, 1988), 732.

imply that some assembly members in particular are giving financial support either to outsiders or to others within their assembly community. Either possibility is economically interesting. My impression is that relationships with outsiders are more in focus from 12:13 onward, so internal economic support is maybe more in view in 12:8. In either case, the first implication of these ministries in 12:8 is that there is not economic equality within the assembly community. Although, in theory, an economically equal group could exist in which some had the gift of sharing and others did not, that would make the rhetoric of 12:8 very strange. It is much more likely that some wealthier members of the group were feeling moved to share with poorer members. A second economic implication is that property was not held in common in the group (as in the Lukan picture of the early Jerusalem assembly).

A third piece of economically relevant information is that the house assemblies have translocal links (interestingly, the chapter does not discuss links between house assemblies in Rome, although that issue may be implicit in Rom 14–15). In principle, translocal links could be a further source of economic stability, especially when a crisis is caused by a local condition such as an earthquake. However, in Rom 12, the only economic effect of translocal links seems to be to place extra financial burdens on the Roman house assemblies: "sharing in the needs of the holy ones, pursuing hospitality" (12:13). Locally, there may be a further economic outflow from the group implied by the enigmatic encouragement in 12:16 to "being carried away to lowly people."

The groups implied by Rom 12 have very difficult relationships with outsiders. They are persecuted (12:14), have evil done to them (12:17, 21), and have enemies (12:20). The rhetoric against taking revenge in these circumstances is so marked that Paul seems to believe that persecution of the assembly communities is actually occurring. As I have discussed elsewhere, this need not be specifically religious persecution. It could be part of the typical negative group interaction that was common in the streets of Rome and elsewhere.[33] However, whatever kind of difficulty is implied by 12:14–21 (and by the "suffering" in 12:12), it will almost certainly have had negative economic consequences. In the "embedded economy" of the first century, almost any trouble ends up being economic trouble, whatever else it involves.

In the economic group context that we have been sketching so far, Paul's rhetoric evokes relationships within the group that have strong potential economic consequences. The group members are "parts of each other" (12:5). They are called to unhypocritical love (12:9), "brotherly love" (12:10; see below),

---

33. Oakes, *Reading Romans in Pompeii*, 123–26.

honoring one another (12:10). What would be the economic consequences of such practices? They might be taken as implying that all the group members had control over the group's economic resources. However, my impression is that Paul is not calling for the kind of radical sharing that results in something like common ownership. Sharing looks more likely to be an ongoing activity within a setting that continues to include some structural inequality. On the other hand, the rhetoric of love presumably implies a quite substantial degree of commitment to mutual economic support within the group. Paul's rhetoric projects a situation of some real rearrangement of access to resources but short of an abolition of existing socioeconomic structures. This probably reflects his experience in at least some of the communities in other cities.

With the Help of Economic Evidence: Ecclesiology for Craftworkers

The previous section, as well as using Rom 12 as an economic source text, was in fact drawing on economic evidence to help interpret the text. For instance, the rhetoric about persecution gives us economically significant data, but we then need to draw in broader first-century evidence about the economic effects of suffering in order to interpret what the persecution might involve. We can, however, go much further in using first-century economic evidence to construct a scenario for reading the chapter. A way of doing this is to construct a socioeconomic model for a house assembly in first-century Rome, then examine how the rhetoric of the chapter interacts with the model.

To construct our model we can begin by considering Roman apartment blocks and craftworkers. Let us follow the common scholarly assumption that typical first-century members of these communities were craftworkers. This is particularly pertinent for Paul's expected hearers in Rome because the house-based assembly that he refers to in 16:5 is hosted by tentmakers, Prisca and Aquila. In the urban landscape of Rome, the most common kind of location for craftworkers who might have space to host an assembly would be a ground-floor workshop in an apartment block. In the *Insula Aracoeli*, for instance, which dates from the Neronian period, we have the classic form of such a block with ground-floor workshops, mezzanine apartments above the workshops, spacious apartments on the next floor up, then increasingly cramped apartments on the higher floors.[34]

---

34. See, e.g., Andrew Wallace-Hadrill, "*Domus* and *Insulae* in Rome: Families and Housefuls," in *Early Christian Families in Context: An Interdisciplinary Dialogue*, ed. David L. Balch and Carolyn Osiek (Grand Rapids: Eerdmans, 2003), 3–18 at 14–15.

A craftworker who rented a workshop and some living space could host a small house assembly, meeting in the workshop. If there were, say, thirty people in the group, that would presumably mean the craftworker's household, a few other complete or partial households, and probably a few individuals whose head of household was not a community member. The absolute numbers are not too important. What matters is the type of socioeconomic structure that emerges.

The house/apartment assembly consists of several components. First there is the host's family, entirely or almost complete. That usually means a male householder who has primary control of all the household's resources. There is then typically a wife, children (young or adult), maybe a couple of slaves, and other dependents such as elderly relatives. There is a clear socioeconomic hierarchy within such a household. The assembly also includes a few other partial or complete households. Each will replicate the kind of socioeconomic structure in the host's household except that the other households will tend to be poorer and smaller. For instance, they are less likely to include slaves. Given that the difficulties of wives of husbands who were not also community members are discussed more than once in New Testament texts (1 Cor 7:12; 1 Pet 3:1), our model house assembly should include some members from non-Christian households. Such people would occupy a curious socioeconomic position: part of the house assembly but with a primary location in an external socioeconomic structure. All in all, the house assembly is quite a complex socioeconomic structure.

The socioeconomic location of the house assembly within Roman life is anchored by the position of the host who will tend to be the highest-status person belonging to the group. During analytical work on housing in Pompeii, drawing on earlier work by Andrew Wallace-Hadrill, Roger Ling, and others,[35] I studied a cabinetmaker's house (I.10.7, called by the Italian archeologists the *Casa del Fabbro*). This house was 310 square meters in size, larger than 70 percent of other dwellings in Pompeii but less than a third of the size of the smallest elite houses. If the tenant occupying this house hosted an assembly, we could locate the probable socioeconomic situations of members of this group as being spread across the bottom 70 percent of household income levels and across the range of slaves and other poor dependents. In Rome, although av-

---

35. Oakes, *Reading Romans in Pompeii*, chaps. 1–2; Andrew Wallace-Hadrill, *Houses and Society in Pompeii and Herculaneum* (Princeton: Princeton University Press, 1994); Roger Ling, *The Insula of the Menander at Pompeii*, vol. 1: *The Structures* (Oxford: Clarendon, 1997); Allison, *Insula of the Menander*, vol. 3.

erage sizes of accommodation would be smaller than Pompeii, it would seem reasonable to assume a roughly similar shape to the socioeconomic structure. This could locate the wealthiest craftworker hosts, such as probably Prisca and Aquila, at a higher income level than more than half the population, although still a long way below the income of the elite. The community members would generally be at economic levels spread out from this point downward.

If we now use this socioeconomic model of a Roman house assembly to help us read Rom 12, it becomes apparent that the rhetoric of the chapter is constructing an idea of the assembly, an ecclesiology, that poses considerable potential challenges for life within the house assembly's socioeconomic structure.[36] At some points, the rhetoric also interacts interestingly with the group's socioeconomic location.

The following points from the chapter look particularly pertinent. In 12:1 the assembly is a family: "brothers and sisters." Also in 12:1 it is a priesthood, offering "a living sacrifice." In 12:3 it is a community where faith is the measure of status. In 12:5 the assembly is "one body in Christ." Moreover, the members are "parts of each other." In 12:6-8 the ministries of the assembly are gifted by God. In 12:10 the assembly is a community of "brotherly love" and of mutual honoring. Finally, in 12:16 it is a community "thinking the same thing" and focused on the poor rather than on grandiose ideas.

If we think of the assembly as a family, as one body in Christ, as a community of love, this is attributing a oneness to the group that would be quite radical if even a single household adopted it as a pattern for relationships within it. However, the house assembly goes beyond this. Several households are involved, as are people who do not belong to a Christian household at all. Economically, first-century craftworker households were primarily free-standing units competing with other households to bring in sufficient income to live and, if possible, to enhance the status of the householder. The ecclesiology of Rom 12 challenges the boundary of the household, presenting a new social structure in which the interests of a wider group take over from household interests.

Conversely, individual members from non-Christian households become part of this new trans-household structure, of which their own household heads are not a part. This must often have caused conflict within these kinds of families.

As well as togetherness, the ecclesiology of Rom 12 involves a reciprocity that challenges the assumptions of household socioeconomic structures: "we

36. For a fuller discussion of these points see Oakes, *Reading Romans in Pompeii*, chap. 4.

are parts of one another" (12:5); the members give honor, presumably to each other (12:10). The assembly includes owners, slaves, men, women, adults, children, wealthier, poorer. First-century households might have a kind of unity, but it was unity based on hierarchy. The slave honored the master but not vice versa. The reciprocity of Rom 12 poses quite a challenge to this. In line with that, self-evaluation within the group is not to be on the basis of status. In 12:3 after Paul warns against overvaluing yourself, he then ties true value somehow to faith, which is not a human achievement but something that "God has distributed."

The ministries of the assembly are organized charismatically (12:6–8). They too are gifts from God (12:6). In principle, this cuts across the socioeconomic order of the household. The householder controls the resources. He therefore gets to allocate the work. In the assembly the ministries depend on gifts from God. Having said this, we have already noticed that "sharing" is a gift that may well be linked to having economic resources at your disposal. It is not clear whether there would be assumptions about some of the other gifts too—for instance, whether teachers might be expected to be literate.

In the rather mysterious 12:16, the assembly is presented as having a socially downward focus, "not thinking high things but getting carried away to the humble." This is a curious contrast, but it probably makes more sense as a pair in the first century than now. In the first century, a contrast between intellectual activity and the lives of the "humble" is a contrast between wealth and poverty. Both high-level education and the leisure to discuss intellectual matters were attributes of the wealthy. The assembly is to be focused on action with the poor rather than academic reflection. All this rather inverts the normal order of the household. The household is primarily to serve the interests of the householder. The effort of the household is focused upward, to benefit the person at the top. The assembly is focused the opposite way.

Finally, two elements in the ecclesiology of Rom 12 interact in interesting ways with the overall social location of the assembly community. The first is the characterization of the members as priests, each offering a living sacrifice, their own body (12:1). Much could be said about that but the point is that, in Rome, priests generally belonged to socioeconomic groups different from those of the house assemblies. In particular, the prominent priesthoods at Rome were occupied by members of the elite. The characterizing of the assembly as a priesthood ascribes to the members a status they would not normally be seen as having.[37]

---

37. Cf. Peter Oakes, "Made Holy by the Holy Spirit: Holiness and Ecclesiology in Ro-

A second element in Rom 12 that may operate in a similar manner is a characterization of the assembly in terms that sound rather like the discourse of some types of elite male groups. This could be said of much of the language of love and mutuality. However, the issue is particularly raised by the term φιλαδελφία ("brotherly love"; 12:10), and by the phrase τὸ αὐτὸ εἰς ἀλλήλους φρονοῦντες ("thinking the same thing as one another"; 12:16). As Alan Mitchell argues in relation to Acts and Joseph Marchal in relation to Philippians, the latter phrase sounds particularly evocative of the interaction of elite male friends.[38] Φιλαδελφία too, although it could evoke a range of ideas and is not even inherently male, could well give the impression of the assembly as the kind of society that might previously have been thought of as arising among men gathered in an association, particularly among elite males.[39] If the ecclesiology of Rom 12 does evoke this kind of setting, its rhetoric is doing unexpected things in addressing a mixed-gender, mixed-status group, none of whom—or almost none of whom—had a socioeconomic location that fitted the normal social setting of such language.

Conclusion

We have looked at three approaches to using economics in the study of Pauline texts and have tried out each of them in relation to Rom 12. The second and third approaches are ones that I draw on fairly regularly in my own work. The first approach is likely to evoke strong positive or negative reactions; however, it does raise important questions for consideration in analyzing what is going on in the rhetoric of New Testament texts. All three approaches deserve serious attention. Paul's letters handle a wide variety of issues, theological as well as social, but, whatever the issue, we should keep in mind that the text is written in a context that, as all human contexts, inescapably involves economics.

---

mans," in *Holiness and Ecclesiology in the New Testament*, ed. Kent E. Brower and Andy Johnson (Grand Rapids: Eerdmans, 2007), 167–83.

38. Alan C. Mitchell, "The Social Function of Friendship in Acts 2:44–47 and 4:32–37," *Journal of Biblical Literature* 111 (1992): 255–72; Joseph A. Marchal, "'With Friends Like These . . .': A Feminist Rhetorical Reconsideration of Scholarship and the Letter to the Philippians," *JSNT* 29 (2006): 77–106.

39. See, e.g., the terminology of ἀδελφοί in association inscriptions cited in Richard S. Ascough, *Paul's Macedonian Associations: The Social Context of Philippians and 1 Thessalonians*, WUNT 161 (Tübingen: Mohr Siebeck, 2003), 76–77.

5 | Urban Structure, Patronage, and the Corinthian Followers of Christ

> To stand at the door of an upper-class Roman house of the late
> republic or early empire is already to glimpse something of the
> centrality of patronage in Roman society. . . . The way the Roman
> house invites the viewer from the front door, unparalleled in the
> Greek world, flows from the patronal rituals so often described
> in the Roman sources: the opening of the doors at dawn to the
> crowd of callers, the accessibility of the dominus to the public,
> his clients and his friends. Patronage was at all periods for which
> we have information central to the way the Roman upper class
> wished to present itself to the world.
>
> —Andrew Wallace-Hadrill

Patronage was indeed central to the way the Roman elite presented itself to
the world. This went beyond what the Romans would have called *patrocinium*.
From a social-scientific viewpoint, patronage was a social relationship central to behavior throughout the preindustrial world (and, of course, it still
lives today). A full social-scientific definition of patronage is complex but its
core characteristics are that it is a nonmarket relationship between socially
unequal people in which dissimilar benefits are exchanged.[1] The most characteristic exchange involves the patron providing access to resources normally
unavailable to the client, and the client providing honor to the patron. This
relationship went beyond Romans to other groups in the empire. Patterns
of Roman elite behavior are replicated in many non-Roman cities. It went
beyond the elite. The house of a cabinetmaker in Pompeii has a stone bench

---

1. S. N. Eisenstadt and Louis Roniger, *Patrons, Clients, and Friends: Interpersonal Relations and the Structure of Trust in Society* (Cambridge: Cambridge University Press, 1984),
48–49.

outside, a structure that archeologists have often taken as a sign of exercise of patronage. Irrespective of that, the size and style of the cabinetmaker's house suggest that, although he himself was almost certainly someone else's client, he probably did exercise some patronage to people further down the scale.[2] Patronage also went beyond affecting just the design of individual houses. It provides a key to understanding many features of the structure of towns and cities in the New Testament period.

The places where most New Testament texts were written and first read out were Greco-Roman urban centers such as Ephesus, Corinth, Antioch, and Rome. We shall consider how the layout of such towns reflected the exercise of patronage. We shall think about how the structure of various particular types of town related to variations in forms of patronage. We shall then reflect on texts from Rom 16 and 1 Corinthians by considering how first-century Corinthian followers of Christ related to their urban environment.

A Patronage Model of First-Century Urban Layout

Andrew Wallace-Hadrill walks his reader into a Roman house.[3] If we did the same for a Greco-Roman town, such as Pompeii, what would we see? Before we reached the town gate we would walk past dozens of elaborate funerary monuments, proclaiming the status and achievements of the town's wealthier families. We would then walk through a substantial gate in an impressive wall, once needed for defense but now lending weight to the impression of the town's status and also enabling some control of activities. Then on into a street lined with shops, bars, and domestic doorways, all mixed together—bakers, shoemakers, bars selling food, grand house entrances, humble doors to upstairs apartments. Graffiti and *dipinti* (painted rather than scratched into the plaster) covered the walls—scurrilous abuse, advertising for house rental or wine or prostitutes, and election propaganda. As we walked into town along the street we would see other streets opening off ours, generally in a grid pattern. Then, suddenly we would reach the end of the street and come out into a dazzling main square—the shaded relative narrowness of the street being replaced by

2. Patronage defined social-scientifically not classically—elite Roman writers would not have talked about patronage operating at such a level. For discussion of this house, see Peter Oakes, *Reading Romans in Pompeii: Paul's Letter at Ground Level* (London: SPCK; Minneapolis: Fortress, 2009), 15–33.

3. The quotation at the start of this chapter is from Andrew Wallace-Hadrill, "Patronage in Roman Society: From Republic to Empire," in *Patronage in Ancient Society*, ed. Andrew Wallace-Hadrill (London: Routledge, 1989), 63–87 at 63–64.

an area bathed in sunlight. This main square was surrounded by impressive buildings, many of them temples, and filled with statues and other honorific monuments. There were practical facilities around the square—usually a market here or nearby—but the main planning of the space was for show.

A basic element of the layout of first-century towns (including large cities) was the presence of a central space, the most obvious feature of which was elite display.[4] Alternatives to a Roman forum, such as a Greek *agora*, would, at this period, also function in this way. In the central space, members of the civic or more distant elite were honored by statues and inscriptions in return for benefaction to the town, especially by provision of buildings and festivals, or by representing the interests of the town in Rome.[5] The design of the forum, and its prominence in the town, proclaimed that the town operated under a patronage system. The statues and inscriptions in the forum showed who the town's main patrons were.

A patronage model of urban structure first sees the town as a central display area for the elite (the patrons) surrounded by the rest of the town (the clients). The civic elite were patrons in three ways. Individually, they each had a network of clients. Collectively, they operated a rotating system of individual patronage of the town as a whole. Particularly when each held a magistracy, they paid for public buildings and events such as games at the amphitheater. Third, the civic elite acted as brokers, on the town's behalf, in dealings with higher, external patrons such as senators and emperors. Many forum inscriptions honor such patrons. Implicitly, they also honor the civic elite who brought the town such patronage.

Ancient writers did not, as far as I know, use patronage language to describe the benefactions made by magistrates in office. It is also controversial, sociologically, to argue that such benefactions constituted patronage (it would be a form with a collective client).[6] The broad argument, however, seems hard to resist, that the centering of a town on a space designed for display of benefaction by, and honoring of, the civic elite represents a patronage system.[7] It proclaims the message, "We are the patrons in this town. Everything good

---

4. Elsewhere in the town, there would also be subsidiary elite display areas at other points of particular benefaction, such as temples and theaters.

5. Richard P. Saller, "Patronage and Friendship in Early Imperial Rome: Drawing the Distinction," in Wallace-Hadrill, *Patronage in Ancient Society*, 49–62 at 54–56; D. Braund, "Function and Dysfunction: Personal Patronage in Roman Imperialism," in Wallace-Hadrill, *Patronage in Ancient Society*, 137–39.

6. See Eisenstadt and Roniger, *Patrons, Clients, and Friends*, 221–22, 245–46.

7. For a definition, see Terry Johnson and Chris Dandeker, "Patronage: Relation and System," in Wallace-Hadrill, *Patronage in Ancient Society*, 219–41 at 220–21.

that is done for it is by our favor. Moreover, we act as the brokers who give the town access to these excellent external benefactors who you see also honored here." The elite domination of the town is ideologically supported by the presentation of the relation between the elite and the town as being a mutually beneficial interchange in which the elite provide benefactions and the town responds with honor.

The center of a typical modern town is not like this. There may be the occasional statue to someone such as a key founding figure but there is no pervasive honoring of the town's elite. Instead, the pervasive image is of shops (in most of the world and in some US cities, such as New York and Philadelphia, in which downtown shopping remains prominent) and other businesses. There is status display to be seen in the impressiveness of shop frontages and corporate headquarters. The function of the status display, however, is primarily advertising. This reflects the difference between modern and ancient societies in distribution of wealth. The modern non-elite customer is the main source of wealth for companies, so the town center is given over to advertising to, and catering for, the customer. In the ancient town, the elite, who controlled the town center, gained most of their income from agricultural rents and production, so their priorities for use of the town center were not the modern ones.

A glance at the pattern of housing in Pompeii reveals that, although some areas have a higher concentration of large houses than others, large houses are generally scattered across the whole town. This suggests a second level of a patronage model of a Greco-Roman town: that, at local level, the town is made up of a set of small patronage networks, each controlled by a member of the elite (or, for very small networks, by someone non-elite but reasonably well off). The classic cross-cultural point of comparison for this is Jacques Heers's study of the division of medieval Italian towns into neighborhoods persistently dominated by the houses of heads of clans.[8] Dominic Perring uses Heers's evidence as suggesting the likely link between "the clan-like ties of *familia* and *clientele*" and the common mixing of rich and poor housing in Roman towns.[9] The comparison can actually be made more securely, without the risky analogy between clan and *clientela*. The elite domination and patronage that Heers demonstrates covers the people in the neighborhood generally, not just the members of the clan that controls it.

8. Jacques Heers, *Family Clans in the Middle Ages: A Study of Political and Social Structure in Urban Areas*, trans. B. Herbert (Amsterdam: North-Holland, 1977), 146–54.

9. Dominic Perring, "Spatial Organisation and Social Change in Roman Towns," in *City and Country in the Ancient World*, ed. John Rich and Andrew Wallace-Hadrill (London: Routledge, 1991), 273–93 at 284.

Particular evidence in favor of the existence of local patronage networks within towns is provided by Henrik Mouritsen's study of the thousands of *programmata*, endorsements of candidates for local elections, found on walls in Pompeii. He maps their locations and finds two patterns for where *programmata* for particular pairs of candidates were situated. The strongest pattern is a preference for main roads, where the *programmata* would be seen most often. There is also a clear secondary pattern that some candidates are represented more heavily in particular parts of the town. In some cases the candidates' actual houses are known. There is a fairly clear pattern of those candidates being especially well represented in the vicinity.[10] As Mouritsen says, it is hard to be sure of the motives behind the placements of all the *programmata*.[11] Local patronal influence, however, does seem an especially likely explanation for preferential use of walls in particular areas for particular candidates.

Our patronage model of urban layout of a Greco-Roman town operates at two levels. At a town level, the patronage model sees the basic layout as being an elite display center, which represents the honoring of the town's patrons, surrounded by the rest of the town, whose population forms the client base for these patrons. Even people who are not, individually, clients to particular elite patrons form part of the town as a client group. The town receives benefactions, such as the provision of games, from various members of the elite in turn. In return the town puts up honorific inscriptions (and, in an ironic social twist, this means, in practice, the elite town councilors putting up inscriptions for each other). At a local level, the patronage model sees the detailed layout of the town as an agglomeration of small patronage networks, typically dominated by a large house or apartment.

Like any model, this one picks out a few key features of the environment and seeks to conceptualize them. Greco-Roman towns had many other features, some of which can usefully be thought of in patronage terms and some of which cannot. Temples are a good example of features that relate closely to patronage. They fit into a patronage model in two ways. First, they act as large honorific monuments for the human patrons who pay for their erection and maintenance. The patron confers both the benefit of provision of the building itself and, by paying for the cult, the benefit of brokerage in relation to the deities as external patrons. Second, temples represent the influence of the

---

10. Henrik Mouritsen, *Elections, Magistrates, and Municipal Élite: Studies in Pompeian Epigraphy*, Analecta Romana Instituti Danici Supplement 15 (Rome: "L'Erma" di Bretschneider, 1988), 50–56, 69, figs. 4–8.

11. Mouritsen, *Elections, Magistrates, and Municipal Élite*, 52.

divine patrons themselves, who are honored at the temples in return for their favor. The temple precinct reminds people of the patronage of both the gods and the elite.

THE PATRONAGE MODEL AND VARIOUS TYPES OF CITY

As well as offering an explanation for some features of the layout of a typical Greco-Roman town, a patronage model offers some suggestions for differences in layout between major types of town.

Rome, from Aristocratic Republican City to Palace City

When Nero built the gargantuan *domus aurea*, sprawling across the center of Rome, we might see it as an attempt to change Rome, in patronage terms, from one type of city to another. Traditionally, the center of Rome—the Forum and its surroundings—had been an area of display for the city's elite as a whole. In patronage terms one might call Rome an "aristocratic republican city." This is effectively the model that we have been describing so far as the typical Greco-Roman one. The aristocratic elite paid for buildings and games and received honor in the Forum. The aristocratic elite were the patrons of the city.

This republican urban structure had been eroded by the building programs of the early Caesars, but it was still significantly present. Nero, however, by replacing much of the center of Rome with a vast complex of magnificent buildings dedicated to the emperor, could be seen as turning Rome into a "palace city." In a palace city, instead of a central display area for the elite in general, it is for display by a single ruler. A large palace dominates the central area. Other forms of honoring are also focused on the ruler. In patronage terms, the urban layout represents the message that "the ruler is patron."

After Nero's death, the Flavian emperors demolished much of Nero's building, returning Rome to a shape more in tune with its republican ideology. Having said this, the longer Rome was under emperors, the more strongly the central area reflected the patronage of them alone.

Athens, the Classical Greek City

The classical Greek city had an ideology of independence. In terms of urban layout, this was represented especially by possession of city walls and an acropolis. This was a fortified hilltop within the city walls. Its ability to provide safety under external attack was warrant of the city's autonomy. The presence of walls and an acropolis in a city layout represent the message: "we have no external patron." Athens, Thessalonica, and many other Greek cities fall into this category.[12] The classical Greek city is probably one key source for the grid layout that characterized many first-century towns. As well as giving a general signal about ability to "civilize" the environment, this also possibly represented something of a democratic ethos: "there are no patrons here." The urban structure is developed rationally, rather than growing up around a palace or other buildings of the elite.[13]

The Roman Colony

One particular form of grid layout was the specifically Roman one, laid out around the crossroads of the *decumanus maximus* and the *cardo maximus*. This pattern, especially prevalent in Roman colonies, had military overtones, originating in the layout of legionary camps. The layout was part of a broader pattern of specifically Roman elements that came to be used in other towns as well as colonies. Many of these elements imitated the city of Rome. The most striking was the presence of a forum, especially when it evoked the position of the Capitoline Hill. At Rome, the temples of the three greatest Roman gods, Jupiter, Juno, and Minerva, stood on this hill at the head of the Forum. At Philippi, the temple of this Capitoline Triad of gods overlooked the forum from the hillside just above it. At Ostia there was no hill available, but the temple was set on a raised platform, built at the head of the forum. The message of such a layout in Roman colonies or their imitators was "Rome is our patron."

The Temple City

A final type of town was a temple city. In such a city, a large temple dominates the central display area or another prominent location. This urban layout rep-

---

12. In Thessalonica's case this was ironic, because the walls and acropolis were built by a Hellenistic king. However, such exceptions prove the ideological rule. The Macedonian kings were strongly hellenized, wanting to engage in Greek life as Greeks. Their equipping of towns with the appurtenances of an independent Greek city was a strong expression of their Hellenistic ideology.

13. For both avoidance and occurrence of patronage in Greece, see Paul Millett, "Patronage and Its Avoidance in Classical Athens," in Wallace-Hadril, *Patronage in Ancient Society*, 5–47.

resents the message "this deity is our patron." Such a message implicitly carries a further one, which would be central to the city's status and economy: "we are the brokers for this deity." The elite of the city controlled access to the benefits that the deity could bring. In the case of a major cult center such as Ephesus or Jerusalem, people would come from distant cities to the central temple, bringing substantial honor and income.

Sjoberg's Preindustrial City

This analysis of types of city allows us also to comment, in patronage terms, on Gideon Sjoberg's classic model of the preindustrial city, known to New Testament scholars particularly through Richard Rohrbaugh's innovative use of it in relation to Luke's Gospel.[14] Sjoberg studied urban patterns across a range of preindustrial cultures. He found a frequent pattern in which a central area of elite residence, with a palace and temple, was separated by a wall from the surrounding city, which was itself physically separated into several sections, with particular areas often relating to particular trades.[15] In terms of our patronage model of urban structure, this is a very sharply marked form of palace city (with the temple presumably subordinate to the palace). The ruler is the sole patron. Moreover, his or her patronage mainly extends only to the elite, who live with the ruler in the central area. Unlike the Greco-Roman model, the elite do not themselves exercise patronage over groups of people around the town.

The strong physical barriers testify to the weakness of patronage links with the non-elite and, conversely, the weakness of non-elite allegiance to the ruler and the rest of the elite. The physical barriers between groups of the non-elite replace one of the subtle functions of a patronage system. The barriers put a limit on the ability of the non-elite to form a coherent group—and thus maybe threaten the elite. Patronage does the same thing. It builds a social system in which vertical social links, between rich and poor, are more important than links between the poor. In a strongly patronal system, the poor tend not to act together as a class. This shape of social system is characteristic of Ernest

14. Richard L. Rohrbaugh, "The Pre-industrial City in Luke-Acts: Urban Social Relations," in *The Social World of Luke-Acts*, ed. Jerome H. Neyrey (Peabody, MA: Hendrickson, 1991), 125-49.

15. Gideon Sjoberg, *The Preindustrial City: Past and Present* (New York: Free Press, 1960), 91-103.

Gellner's model of the "agro-literate state," in which the hierarchical elite rule "laterally insulated communities of agricultural producers."[16]

The Sjoberg model is rooted in a range of cultures, so it is interesting that typical Greco-Roman towns differ sharply from it. In historic cultural terms, Greco-Roman towns may be rather unusual. Such towns were the main centers of production of New Testament texts. There are New Testament texts, however, where we find cities more like the Sjoberg model. They probably appear in several of Jesus's parables, in which powerful rulers hold sway over their populations. Rohrbaugh's study shows how Sjoberg's model can fruitfully be put to work on these texts.

CORINTHIAN FOLLOWERS OF CHRIST AND A PATRONAGE MODEL OF URBAN STRUCTURE

In Rom 16, three Corinthians are named and something is indicated about each of their social situations. A range of social circumstances are also discussed in 1 Corinthians. Several scholars, most notably John Chow,[17] have considered this letter in relation to patronage issues. If we, however, take texts in 1 Corinthians that, explicitly or implicitly, put the Corinthian Christ followers at various places in the city, and then consider these in relation to our patronage model of urban structure, some further interpretative possibilities emerge.

We will apply the general patronage model for the structure of a Greco-Roman city to Corinth. Corinth was also a Roman colony and, to an extent, it fits the more specific Roman colony patronage model, in which elements of the urban structure (especially the grid pattern, laid out at the colonial foundation in 44 BCE and prominent buildings such as the Julian Basilica) testify to the whole city, including the elite, being client to Rome as patron. Consideration of this model will affect our handling of one scenario for the eating of idol meat in 1 Cor 8–10. We must, however, not overstate the significance of this model for understanding Corinth. The effect of Corinth's colonial identity on its urban structure is rather ambiguous. Most notably, although the forum occupies a space formed by the grid laid out at colonization, the buildings in the forum are aligned differently. Some monumental Greek constructions in

16. Ernest Gellner, *Nations and Nationalism*, 2nd ed. (Oxford: Blackwell, 2006), 9–10, fig. 1; applied to cities in Ian Morris, "The Early Polis as City and State," in Rich and Wallace-Hadrill, *City and Country in the Ancient World*, 24–57 at 46–47 and fig. 6.

17. John K. Chow, *Patronage in Corinth: A Study of Social Networks in Corinth*, JSNTSup 75 (Sheffield: JSOT Press, 1992).

the forum survived from classical Corinth (sacked by Romans in 146 BCE). Moreover, even the new Roman buildings are more closely aligned to some of the Greek structures than to the colonial street grid.[18] In layout terms, there is some qualifying effect on the sense of Rome as the city's sole patron. Greek cultural reference points are also given some honor. In many ways, Corinth is more like a general Greco-Roman city than like a typical, overwhelmingly Roman colony such as Philippi or the many colonial foundations in the west of the empire.

The Corinthians of Romans 16

Three of the Corinthians named in Rom 16 can be related fairly confidently to our patronage model. Phoebe, a διάκονος ("deacon") of the church in Cenchreae and a προστάτις ("benefactor") to many, including Paul (16:1-2), is presumably a local patron in an area of the eastern port settlement of Corinth, about ten kilometers from the city center. Similarly, Gaius, "the host to me and to the whole church" (16:23), must have a fair-sized house and reasonable financial resources. He seems likely to be a local patron in an area of Corinth.

As we have seen, this does not mean that Phoebe and Gaius were necessarily (or even probably) elite, in the sense of being at the social level of civic patrons of Corinth. The Pompeian cabinetmaker probably exercised some low-level patronage and could rent a house of sufficient size to host a meeting of a few dozen, which was conceivably the extent of the Corinthian "whole church." Having said this, his patronage would have been rather limited. It could not have made the cabinetmaker the patron of the local area. His house is right next to the vast House of the Menander, whose owner was of senatorial level and was probably landlord and patron to the cabinetmaker. If there are cases where someone at the upper end of the social range of craftworkers acted as a local patron, this would probably be local in the sense of being a network that included a number of people from a particular area, rather than the craftworker being the area's main patron. In fact, one of the main patronal functions of such a low-level patron would be as broker for access to an elite patron to whom the craftworker was client.

Romans 16 does not show that Phoebe and Gaius were elite, although it does suggest that they were each at the center of some local patronage network.

18. David Gilman Romano, "Urban and Rural Planning in Roman Corinth," in *Urban Religion in Roman Corinth: Interdisciplinary Approaches*, ed. Daniel Schowalter and Steven J. Friesen (Cambridge: Harvard University Press, 2005), 25-59.

Paul's indication of their social status could function for the Roman hearers as an indication of the success of the gospel in Corinth in making inroads into society in some parts of the city.

Erastus, the οἰκονόμος ("steward") of the city (16:23), has been subject of long debate: whether he was of high or low status; whether he is the archeologically attested Erastus the aedile, who dedicated a pavement in Corinth in or around the first century CE.[19] Irrespective of the answer to these questions, we can think about the Erastus of Rom 16 in relation to urban layout. Whereas Phoebe and Gaius are probably local patrons, Paul asserts that Erastus relates to the urban center. A follower of Christ is presented as having some sort of responsibility for the city as a whole. The Christ movement has penetrated to the heart of the city. It is curious that Paul points this out. Possible analogies are his assurances to the Philippians that the gospel has spread "among all the Praetorium" (Phil 1:13) and that there are followers of Christ in Caesar's household (4:22)—the imperial slaves and freed slaves. A likely intended function of these assurances is to encourage the Philippians as they undergo suffering: the gospel can survive and prosper even in the empire's central places. The reference to Erastus's position could be intended to offer some encouragement to the hearers of Romans.

Taking Cases to the Judges of Corinth (1 Cor 6:1–11)

In 1 Cor 6:1–11, Paul criticizes the Corinthians about lawsuits. Very surprisingly, the main focus of the criticism is not on the fact of lawsuits between believers: "Does one of you dare, having a grievance against another, to take it to be judged by the unrighteous and not by the holy ones?" (6:1). The key issue is about who is judging. In terms of urban layout, the Corinthians are going into the elite display center, where the matter will be judged in one of the basilicas or other spaces around the forum. This is the zone of elite urban patronage. By coming here for resolution of disputes, the followers of Christ put themselves under the patronage of the city's elite, as judges, advocates, or juries.

Paul rejects the structural implication. Even the lowest-status follower of Christ is more suitable than an outsider to adopt the patronal position of

19. For the two sides, see Andrew D. Clarke, *Secular and Christian Leadership in Corinth: A Sociohistorical and Exegetical Study of 1 Corinthians 1–6*, Ancient Judaism and Early Christianity 18 (Leiden: Brill, 1993), 46–56; and Justin J. Meggitt, *Paul, Poverty, and Survival*, Studies in the New Testament and Its World (Edinburgh: T&T Clark, 1998), 135–41.

resolving a dispute (6:4–5). Paul trumps the city's social structure by appeal to a larger structure, that of the universe. In the lawcourts of the universe as a whole, the assembly of Christ's followers lies at the heart of the system. They, and not the first-century social elite, will act as judges of the world and even of angels (6:2–3).

Places Where People Eat Idol Meat (1 Cor 8–10)

In 1 Cor 8–10, Paul deals with an issue raised by the Corinthians about food offered to idols. Geographically, he considers three scenarios. First, there are people who are "reclining in an idol temple" (8:10). This is probably the same situation as is characterized in 1 Cor 10:21 as "sharing in the table of demons." Second, there are people buying meat in the meat market, presumably to eat at home (10:25). Third, there are people who are invited by a nonbeliever to eat with them, presumably at their home (10:27).

The first scenario worries Paul most. He is concerned about people who are participating in meals held in Greco-Roman temples (8:1, 7, 10; 10:19–22). In terms of our patronage model of urban layout, one of two possible events is happening. Either the people are going to the forum and its vicinity, to take part in religious meals sponsored at a civic level, or they are taking part in meals in temple areas away from the center, such as the slopes of the hill of the Acrocorinth or individual locations around the town.[20] In both cases there is a double patronage at work, although the specific shapes differ somewhat.

The double patronage is of human sponsor and sponsoring deity. For a cultic meal in the urban center, the participants implicitly put themselves under the patronage of the civic elite. There will usually have been one person who has paid for the particular festival. This, however, will often have been done as part of his holding of a municipal office, so there was also a sense of the meal as a civic function. For a cultic meal in the urban center, the deity who was viewed as divine patron of the event would tend to be one strongly tied to the city's identity. For the Roman colony of Corinth, this especially meant the imperial family or the definitively Roman gods such as the Capitoline Triad or Roma herself. As participants put themselves under the patronage of such a deity, they were not only expressing allegiance to a god, they were also expressing allegiance to Rome as a divine superintending power. Clearly, we must not overstate the commitment expressed by eating a meal, but to go to

20. For temples in Corinth, see Nancy Bookidis, "Religion in Corinth: 146 BCE to 100 CE," in Schowalter and Friesen, *Urban Religion in Roman Corinth*, 141–64.

the urban center and participate in one of the civic religious meals did carry at least a symbolic commitment to patronage of the local elite, the deities in question, and Rome as a divine governing force.[21]

The other possibility is that the criticized group is dining at one of the local temples around the city. In this case we should think in terms of local patronage networks. Human patronage of a temple could be a key public element of patronage of a local area. The deity who, in a sense, was viewed as host of the meal, might also be seen as patron of the area. It could be useful to think of the area around a local temple as being like a temple city, writ small.

In either situation, followers of Jesus who participated in cultic meals in Corinth placed themselves, at least symbolically, under both human and divine patronage. Paul was bound to disapprove of the latter. His reaction to the issue of lawsuits in 1 Cor 6 means that he was also likely to have concerns about the former.

Eating a meal at home, using meat bought at the market, raised none of these issues of patronage. Although market buildings often carried dedicatory inscriptions celebrating the person who paid for the building, it would be going too far to say that people would see goods bought in the market as being bought under that person's patronage. Similarly, the meat itself was presumably not advertised as coming from the temple of a particular deity, even if some was the surplus from a festival meal that involved a sacrifice. Away from the temple, the meat was not provided under the deity's patronage. In fact, Paul may make a counterassertion to any such idea: "The earth belongs to the Lord—and everything in it" (1 Cor 10:26, citing Ps 24:1). If there is any patron for the general providing of meat, it is God, not a Greco-Roman deity to whom it may have been offered.

For some types of Corinthian followers of Christ, one of the most likely occasions for being invited to someone's house to eat (1 Cor 10:27) would have been if they had a patron. The invitation would then be a patronal benefit to the client. This practice was an element of traditional Roman patronage. Clients in that kind of relationship might tend to be at the upper end of the non-elite. This means that most Christ followers would be excluded, as being too poor. Eating at the house of a local patron would not have an obvious link to issues of idol meat. Paul is relaxed about such meals (10:27). This may also mean that he is happy for Christ followers to continue to accept local patronage from nonbelievers. In the gospel accounts, Jesus and his followers accept invitations to meals from all sorts of people. His one caveat occurs when the host draws attention to the temple

---

21. Cf. Chow, *Patronage in Corinth*, 147–57.

origins of some meat. The follower of Christ should then decline it (10:28). There is, however, no patronage issue here, as far as I can see.

When You Gather Together as an Assembly (1 Cor 11:17–34)

Our final example is the problem about communal meals, criticized by Paul in 1 Cor 11:17–34. Since the groundbreaking work of Jerome Murphy-O'Connor, scholars have given much thought to the possible concrete realities of this situation, as it would work out in a Roman domestic setting.[22] This work is very valuable, revealing a wide range of points at which the norms of Greco-Roman household structure and behavior would raise difficult issues for a socially mixed community that ate together.

Our model suggests that we may be able to take this one stage further. The implicit geographical note here is the gathering together (11:18). The group of Christ followers from across the city comes to a single place. The host of this meal clearly has accommodation of some size. This makes it rather likely that he or she will be patron of a local network. If that is the case, then the behavior that Paul criticizes becomes quite easily explicable. Although patronage involved transfer of benefits—such as provision of a meal—between patron and clients, the relationship was founded on structural inequality. If a patron participated in a meal with clients, we would expect the meal to reflect the structural inequality. Patrons stop being patrons if they do not generally eat more food, and more expensive food, than clients. This is sharpened by the patron's need to project his or her status beyond the people gathered at the meal. The patronal network might extend across several blocks of houses. Maintenance of the patron's position required maintenance of appropriate status relationships. Paul's challenge to social differentiation in provision of communal meals could cause difficulties for maintenance of patronal relationships, both with fellow believers and with other people in the local area. Paul's instructions would stop the meetings of the assembly from being occasions for demonstration of structural inequality—the structural inequality that was, and is, inherent in patronage.

---

22. Jerome Murphy-O'Connor, *St. Paul's Corinth: Texts and Archaeology*, 3rd ed., Good News Studies 6 (Collegeville, MN: Liturgical Press, 2002); David G. Horrell, "Domestic Space and Christian Meetings at Corinth: Imagining New Contexts and the Buildings East of the Theatre," *NTS* 50 (2004): 349–69.

6 | Jason and Penelope Hear Philippians 1:1–11

This chapter is based on part of my thesis "Philippians: From People to Letter,"[1] the first half of which is a study of the church at Philippi. One chapter in the thesis models the development of the Roman colony of Philippi. The next considers the social structure of a church likely to arise in that context. A further chapter discusses evidence in the letter of suffering in the church. It then considers what this was likely to involve. I conclude that the most likely form of long-term suffering in Philippi would be economic suffering caused by breakdown of some relationships with non-Christians. The breakdowns would largely be caused by non-Christians seeing that converts have stopped honoring the gods.[2] Such suffering would tend to be more acute among the poorer, more dependent, Christians.

In the second half of the thesis, I imagine how certain aspects of the letter were likely to sound to Philippian Christians. I consider Christ's accession to lordship in the light of the Philippians' experience of imperial ideology. I also consider the relationship between the themes of suffering and unity, as they would be heard by Philippians listening to 1:27–2:11. Before either of these investigations, I try sharpening my perception of the material on suffering in the letter by listening to the letter from the viewpoints of two imaginary hearers. One of them has suffered a great deal, the other has suffered very little. The imaginary hearers are reconstructed from my social data about types of people likely to be in the church. They are essentially vehicles for helping me to use the social data in engaging my imagination in the study of the text.

---

1. Peter Oakes, "Philippians: From People to Letter," DPhil thesis, Oxford University, 1995, supervised by N. T. Wright.

2. See Martin Goodman, *Mission and Conversion: Proselytizing in the Religious History of the Roman Empire* (Oxford: Clarendon, 1994), 105; Robin Lane Fox, *Pagans and Christians in the Mediterranean World from the Second Century AD to the Conversion of Constantine* (Harmondsworth: Viking, 1986), 38, 95, 98.

JASON AND PENELOPE

Jason is a Greek of Macedonian descent. He is married to Chloe, who is also a Greek Christian. They have four young children. Jason's forebears farmed near Philippi, but his own profession has been as a goldsmith, working for his cousin. He was spared any agonizing over whether to continue doing work for temples because, as soon as his cousin found out that Jason had become a Christian, he sacked him. For the last eighteen months, Chloe and Jason have faced a desperate financial struggle, keeping their family alive through Jason doing casual farm-laboring, mainly for other Christians, and Chloe doing some very poorly paid work as a waitress in her second cousin's tavern. Six months ago, Jason was involved in a fight after a discussion with some former friends. He ended up with a night in jail and, since then, has found casual labor harder to find—even from Christians. Jason thinks of himself as something of a hero. To their great regret, he and Chloe did not manage to send any money to Paul.

Penelope, along with her husband, Isidoros, was one of the most generous contributors to Paul's gift. She and Isidoros moved to Philippi from Asia and run a business importing fine Italian pottery—made in one of the areas from which many of the colonists' grandparents came. When a number of their customers found out that Penelope and Isidoros had become Christians, sales dropped by 20 percent and, on one morning, thirty-nine pots were smashed. However, much of the business is from farmers in the countryside, and people have tended to forget or have decided that they do not mind too much. Neither Penelope nor Isidoros gets involved in any high-profile (or even rather low-profile) attempts to persuade others to become Christians, and Isidoros, who rents some land near the town, has become rather less ready to employ certain people in the congregation. However, the couple are regular attenders of church meetings and were, as noted above, among the most generous contributors to Paul's gift. Penelope is a little unsure of how good a Christian she is, in the light of the heroics of people such as Jason (and Paul).

Jason was pleased that there was no direct reference to the gift in 1:1–11: he had been very disappointed that they had not managed to contribute to it. Instead, Paul, knowing the difficulties at Philippi, had focused on their fellowship with him in their continuing faithfulness to the gospel (1:5), faithfulness even to the extent of sharing Paul's chains (1:7)—which was generous of Paul since none of them was facing a trial for his or her life. Paul encouraged them by promising that God would sustain them through their difficulties right through to Christ's return (1:6). He also acknowledged the value of their ministry of evangelism in Philippi (1:7)—although Jason was slightly galled by the insistent πάντας (1:4, 7 [twice], 8), especially at this point (end of 1:7). Did Paul not realize that one of the main problems at Philippi was that people like Isidoros were not pulling their weight? Jason was also caused to reflect a little by the prayer for increased love (1:9), but decided that Paul was *probably* thinking about the wealthier Christians failing properly to help people like him and Chloe. Jason was encouraged by 1:10, feeling that he had weighed the importance of various things and had gone for the things that really counted. (In this, he was slightly fooling himself, since the differences between what had happened to him and to Penelope arose principally from the difference in their prior social circumstances, rather than from some difference in how they acted when they became Christians.)

Penelope was pleased by Paul's warm expression of gratitude for the gift in 1:1–11. He clearly continued to value highly his relationship with the Philippian community. He recalled their friendship with him and financial support of his mission (1:5) and expressed his confidence that God would enable them to continue their support (1:6). He saw them as being thus involved in everything that he did or suffered for the gospel (1:7). As the word πάντας came up at the end of 1:7, a momentary uncharitable thought went through Penelope's mind, about those who had not contributed to the gift. But she realized that neither she nor Paul would dream of regarding those less well off in the church as not having participated fully, in some sense, in the gift to him. She wondered whether the prayer for ἀγάπη (1:9) was directed toward Euodia and Syntyche: she knew that Paul knew about them. Penelope was a little disturbed by 1:10. In the light of the more zealous activities of people like Jason, were she and Isidoros really making the most important things their priority?

Jason had been waiting to hear a letter from his suffering hero. In 1:1–11 he heard Paul expressing warmth toward the Philippians as they shared with him by going through the same suffering. Penelope had been waiting to hear from the missionary she supported. In 1:1–11 she heard Paul expressing appreciation for their financial support. Each hearer "filled in" relatively open terms in the text from their own perspective.

If my two hearings are plausible, this has implications for four contexts: Philippi, reception in the modern context, Paul's writing of the letter, and the general study of the text.

What would happen in Philippi? This might depend on how closely Penelope and Jason were in communication. If they were in different house churches, the divergence in the hearings might go unnoticed, especially if each person was in a house church whose members shared their kind of perspective. If Penelope and Jason communicated and realized the divergence, there might be an authoritative figure who would express the community's standard interpretation. This might or might not correspond with Paul's intention. It would be more likely to do so if the authoritative figure was Epaphroditus or someone else close to Paul. An alternative scenario would involve Jason and Penelope agreeing that Paul intended both hearings: that he had left the text deliberately open. Such a decision would reflect the hearers' expectations about Paul—as would many features of their hearings anyway. Jason and Penelope could also simply disagree about Paul's intention.

It is interesting to note that thoughts about Paul's intentions seem likely to be more important in a process of arbitration than in the original hearing. Although the hearers' expectations about Paul are always important as they hear, the hearers' own perspectives are a very strong factor too. In a process of arbitration, the hearers' perspectives must, conventionally, be subordinated. A factor agreed by both parties must dominate. The most obvious role remaining for the hearers' own perspectives would be in motivating them to defend their original hearing.

Leaving aside the issue of arbitration, there is the question of the function of the passage as it is heard. Jason and Penelope each hear the passage in their way, and the passage seems to function well for each of them. It functions to bind each of them closer to Paul as he identifies with each at an appropriate point. It also functions to encourage each in their particular Christian walk: Jason as he stands firm under suffering; Penelope as she applies her money to the relief of need.

If, after arbitration, Penelope decides that the passage should be heard in Jason's way, the passage stops functioning effectively for her in the way that it did. It will start functioning in a different way—probably by making her think that she ought to be behaving more like Jason does, which she would expect to result in suffering. If Jason, who has not contributed to Paul's gift, decides that the passage should be heard in Penelope's way, it would probably become dysfunctional. Jason would hear Paul thanking people other than him in the church for their gift. At best, Jason is likely to be only a spectator of the passage. At worst, the passage might distance Jason from Paul somewhat. This would be the opposite of the function that Paul clearly intends for all the Philippian hearers.

Considering reception in the Philippian context sheds light on the issues involved in reception in the modern context. All the same issues seem to be present, although various factors differ in degree. This difference is most pronounced in the factor of communication between people or groups who hear the text in different ways. In the modern context (and in any context since the letter was first heard widely), lack of communication is endemic. This is, first, because the hearers of the text will belong to groups far more separated from each other—physically, culturally, and in terms of experiences—than two house churches in Philippi. Another factor hampering communication is distrust and dismissal. Some groups will think that hearings by some other groups are not worth listening to.

There are also two specific areas of change between Philippi and now. First, there is now no Epaphroditus who may have discussed the letter with Paul as he wrote it. Also, none of us knows Paul personally, as many Philippians did. This places a limit on the point we can reach in appeal to Paul's intention as arbiter. This limitation is counteracted to an extent by our possession of the wider corpus of Paul's letters. Another resource that we have is centuries of traditions of hearing of the passage by others. A second area of change is in the balance between modes of receiving the passage. I would imagine that most people still hear the passage read out, rather than reading it themselves. However, when it is read out it would tend then to be expounded by a preacher. Even if some explanation of the letter was given in Philippi, it is unlikely to have been such a decisive shaping of the hearing as is produced by preaching. Also, many do read the passage. This differs from Jason's and Penelope's hearings primarily in its inherent individualism. This difference, however, should not be exaggerated. People read against a background of group norms on how such passages—or this specific passage—should be read. Conversely, Jason and Penelope each hear as individuals, as well as part of a group. In particular, each Philippian hearer has his or her own combination of life experiences that will shape his or her perspective.

Reception in the Philippian context sheds light on the modern context. It also sheds light on Paul's writing of the letter. It does this by raising a number of fresh issues about what Paul may be doing.

A particularly striking conclusion about Jason's and Penelope's hearings is that the text performs the same functions for each of them precisely by their hearing it in different ways. The functions it performs are drawing the hearer closer to Paul and encouraging the hearer in his or her own kind of Christian walk. This works for Jason via references to suffering and for Penelope via references to financial giving. This raises the question of whether Paul might have meant this to happen. He could have chosen, say, "fellowship in the gospel from the first day until now" (1:5) as a deliberately open expression that could function successfully for various hearers, who might have differing ideas of what "fellowship in the gospel" consisted of.

Alternative possibilities are raised by considering the overall flow of Paul's rhetoric (informally or formally understood) through the letter and then placing 1:1–11 within that flow. One such possibility begins from the observation that, if there are both sufferers and nonsufferers in the church, Paul has, by 1:27–30, decisively placed himself on the side of the sufferers. I would argue that the central issue of the letter is involved with this (notice the pervasive theme of suffering: 1:12–26, 27–30; 2:6–8, 17–18, 25–30; 3:9–11; 4:11–13; these are only the explicit passages). If the central issue does involve some sort of taking sides on Paul's part, and if he wants to present the issue directly only from 1:27 onward—having prepared the ground first—then Paul may well want to leave his language very open in 1:1–11 so as to draw both parties with him into the heart of the letter.

Finally, all this has implications for the general study of the text. If we are going to describe the attributes of a particular text, we need to observe its various features. Jason and Penelope provide two angles from which to observe the text. As with a three-dimensional object, different features become visible when the object is viewed from different angles. Each fresh type of hearer can potentially make us aware of previously unobserved features of the text. This is true for various types of modern hearer as well as for various reconstructed types of ancient hearer. Of course, as with viewing objects, some angles may reveal less than others and some objects look similar from several viewpoints.

Which features of the text count as interesting will depend on the objectives of the reader. Features observed via Jason and Penelope ought to be of interest to most readers. They raise important questions for our understanding of the life of people in early churches undergoing suffering. They raise important questions about who Paul expected as his hearers and how he addressed their situation. They make us ask questions about the concrete ways in which the New Testament texts were first (and are now) heard—questions that we would otherwise leave too blurred.

An Assessment of Scholarly Views on Philippians 1:7

A cogent objection to the above reading would arise if Phil 1:7 could be shown to fit unambiguously either a Jason- or a Penelope-type hearing. Scholars have argued vigorously for each option, with the recent majority favoring the "financial-support" model over the "suffering" one. Of the two I would see the suffering model as the more likely to reflect Paul's intention. However, the points on which the decision turns seem sufficiently unclear to allow the likelihood of the passage being heard in different ways by different Philippians.

Καθώς ἐστιν δίκαιον ἐμοὶ τοῦτο φρονεῖν ὑπὲρ πάντων ὑμῶν διὰ τὸ ἔχειν με ἐν τῇ καρδίᾳ ὑμᾶς, ἔν τε τοῖς δεσμοῖς μου καὶ ἐν τῇ ἀπολογίᾳ καὶ βεβαιώσει τοῦ εὐαγγελίου συγκοινωνούς μου τῆς χάριτος πάντας ὑμᾶς ὄντας. (Phil 1:7)

Ernst Lohmeyer makes this verse a key text in his commentary. He argues that the only thing that can give an objective basis to συγκοινωνούς is if the Philippians, like Paul, are suffering. The warmth of the friendly language in the letter arises precisely because the Philippians are sharing with Paul in this way.[3] J. B. Lightfoot links 1:7 with 1:29–30 and explains συγκοινωνούς as "if I have suffered, so have you; if I have labored actively for the gospel, so have you." He takes τῆς χάριτος in the sense of 1:29: God granting, as privileges, both preaching and suffering.[4]

A wide range of scholars disagree with these two great exegetes, arguing that, instead of 1:7 referring to the Philippians' suffering, it refers to the Philippians' financial and other support of Paul. F. W. Beare writes: "The words are simply a grateful recognition that they are with him by their sympathy and by their prayers, and sustained themselves by his cheerful steadfastness."[5] G. B. Caird's view is that "by their help and sympathy they have taken partnership shares in his commission."[6] Joachim Gnilka's perspective could be somewhat wider. He sees here an active element in their participation in the gospel—but he also thinks that the verse refers to their sending money.[7] Peter O'Brien ties the grace directly to the giving: "It must mean that God in his grace had prompted the Philippians to alleviate Paul in his imprisonment."[8] This demonstration of God's grace at work in the Philippians gives Paul grounds for confidence in the Philippians' position (1:3–6).[9]

The vocabulary and syntax of 1:7 seem to leave open the options of seeing a reference either to the Philippians' suffering or to their giving. For help in

3. Ernst Lohmeyer, *Der Brief an die Philipper* (Göttingen: Vandenhoeck & Ruprecht, 1928), 26.

4. J. B. Lightfoot, *Saint Paul's Epistle to the Philippians* (London: Macmillan, 1885), 85.

5. F. W. Beare, *A Commentary on the Epistle to the Philippians* (New York: Harper, 1959), 53.

6. G. B. Caird, *Paul's Letters from Prison: Ephesians, Philippians, Colossians, Philemon*, New Clarendon Bible (Oxford: Oxford University Press, 1976), 108.

7. Joachim Gnilka, *Der Philipperbrief*, Herders Theologischer Kommentar zum Neuen Testament 10.3 (Freiburg: Herder, 1968), 49.

8. Peter T. O'Brien, *Commentary on Philippians*, New International Greek Testament Commentary (Grand Rapids: Eerdmans, 1991), 70.

9. Note the flow of O'Brien's argument up to the "it must mean" sentence.

deciding on Paul's intention here, we need to go further afield, to 1:29–30 and to Paul's general theology and self-understanding.

Following Lightfoot's lead, 1:29–30 offers a possible explanation of 1:7. The Philippians share in χάρις because their suffering ἐχαρίσθη. In this they are sharers with Paul because they are τὸν αὐτὸν ἀγῶνα ἔχοντες. A reasonable explanation of the language of 1:7 that is available in the same letter must generally be preferred over one that has to be constructed from supposition.

One might respond that συγκοινωνούς is equally explained in Philippians under the financial-support reading of 1:7. One could cite 4:14: συγκοινωνήσαντές μου τῇ θλίψει.[10] However, there is a crucial difference in syntax between 1:7 and 4:14. Philippians 4:14 follows Rom 12:13: ταῖς χρείαις τῶν ἁγίων κοινωνοῦντες.[11] In both verses, κοινωνέω is about providing for someone rather than about receiving along with someone or from someone. Philippians 1:7, on the other hand, is like Rom 15:27: εἰ . . . τοῖς πνευματικοῖς αὐτῶν ἐκοινώνησαν τὰ ἔθνη, in which the nations receive a share in the spiritual things.[12] In Phil 1:7, the Philippians definitely receive a share in the grace. Any attempt to make συγκοινωνούς of 1:7 perform both functions, meaning "shared" in the sense of "provided" (which is the meaning in 4:14) and "shared" in the sense of "receiving," looks like exegetical sleight of hand. Philippians 1:7 seems unequivocally to mean "received, alongside me, a share of grace." Even if Paul is thinking about financial support rather than suffering, we cannot draw in 4:14 as an explanation of his language.[13]

As well as explaining Paul's language in 1:7, 1:29–30 may explain his overall argument in 1:3–7. Philippians 1:29 provides a reason for something in 1:28: either for the Philippians receiving salvation or for their stand acting as ἔνδειξις of destruction and salvation. Taking the former option, that the Philippians had been granted to suffer for Christ would be the reason for Paul's confidence in their salvation. The relevance of this to 1:3–7 is fairly direct. Philippians 1:7 begins: καθώς ἐστιν δίκαιον ἐμοὶ τοῦτο φρονεῖν. The referent of τοῦτο must be

---

10. J. L. Houlden loosely suggests this in *Paul's Letters from Prison*, Pelican New Testament Commentary (Harmondsworth: Penguin, 1970), 53–54.

11. Lightfoot (*Philippians*, 174) sees the usage of κοινωνέω as indicating that of συγκοινωνέω.

12. Cf. J. D. G. Dunn, *Romans 9–16*, Word Biblical Commentary 38B (Grand Rapids: Zondervan, 1988), 743; J. B. Lightfoot, *Saint Paul's Epistle to the Galatians* (London: Macmillan, 1880), 218 (on Gal 6:6).

13. In contrast, a good parallel to 1:7 would be a verse that is remarkably similar to 4:14, Rev 1:9: Ἰωάννης . . . συγκοινωνὸς ἐν τῇ θλίψει.

1:6 or, probably, 1:3–6 as a whole[14]—Paul's joy and confidence in the Philippians and their future. There seems to be a pattern of argument that is included in both 1:3–7 and 1:28–30: the Philippians have χάρις, which is in common with Paul and which is grounds for confidence in their salvation. Especially when we note that in each case χάρις is connected with suffering, the parallel with the argument in 1:28–30 looks very strong.

The parallel with 1:28–30 also makes 1:3–6 seem a very Pauline argument. The financial-support model of 1:7 struggles to do this. The argument using the financial-support model is something like, "You have supported me (and the work of the gospel) financially, therefore you share with me in grace, therefore I am confident of your salvation." One feels rather sorry for the Corinthians who were so forcefully denied this road to assurance! Using the suffering model of 1:7, we have, "You have suffered, therefore you share with me in grace, therefore I am confident of your salvation." Romans 8:17 comes to mind, as do other parts of Philippians, especially 3:9–10. The picture is of a faithful Pauline church being seen by Paul as following his own road of suffering for the gospel. This gives Paul joy and confidence in their salvation. The financial-support model would seem less likely to flow from the pen of Paul.

G. F. Hawthorne's view of 1:7 is, from a general Pauline perspective, particularly problematic. He sees "grace" as referring to "Paul's apostolic commission to preach the gospel handed him by God . . . and in which the Philippians have shared by making it financially possible for him to carry out this work of evangelism . . . Paul sees himself as an extension of the Philippian Christians."[15] Clearly, if we were to replace "Philippian" with "Corinthian," the sentence would appear very dubious. It is, however, far from certain that putting "Philippian" back into the sentence really clears the problem. In fact, it may be that an objective behind 4:11–13 is for Paul to refute Hawthorne's conclusion.[16] Paul says to the Philippians: I value my close relationship with you, but I am not an extension of you. It is noticeable, both in Acts and in his letters, how little Paul seems to operate as the fieldworker of any church, notably the church at Antioch. In marked contrast to modern missionary practice, Paul the apostle is not responsible to a sending church. The Jerusalem leaders have some sort of an originating and authoritative role in his thinking, but Paul certainly does

14. Jean-François Collange, *The Epistle of Saint Paul to the Philippians*, trans. A. W. Heathcote (London: Epworth, 1979), 47; O'Brien, *Philippians*, 66.

15. G. F. Hawthorne, *Philippians*, Word Biblical Commentary 43 (Grand Rapids: Zondervan, 1983), 23.

16. See Hawthorne, *Philippians*, 195.

not act as though he is a fieldworker answerable to them. It seems unlikely that Paul saw himself as "an extension" of any group.

Finally, O'Brien raises the objection that the addition of μοῦ to τοῖς δεσμοῖς excludes the possibility of the Philippians' suffering in 1:7.[17] This does not seem forceful. If Paul wanted to say that the Philippians' sufferings should be categorized with his, then μοῦ seems quite natural.

O'Brien's verdict on Lohmeyer's reading of 1:7, "this view has rightly been rejected by New Testament exegetes,"[18] while reasonable given the extremeness of Lohmeyer's martyrological reading of the letter, needs revision when discussing the more general suffering model of 1:7 as presented by Lightfoot. From the point of view of Paul's intention, my exegetical sympathies are, therefore, more with Jason's reading than Penelope's. However, if the scholars are reasonable in being divided on the interpretation of 1:7—that is, if 1:7 may, with only a slight interpretative push (such as whether the first μοῦ makes a difference), be understood in two differing ways—then the strong possibility is raised that the differences in life experiences of the various first hearers will have led them to interpret the verse differently.

17. O'Brien, *Philippians*, 70.
18. O'Brien, *Philippians*, 70.

PART III

EMPIRE

7 | Remapping the Universe: Paul and the Emperor in 1 Thessalonians and Philippians

A considerable number of scholars have asserted the existence of links between texts in either 1 Thessalonians or Philippians and the Roman Empire, the Roman emperor, or the Roman imperial cult. These assertions have taken a wide variety of forms. It seems a good time to take stock of the issues involved and how one might go about assessing them.

The issues turn about two poles. The first is parallel terminology. Various claims have been thoroughly rehearsed about language in the letters that is similar to language used in Roman imperial ideology, expressed in cultic or other forms.[1] We need to consider what degree and type of significance to give to such similarities of language (or of concept). The second pole is structural relationship. Claims have been made about systemic conflicts or parallels between early Christianity and Rome. For example, claims about Christ's authority may conflict with some authority claims made by emperors. We need to consider the nature of any conflict or comparison.

These topics clearly go beyond 1 Thessalonians and Philippians.[2] However, these two letters provide well-focused examples for considering the issues and attempting to give some definition to them. Our method will be to take the three exegetical points that dominate discussion of the topic and on which there is fairly broad agreement. In each case I shall ask: What is the significance of the possible link with Rome? The first example is the terminology used about Christ's arrival in 1 Thess 4:15–17. The second is the phrase "peace and security" in 5:3. The third is the depiction of Christ's authority in Phil 2:9–11. To prepare for considering these, I will set out some options for the relationship

---

1. For some of the claims and for the meaning of "ideology," see below.
2. See Peter Oakes, "A State of Tension: Rome in the New Testament," in *The Gospel of Matthew in Its Roman Imperial Context*, ed. John Riches and David Sim (London: T&T Clark, 2005), 75–90, included as chap. 9 of the present volume.

between Christian discourse or practice and Roman discourse or practice. Then I will look at some basic data about relevant features in the social context or in early Christian beliefs or practice. Some of these will then need further discussion to set up a couple of the criteria that are significant for discussion of the texts. Finally, I will consider the texts themselves.

Christianity and Imperial Ideology: Four Options

There is inevitably some interaction between first-century Christianity and Roman imperial ideology. Such interaction presumably consists of some combination of four broad possibilities: Rome and Christianity follow common models, Christianity follows Rome, Rome conflicts with Christianity, and Christianity conflicts with Rome.

This terminology is shorthand. By "Rome" I mean, primarily, Roman ideology, that is, Roman discourse that sustains certain power relations.[3] The power relations in question are those of Roman society. They have both external and internal dimensions. Externally, they constitute Rome's dominant position over against any competing powers. Internally, they constitute a hierarchy that runs from the emperor down to the most marginal inhabitants of the empire. Alongside ideology, I am including practices that maintain the power relations in question. By "Christianity" I mean the discourse and practices of particular early Christians or particular early Christian groups. Discourse and practice varied. I am interested in any occasions where such discourse or practice intersected with Roman discourse or practice. So, my phrase "Christianity conflicts with Rome" means "some element of the discourse or practice of one or more early Christians conflicts with some element of the discourse or practice involved in the maintenance of the power relations of Roman society."

Option 1: Rome and Christianity Follow Common Models

This covers cases in which Roman discourse and Christian discourse independently borrow terminology from the same source. This is obviously the case for many elements, especially linguistic ones. For example, there were κύριοι around before Greek-speaking Romans or Christians referred to them. Similarly, patterns of behavior by, and toward, rulers, had elements that were

---

3. John B. Thompson, *Ideology and Modern Culture: Critical Social Theory in the Era of Mass Communication* (Cambridge: Polity Press, 1990), 7, 56.

already millennia old. More immediately, both Roman and Jewish—and hence Christian—discourse about rulers was affected by experience of Hellenistic monarchs. Paul's Greek readers, in particular, would have their expectations shaped by that period of history. For example, scholars such as E. Peterson see the language of παρουσία and ἀπάντησις in 1 Thess 4 as relating to Hellenistic practice.[4]

Where elements of Christian and Roman discourse stem independently from common models, then nothing is directly implied about Christianity's relationship to Rome. The coincidence in terminology does not arise from such a relationship. The effects of the coincidence might include conflict (as Adolf Deissmann argues to be the case with the political effects of the early Christians' adoption of Septuagintal language of lordship).[5] However, our interest is in the origin of parallel terminology. If a parallel stems from the use of a common model, then it does not give us direct evidence about the relationship between Christianity and Rome.

Option 2: Christianity Follows Rome

This covers cases in which Christian expressions and practices follow, to some extent, Roman ones. The reality is that certainty about independence of influence, as discussed in option (1), can rarely be achieved. The word κύριος predates the Roman Empire. Christians would have used it even if Rome had never existed. However, all Christians had, in reality, experienced Roman κύριοι. The experience must have stamped Christians' usage. Similarly, the patterns that Greek cities developed for the greeting of arriving officials may have been fairly fixed since Hellenistic times. Even so, a Greek hearer of Paul's day will have been used to such rituals being performed for visiting officials from Rome.

Fundamentally, options (2), (3), and (4) are all cases of Christian discourse following elements of Roman discourse. However, the three options are worth enunciating separately because the modes in which one discourse picks up elements of another can vary sharply, from admiring imitation to violent conflict. Option (2), properly speaking, relates to areas in which Christianity may imitate Rome (although without this necessarily involving admiration).

4. E. Peterson, "Die Einholung des Kyrios," *Zeitschrift für systematische Theologie* 7 (1929–30): 682–702.

5. Adolf Deissmann, *Light from the Ancient East: The New Testament Illustrated by Recently Discovered Texts of the Graeco-Roman World*, trans. L. R. M. Strachan (London: Hodder & Stoughton, 1927), 342.

Scholars such as Richard Ascough argue that the Macedonian Christian communities functioned in ways analogous to those of *collegia* ("associations").[6] Associations had hierarchies that reflected, to some extent, those of cities. In a Roman colony such as Philippi, the hierarchy of the city reflected, in turn, that of Rome. Roman power relations might thus be partially replicated in those of a Christian community.

Option 3: Rome Conflicts with Christianity

Gordon Fee writes that Phil 2:9–11 "places Christ in bold contrast to 'lord Nero.'"[7] The reason why discourse about Christ is expressed in terms relating to Nero is because, in Fee's view, the Christians are being persecuted by the Roman authorities at Philippi. The conflict is about the imperial cult.[8] Therefore Paul reacts by producing discourse that pits Christ against the imperial cult. Roman action against Christians can produce Christian discourse that is cast in Roman terms. This is the kind of case covered by option (3). Elements of the book of Revelation give a large-scale example of this.

Of course, Rome was scarcely aware of Christianity in Paul's day, so ways in which Rome caused trouble for Christians would generally be accidental. They would be aspects of general Roman life that just happened to lead to difficulties for the lives of Christians. For example, my reading of Philippians sees various norms of Greco-Roman society, especially the preservation of status and the avoidance of "troublemakers," as being opposed to the behavior needed by the suffering Philippian church. I see part of Paul's reaction to this as being to deliberately place Christ above the Roman emperor in 2:9–11. I see the main point of this as stemming from the emperor being the symbolic head of Greco-Roman society. If Christ is above the emperor, then Christ's imperatives of humility and unity outweigh society's imperatives that work against these and hence against the survival and health of the Philippian Christian community.[9]

Option (3) covers essentially reactive discourse. The discourse reacts to opposition by expressing itself in terms drawn from the source of opposition.

6. Richard S. Ascough, *Paul's Macedonian Associations: The Social Context of Philippians and 1 Thessalonians*, WUNT 161 (Tübingen: Mohr Siebeck, 2003), 3, 160–61, 190.

7. Gordon D. Fee, *Paul's Letter to the Philippians*, New International Commentary on the New Testament (Grand Rapids: Eerdmans, 1995), 197.

8. Fee, *Philippians*, 31–32.

9. Peter Oakes, *Philippians: From People to Letter*, SNTSMS 110 (Cambridge: Cambridge University Press, 2001), 204–7.

This is part of the complex area explored by scholars such as James C. Scott, in which subordinate groups produce discourse that relates to discourse of the dominating power.[10]

Option 4: Christianity Conflicts with Rome

In option (4), Christians use Roman terminology because they want to oppose something Roman. Dieter Georgi, for example, argues that Jesus's rule "puts an end to the hegemonic claims of all alienating and murderous power and violence together with their law."[11] This leads to Paul presenting Jesus's exaltation in Phil 2:9-11 in terms evoking ideas of Roman imperial apotheosis.[12] A substantial number of scholars have argued that various strands of early Christianity were opposed to the domination and injustice that were central to Roman society. Among the scholars working in this area, Klaus Wengst, Richard Horsley, Neil Elliott, and Warren Carter spring particularly to mind.[13]

There are other more specific areas in which Christian discourse may conflict with an aspect of Roman discourse. J. R. Harrison has argued that people in Thessalonica were under the influence of an "imperial gospel," whose eschatology proclaimed that Augustus had arrived as the ultimate savior. Paul responded by combining Jewish apocalyptic with "a radical subversion of Roman eschatological imagery and terminology." "Above all, the imperial eschatology was stripped of its ideological power: its honorifics and conventions were transferred to the risen and returning Lord of all."[14] Christian eschatology is seen as conflicting with Roman eschatology. This conflict then gives rise to parallels in terminology.

It is a short distance from this to seeing Christology as conflicting with Roman imperial ideology. Tom Wright emphasizes the idea that the gospel involves proclamation of the lordship of the Messiah, a proclamation that

10. James C. Scott, *Domination and the Arts of Resistance: Hidden Transcripts* (New Haven: Yale University Press, 1990).

11. Dieter Georgi, *Theocracy in Paul's Praxis and Theology*, trans. D. E. Green (Minneapolis: Fortress, 1991), 76-77.

12. Georgi, *Theocracy in Paul's Praxis and Theology*, 73.

13. Klaus Wengst, *Pax Romana and the Peace of Jesus Christ*, trans. J. Bowden (Philadelphia: Fortress, 1987); Richard Horsley, ed., *Paul and Empire: Religion and Power in Roman Imperial Society* (Harrisburg, PA: Trinity, 1997); Neil Elliott, *Liberating Paul* (Maryknoll, NY: Orbis, 1994); Warren Carter, *Matthew and Empire: Initial Explorations* (Harrisburg, PA: Trinity, 2001).

14. J. R. Harrison, "Paul and the Imperial Gospel at Thessaloniki," *JSNT* 25 (2002): 71-96 at 92-93.

relativizes the claims of all other lords, especially Caesar.[15] As noted above, Christ's enthronement in Phil 2:9-11 seems deliberately to eclipse that of the emperor. This is particularly seen in the scope of the submission to Christ, which includes the emperor's realm but goes beyond it.[16] Early Christians cast their claims about Christ's universal sovereignty in such a way that they could not be waved away as myths about goings-on in the heavens. They were concrete enough to pose a challenge on earth.

Having said that, there was clearly also a challenge in the realm of the divine. Fee sees persecution of Christians at Philippi on account of the imperial cult. Looking at the other side of that, he sees the Christians as refusing to participate in the imperial cult.[17] The imperial cult was an important element of Roman imperial ideology. This does not make it any less a cult, but it does invest it with forms of significance that even the worship of the Capitoline Triad (Jupiter, Juno, and Minerva, the classic gods of Rome) did not have.

Finally, Christians opposed various specific elements of Greco-Roman discourse or practice. An obvious case is opposition to, and disparagement of, other cults besides that of the emperors. Such opposition could tend toward condemnation of Greco-Roman society as a whole. This seems likely in Rom 1:18-32. Certain practices could also be seen as particularly characteristic of the ruling group in Rome. Bruce Winter has argued that in Rom 12-15 Paul is "a radical critic of the prevailing culture of privilege in Rome's society." Winter sees this as causing Paul to use language and concepts from Roman law and society to express this critique.[18]

The idea of Christian conflict with Rome could be elaborated further, but the possibilities are raised usefully by the five issues noted above: Rome's domination and violence, eschatology, Christology, imperial cult, and specific aspects of discourse and behavior.

So, if we notice a parallel between an element of Christian discourse or practice and that of Rome, I am suggesting that we have four basic interpretative options: (1) the parallel is a coincidence arising from Roman and Christian use of the same prior model; (2) Christians are borrowing some aspect of Roman discourse or practice (without that involving conflict between Christianity and Rome); (3) the Christian discourse uses Roman language as part of

15. N. T. Wright, *What Saint Paul Really Said* (Oxford: Lion, 1997), chap. 3.

16. Oakes, *Philippians*, 148-50.

17. Fee, *Philippians*, 197.

18. Bruce Winter, "Roman Law and Society in Romans 12-15," in *Rome in the Bible and the Early Church*, ed. Peter Oakes (Carlisle: Paternoster; Grand Rapids: Baker Academic, 2002), 67-102 at 99.

a reaction against trouble caused by Rome; or (4) Christians write in Roman terms in order to oppose some aspect of Roman discourse or practice.

Basic Contextual Data

Having set out some options, we can pull back and look at some generally agreed features of the context in which 1 Thessalonians and Philippians were written. The context includes aspects of the life of Thessalonica and Philippi. It also includes some general characteristics of the ideas and practice of early Christians in general and of Paul in particular. After setting out such data, I will consider implications that give us some directions in considering 1 Thessalonians and Philippians.

The first basic point is that the imperial cult was practiced in both Thessalonica and Philippi. I would assume that there was some expression of the imperial cult in every town of any size in the eastern Roman Empire, with the possible exception of exclusively Jewish areas. I therefore doubt whether the point needs proving as such for the two cities that we are looking at. However, the practice of the cult can be clearly demonstrated at both Philippi and Thessalonica. At Philippi, the excavation of the forum has revealed a prominent temple to the imperial family and, of particular relevance to Paul's day, a large monument connected with the cult of Livia, who was deified by Claudius.[19] At Thessalonica, no remains of an imperial-cult temple have been found. However, this is not surprising since only small areas of the city have been excavated. What we do have is ample inscriptional and coin evidence of the cult. The most notable is the city's extraordinarily early coin issue featuring Caesar as ΘΕΟΣ.[20] The city's position as provincial capital brings the point home further. By analogy with what happened in the nearby province of Asia,[21] we can be confident that part of Thessalonica's action to reinforce its leading position in the province of Macedonia would have been to go to the greatest lengths in the practice of the imperial cult.

---

19. M. Sève and P. Weber, "Un monument honorifique au forum de Philippes," *Bulletin de Correspondance Hellénique* 112 (1988): 467–79.

20. Christoph vom Brocke, *Thessaloniki—Stadt des Kassader und Gemeinde des Paulus*, WUNT 125 (Tübingen: Mohr Siebeck, 2001), 139, citing I. Touratsoglou, *Die Münzstätte von Thessaloniki in der römischen Kaiserzeit (32/31 v. Chr. bis 268 n. Chr.)*, Antike Münzen und geschnittene Steine 12 (Berlin: de Gruyter, 1988), 140.

21. S. R. F. Price, *Rituals and Power: The Roman Imperial Cult in Asia Minor* (Cambridge: Cambridge University Press, 1984), 126–32.

Looking more broadly, the commitment of both Thessalonica and Philippi, as cities, to Roman imperial ideology is unquestioned. The battle of Philippi marked a key point for each city. Thessalonica had been isolated in backing the triumvirs against Brutus and Cassius. Octavian and Antony's victory brought a declaration of freedom for the city.[22] It was already the provincial capital, and its fresh political success must have strengthened its position further. As noted above, the city's gratitude was especially expressed in its coin issues. Philippi, on the other hand, had been Brutus and Cassius's forward base for the battle. It suffered the catastrophe of Roman colonization, a process that reached its most brutal peak, there and in Italy, in the aftermath of the battle.[23] However, the name "Philippi" is attached to a location, not to a group of people. Disaster for the Greek farmers of Philippi and for their ruling council, who entirely lost their political control, meant benefit for the Roman veteran soldiers who settled there and took over the running of the city. The new regime at Philippi looked back to the battle as the city's great rebirth. Roman Philippi was at least as attached to Roman ideology as Thessalonica was. In fact, for Philippi, their cultural survival as a Roman enclave depended on promotion of that ideology and of the elements of "Roman-ness" that went with it. Their efforts can be seen in the provision of a Latin library and of a troupe of Latin-speaking mime actors.[24] Since the Romans were probably in a minority even in Philippi,[25] they had to hold tightly to Rome.

Looking beyond the two cities, an important piece of basic data is the general one that the Roman Empire provided the main perceived structure of world order around the Mediterranean. Any movement that challenged the status quo of the social structure would, to some extent, be challenging Rome. Linked to Rome's actual control of society is the consequence that Roman ideology provided the most common terminology of first-century discourse about authority structures. Any first-century writer dealing with issues of authority was likely to use language and concepts drawn from that source, whether or not Rome was in view.

Turning to the context of Christian ideas and practices, the first basic point

22. Vom Brocke, *Thessaloniki*, 16–18.

23. Lawrence Keppie, *Colonisation and Veteran Settlement in Italy, 47–14 B.C.* (London: British School at Rome, 1983), 60; E. T. Salmon, *Roman Colonization under the Republic* (London: Thames & Hudson, 1969), 137–38; Oakes, *Philippians*, 26–27.

24. Paul Collart, *Philippes, ville de Macédoine: Depuis ses origines jusqu'à la fin de l'époque romaine* (Paris: Ecole Française d'Athènes, 1937), 272–73, 338–39.

25. Peter Pilhofer, *Philippi*, vol. 1: *Die erste christliche Gemeinde Europas* (Tübingen: Mohr, 1995), 90; Oakes, *Philippians*, 35–39.

is that Christians did not, in principle, honor any of the Greco-Roman gods. First Corinthians 8–10 shows that cultic practice did not always match the rhetoric (a very paradoxical mismatch in 8:4, since the basis of cultic participation was disbelief in the gods' existence!). However, Paul certainly believed the Thessalonians to have given up Greco-Roman cults (1 Thess 1:9). The Christian failure to honor the gods would have included central Roman deities, such as Jupiter and also the deified Caesars.

A second area of Christian belief was the current authority ascribed to Jesus. As well as Paul (e.g., Phil 2:9–11), this is seen, for example, in both Matthean (Matt 28:18) and Lukan (Luke 22:29) strands of tradition. Such ascription of current authority had the potential to conflict with Roman imperial claims and, hence, possibly to support lines of interpretation such as those of Georgi or Wright, mentioned above.

Picking up another of the issues above, a further piece of basic data is that early Christian eschatology does seem to have consistently expected an intervention by God, involving the return of Jesus, that would constitute a radical change in the authority structure of the world. Again, this is attested in many strands of tradition other than the Pauline one. Also again, this clearly gave potential for conflict with discourse that sustained current structures, notably Roman rule.

Turning to Christian practice, a feature of this was that it sometimes transgressed the norms of Greco-Roman society. It is notable in 1 Corinthians that Paul actually supports (and in some cases presumably instituted) many of the social practices in the Christian community at Corinth. The conduct of Christian gatherings cut across many expectations of household behavior, especially in relation to gender and other status-related roles (1 Cor 11–14).

A final piece of basic contextual data for our letters, although this time a contested one, is that, prior to receiving the letters, the Christians in both Thessalonica and Philippi had undergone suffering, brought about by their fellow townspeople. Abraham Malherbe (for 1 Thessalonians) and J.-F. Collange (for Philippians) have argued that much of the evidence should be interpreted in terms of mental struggle and ideas.[26] However, as Todd Still and others, including myself, have argued, the key passages are most naturally taken in terms of tangible suffering (in my view, particularly economic suffering).[27]

---

26. Abraham J. Malherbe, *The Letters to the Thessalonians: A New Translation with Introduction and Commentary*, Anchor Yale Bible 32B (New York: Doubleday, 2000), 127–28; J.-F. Collange, *The Epistle of Saint Paul to the Philippians*, trans. A. W. Heathcote (London: Epworth, 1979), 14, 71–72.

27. Todd D. Still, *Conflict at Thessalonica: A Pauline Church and Its Neighbours*, JSNTSup 183 (Sheffield: Sheffield Academic Press, 1999), chap. 9; Oakes, *Philippians*, chap. 3.

To summarize, the basic contextual data that I have drawn attention to is the following: imperial-cult practice took place in both Thessalonica and Philippi; both Thessalonica and Philippi as cities were particularly strongly committed to Roman imperial ideology; the Roman Empire provided the basic structure and discourse of authority in the Mediterranean world; early Christians did not honor the Greco-Roman gods; early Christians saw Jesus as holding current authority; they expected an intervention by God, involving the return of Jesus, which would radically change the world's authority structures; some Christian practices cut against Greco-Roman social norms; Christians in both Thessalonica and Philippi had suffered at the hands of fellow townspeople.

SOME IMPLICATIONS OF THE BASIC DATA

We need one more step before finally looking at features of the two letters. That step is to think about the general implications of the basic points on the imperial cult, Christology, and eschatology in order to consider the criteria for assessing such issues in the two texts.

The imperial cult was clearly a problem for early Christians even before it came into use in trials of Christians as a test of apostasy, presumably at around the time when Pliny the Younger was using it, in the early second century. The Christians' fundamental attitude to the imperial cult was presumably the same as that to other cults: they were non-Christian and not to be practiced. However, the nature of the imperial cult must in fact have set it somewhat apart from other cults.

What did practice of the imperial cult involve? The two essential activities were the maintenance of a shrine and the celebration of festivals. The maintenance and beautification of a prominent imperial-cult temple provided an ongoing communication of the importance of the imperial gods to the existence of a town and, indeed, the world. Daily life went forward under the imperial aegis. The people actively involved in this temple maintenance would be wealthy Philippians or Thessalonians who might contribute gifts for the temple's upkeep and adornment. Festivals occurred several times a year. Again, the people most actively involved would be wealthy citizens who sponsored a festival's games, or a feast, or a handout of food or money on the occasion.[28]

---

28. Steven Mitchell, *Anatolia: Land, Men, and Gods in Asia Minor*, vol. 1: *The Celts in*

Priests and, sometimes, other people would offer sacrifices.[29] Civic officials more generally would take part in processions or meals. Other groups might take part in these too.[30] Citizens of Thessalonica or Philippi might be recipients of handouts at the festival.[31] The population as a whole might wear celebratory clothing and might attend the free shows at the theater or amphitheater.[32]

Simon Price places considerable stress on the universality of participation in imperial-cult activities. His aim is to counter the earlier scholarly view that the cult was an elite concern, with which the rest of the population was not really engaged.[33] Price seems to be correct in opposing this view. There is little doubt that people generally will have gladly joined in the celebration of the festivals, especially where handouts or shows were available. Moreover, this presumably represented a genuine expression by the people of their understanding of the significance of the emperor and his family.[34] However, Duncan Fishwick draws attention to the fact that participation in such cultic activity was not generally obligatory.[35] This is inevitable given that Greco-Roman cities, like most cities throughout history, were relatively chaotic places. For example, I cannot imagine the city authorities of Ephesus going round the city's thousands of beggars, migrant workers, and other marginal inhabitants, checking that they had the means and the inclination to participate in the festivities. Inscriptions detailing ambitious plans by a city to honor the emperors seem unlikely to have often translated into activity that was truly universal, or even nearly so. The aim of the inscriptions was to enhance the city's standing and fortunes. Actual implementation would seem likely to be in terms of a general impression of public celebration rather than the kind of rigorous application of detail that would clearly cause trouble for Christians. After all, Christians were happy to affirm political loyalty to the emperors, so they were presumably happy to celebrate, say, the anniversary of the date of his accession.

Anatolia and the Impact of Roman Rule (Oxford: Clarendon, 1993), 108, table 8.1. This is a particularly useful chart of donations by a series of imperial-cult priests.

29. Duncan Fishwick, *The Imperial Cult in the Latin West*, vol. 2.1 (Leiden: Brill, 1991), 528–32.

30. Price, *Rituals and Power*, 110–12.

31. Fishwick, *Imperial Cult*, 584–87.

32. Fishwick, *Imperial Cult*, 574–84.

33. Price, *Rituals and Power*, 107–8.

34. Price, *Rituals and Power*, 235, 238–39, 247–48.

35. Fishwick, *Imperial Cult*, 530–31.

Even the strict Tertullian affirms that Christians would, in a restrained way, honor imperial festivals.[36] Many Christians probably went much further.

James Harrison and others draw attention to oaths of loyalty sworn by the inhabitants of towns on the accession of an emperor. Harrison's example is the oath for Caligula at Aritium,[37] but he is also looking back to the work of E. A. Judge and Karl Donfried.[38] The oath at Aritium seems to be a political commitment rather than, per se, a commitment to participate in the imperial cult. The imperial gods enter the oath as part of a self-curse formula: "If . . . I swear falsely . . . may Jupiter Optimus Maximus and the deified Augustus and all the other immortal gods punish me."[39] Presumably Jews might swear such an oath but with the self-curse formula relating to their God. Harrison draws attention to Augustus's assertion that all Italy swore allegiance to him after Actium.[40] That oath would certainly not have involved commitment to offering cult to Augustus. He would not have wanted to take Italians so far from their traditional religious norms. The accession oaths were not, in the early Principate at least, commitments to offer cult to the reigning emperor.

I would also expect that, if a population as a whole was called to swear an oath of loyalty, this would be a corporate act, rather than a public affirmation by individuals. Admittedly, Clifford Ando makes the effective point that each Roman was individually linked into the ideological (including cultic) system through events such as censuses and registration of births.[41] However, oaths of loyalty seem much more likely to have been administered to the population in the theater, as part of a festival, rather than individually. The logistics of individuals swearing would seem impractical. If fifty thousand Thessalonians took a minute each, it would require 170 officials to sit for five hours (going rapidly insane), not to mention the other people required for crowd control and checking of registration (which would itself be unworkably complex if it attempted to be universal). Even if this was scaled down by concentrating on heads of household, the complexity of the exercise would surely prevent any city from trying it twice. In any case, a likely model for action would be the

36. Tertullian, *Apology* 35.

37. Harrison, "Paul and the Imperial Gospel," 80, citing *CIL* 2.172.

38. E. A. Judge, "The Decrees of Caesar at Thessalonica," *Reformed Theological Review* 30 (1971): 1–7; Karl Donfried, "The Cults of Thessalonica and the Thessalonian Correspondence," *NTS* 31 (1985): 336–56 at 349–50.

39. Harrison, "Paul and the Imperial Gospel," 80.

40. Harrison, "Paul and the Imperial Gospel," 79, citing Augustus, *Res gestae* 25.

41. Clifford Ando, *Imperial Ideology and Provincial Loyalty in the Roman Empire* (Berkeley: University of California Press, 2000), 351–62.

political process at Rome. In the imperial period, political action of the populace as a whole was generally limited to group acclamation of the emperors and their acts.

For most Christians, the imperial cult was probably a less pressing issue than other cults in which they had previously participated. At Philippi, even though the imperial-cult temple occupied a prominent place in the forum, the cult has only a minor place in the overall collection of inscriptions that testify to the religious life of the people of the city.[42] If you were a shopkeeper and, like many shops in Pompeii, your shop had a very visible shrine on the wall, with a shelf on which offerings would regularly be placed,[43] then your conversion to Christianity would produce extremely difficult decisions. A painted-out shrine picture, or even the cessation of offerings, would presumably cause outrage among family, friends, customers, and fellow traders. For the ordinary inhabitant of the town, the imperial cult did not impose such sharp decisions. Few would object if you failed to turn up for a festival handout, if there was one. Neither would you be compelled to attend the free shows, although in both cases your family would notice. If a festival for the accession of a new emperor involved a show during which an oath of allegiance was to be sworn, then maybe you would have to attend. However, a Christian might not have a great problem with attendance at a mass-audience, generally passive, activity. If an oath was to be sworn, I imagine that a Christian would join in the crowd's pledging of allegiance but omit or amend any self-curse formula relating to the gods.

On the other hand, the imperial cult raised two particular problems. The first was that everyone participated in it. It was not a sectional interest like the cults of, say, Isis or Silvanus. All gentile converts to Christianity would previously have taken part. If a magistrate or counselor was a Christian, the problem of avoiding participation in imperial-cult events would probably have been insurmountable (the same would be true of some other civic cults too). The second problem was that the imperial cult was an expression of Roman imperial ideology. To dishonor the imperial gods was, of course, to dishonor the emperor. The imperial gods and the emperor and his family were one and the same. If you abandoned the cult of Isis, your family and other associates might be angry with you. If you were seen to dishonor the imperial cult, you were rebelling against Rome.

---

42. Peter Pilhofer, *Philippi*, vol. 2: *Katalog der Inschriften von Philippi*, WUNT 119 (Tübingen: Mohr, 2000). The *kultisches* index offers a good way into the collection.

43. As seen, for example, in the bar in Region I Block 8.

A further consequence of the link between the imperial cult and Roman ideology was that if Christian ideas, such as Christology and eschatology, challenged Roman ideology, then they also challenged the imperial cult. This poses a methodological difficulty in looking for evidence of the imperial cult in our two letters. The kind of evidence that Fee uses, in detecting language in Philippians that relates to the cult,[44] is language of lordship that relates more immediately to ideology rather than cult. I am inclined to see the imperial cult in a text only if the issue giving rise to the text appears to be specifically cultic. We will need to assess these possibilities.

This takes us on to Christology. The point has been made above that discourse on Christ's sovereignty almost inevitably uses terms and concepts found in Roman imperial ideology, whether or not Christ is really being compared with the emperor. To detect such actual comparison in 1 Thessalonians and Philippians we need to look for details that go beyond general discourse: for example, details such as the form of accession to power (or possibly apotheosis). Similarly, to decide whether Christ is being seen as specifically relativizing the emperor's authority, we ought to look for details that suggest reference to the emperor's sphere of rule. For example, if a passage described Christ as the victor, entering the city in a triumphal chariot, ruling over the Mediterranean and to the ends of the earth, then no one would doubt that there was a deliberate comparison to, and relativization of, the Roman emperor. The cases in our two letters are harder to judge.

Similar issues arise in assessing eschatology. Any eschatological scheme that involves a world-changing intervention by God has implications for every current holder of power. It affects the emperor of China as well as the emperor of Rome. Paul presumably knows nothing of China. That his eschatology has implications for China does not mean that his writing consciously relates to China and its power structures. The same could, to an extent, be true of Rome. Paul could simply be expressing a version of an essentially pre-Roman eschatology (an Isaianic one, for example), without shaping it in relation to Rome. As with Christology, we would need to find more details to relate the Pauline texts to Rome. Alternatively, we would need arguments that suggested that Paul specifically had Rome in view when expressing his eschatology.

Finally, we can move to the two letters in question.

44. Fee, *Imperial Cult*, 31.

1 Thessalonians

Let us assume the validity of the two most pertinent, exegetical contentions about 1 Thessalonians, namely, that Christ's return is portrayed in language (παρουσία, ἀπάντησις) appropriate to an arriving political leader (4:15–17) and that the attitude of non-Christians, who face destruction at the arrival of Christ, is described using a Roman imperial slogan (5:3). What combination of our four options should these be seen as expressing, and in what way?

In the case of the arrival and meeting in 4:15–17, option (1) is clearly possible. Both the Roman and Pauline language could be Hellenistic in origin. However, if we think about Paul's experience, option (2) is at least as likely: Paul could be thinking of an arriving Roman official. Harrison combines options (3) and (4). Paul uses imperial language of παρουσία and ἀπάντησις because he is reacting to persecution of the Christians (which, Donfried argues, quite likely arose because of problems about swearing an imperial loyalty oath)[45] and because he is opposing the Roman imperial eschatology (of the Golden Age, ushered in by the savior Augustus), which was prevalent in Thessalonica:[46] Rome conflicts with Christianity, and Christianity conflicts with Rome.

The "political" terms παρουσία and ἀπάντησις occur near the beginning and end of 4:15–17. They are not particularly emphasized. In fact, each is somewhat overshadowed by surrounding phrases that relate more closely to the main topic of the passage, the relative fates of living and dead Christians: "we who are alive, who remain . . . will certainly not precede those who have fallen asleep" and "we who are alive, who remain, will be snatched up together with them" (4:15, 17). A further difficulty for reading great significance into the two political terms is that they sometimes occur in nonpolitical senses.[47] A third difficulty is that 4:17 does not fully fit the pattern of civic greeting because, in this verse, the Christians appear to stay in the air, which would be the equivalent of staying outside the city after greeting an official. What happens long term is unclear but, if Paul intended a parallel with civic greeting, we might have expected the Christians to lead Christ down to earth. Seth Turner argues that the parallel with civic greeting implies the return of Christ and the Christians to earth. He further argues that this is confirmed by the promise of the renewal of creation in

---

45. Harrison, "Paul and the Imperial Gospel," 82; Donfried, "Cults of Thessalonica," 349–50.

46. Harrison, "Paul and the Imperial Gospel," 92.

47. For παρουσία ("arrival"), e.g., 1 Cor 16:17; Phil 1:26. For ἀπάντησις ("meeting"), e.g., Matt 25:6.

Rom 8:19–23.[48] Turner's first argument assumes, of course, the very point at issue for us. His second argument is too tenuous to bear any weight. It is in another letter. It is far from clear in Romans that the renewal of creation is a process enacted following the return of Christ and the Christians to earth. Finally, Paul speaks of the "whole creation." This seems likely to mean a new heaven as well as a new earth (Rev 21). Philippians 2:10 certainly shows a concern beyond the earth. If the whole universe is to be renewed, this would be no evidence for a return specifically to earth. Of course, many New Testament texts do indicate belief in a return of Christ to earth (most clearly Acts 1:11; most pertinently 1 Thess 1:10). However, it seems very unsafe to use these to determine the inter-pretation of Paul's description of the rapture in 1 Thess 4.

However, the arrival of Christ is portrayed very emphatically in 4:16. The portrayal goes beyond what is needed to explain the relative fates of the living and the dead. A range of Jewish apocalyptic imagery emphasizes the majesty of Jesus's arrival. The Christology and eschatology are powerfully brought home. In the context of suffering at Thessalonica, such a message presumably brought reassurance of the security of the Christians' position, under the sovereign lord who would arrive in power. If παρουσία and ἀπάντησις do have any political weight here, it is probably given to them by the unexpectedly weighty apoca-lyptic of 4:16. The two terms may become political translations of apocalyptic into a form understandable to a Greek audience: political hooks on which the audience can hang the apocalyptic imagery.

However, these political hooks are not prominent terms in Roman escha-tology or, indeed, Roman ideology in general. Harrison has a stronger case with ἐπιφάνεια in 2 Thess 2:8, but that is not at issue here. Παρουσία and ἀπάντησις could relate to the arrival of a Roman emperor visiting a town but they do not relate to the arrival of say, Augustus, on earth to initiate the Golden Age.[49] Paul may be implying that the key arrival in Thessalonica to wait for is not that of the emperor but that of Jesus. However, if so, he is doing it without any emphasis on the emperor (the case would change sharply if some of the trumpet blowing and other activities could be shown to relate to imperial practice). The language of παρουσία and ἀπάντησις seems likely to be drawn from experience of Roman practice, but the passage does not seem to be a conscious challenge to Roman eschatology.

48. Seth Turner, "The Interim, Earthly Messianic Kingdom in Paul," *JSNT* 25 (2003): 323–42 at 331.

49. Harrison, "Paul and the Imperial Gospel," 82–92. Notice the contrasting types of evidence relating to ἐπιφάνεια on the one hand and παρουσία and ἀπάντησις on the other.

The equation could change in the light of 1 Thess 5:3. However, I doubt that it does because, even though 5:3 is likely to relate to Roman eschatology, the idea of eschatology involved is very different from anything that might be perceived as a point of comparison for 4:15–17. These verses are about a future visit; 5:3 seems to evoke a slogan of a current Golden Age.

As Christoph vom Brocke, James Harrison, and others demonstrate, εἰρήνη καὶ ἀσφάλεια ("peace and safety") is a very powerful evocation of the central ideology of the new age brought in by Augustus. Vom Brocke particularly brings this home with his quotation of an inscription from Turkey that uses this very phrase in relation to Pompey,[50] who was a significant model for the development of the ideology of the emperor.[51] The imperial propagation of the centrality of *pax* and *securitas* in the legitimation of the empire[52] makes 5:3 look deliberately evocative of Roman ideology. Alternative derivations from Jeremiah or Epicurean philosophy[53] offer much less close or widely known parallels.

In 5:3 Paul is emphasizing the unexpectedness of the day of the Lord. He is not specifically attacking the Roman Empire. However, he seems deliberately to be denying the central assertion of Roman imperial ideology. He asserts that the empire cannot guarantee peace and safety. Its claim to do so will be disproved by the arrival of Christ. The implication seems to be that the Thessalonians should not put faith in the imperial promise of peace and safety. In their experience of persecution they should stay faithful, trusting in Christ's security rather than that of the state. Paul undermines the value of the status quo in order to enhance allegiance to an alternate reality. This is, as Harrison argues, a challenge to Roman eschatology. This is Christianity against Rome. However, it is neither Christianity seeking Rome's overthrow nor Christianity arguing against participation in the imperial cult. It is Christian hope being asserted to be superior to Roman hope in order to sustain suffering Christians.

PHILIPPIANS

The points of contact between Philippians and Rome are more numerous than is the case for 1 Thessalonians. Paul is imprisoned by the Roman authorities.

50. Vom Brocke, *Thessaloniki*, 179n64.
51. Oakes, *Philippians*, 141.
52. See, for example, the *Paci Augustae* coins of Claudius and the *Securitas Augusti* ones of Nero; vom Brocke, *Thessaloniki*, 177–79.
53. Malherbe, *Thessalonians*, 303–5.

The Philippians are also suffering. As a predominantly Greek-speaking group in a Roman colony, any suffering that involved the civic authorities would be perceived as having a specifically Roman dimension. Paul notes the spread of the gospel "in the Praetorium" (1:13)[54] and among Caesar's household (4:22). He asserts that the needs of the gospel work will determine the outcome of the Roman judicial process that he is facing (1:22–26).[55] Christ is presented as becoming emperor of the universe (2:9–11), and this is done in a way that fulfills the Isaianic vision of God's sovereignty over the nations.[56] The Philippians are told that they belong to an alternative state (πολίτευμα, 3:20) that determines their ethics (as Roman citizenship was supposed to determine that of Romans).[57] They await the arrival of their σωτήρ ("savior") from this state, who will save on the basis of his imperial power (3:20–21).[58]

Is the imperial cult in view? The strongest likelihood of it would be in 2:6–11, but I cannot see it there. The event in 2:9–11 looks to be an accession to imperial authority rather than an apotheosis. Jesus becomes a ruler of those on earth as well as of those in the heavens. His enthronement prepares for his saving return in 3:20–21, which is like the action of a ruling emperor rather than a dead one who has been divinized. Furthermore, 2:6–11 is, in Philippians at least, the reinforcement for 1:27–2:4. These verses, rather than 2:6–11 itself, are the best location for understanding the issues at Philippi, to which 2:6–11 is part of Paul's response. Philippians 1:27–2:4 gives no impression of a problem relating specifically to the imperial cult. The verses are about the church holding together, faithful to the gospel, while suffering. Their punch line is about mutual concern and support (2:4). It therefore seems better to see 2:6–11 as addressing these broad issues rather than a particular one such as the imperial cult. If 2:6–11 addresses the broad issues, then the parallels and contrasts that there appear to be to imperial ideas are likely to relate to the emperor in general, rather than to the emperor as specifically a cultic figure. Paul replaces the emperor with Christ as the new decisive power. This would be an effective element of a rhetorical strategy aimed at sustaining the Christians in a hostile environment.

There is an element of option (1) here (independent use of common mod-

54. Oakes, *Philippians*, 66.
55. Peter Oakes, "God's Sovereignty over Roman Authorities: A Theme in Philippians," in *Rome in the Bible and the Early Church,* ed. Peter Oakes (Carlisle: Paternoster; Grand Rapids: Baker Academic, 2002), 126–41 at 132–33, included as chap. 10 of the present volume.
56. Oakes, *Philippians*, 147–74.
57. Oakes, *Philippians*, 138.
58. Oakes, *Philippians*, 138–45.

els). Paul draws on the Isaianic description of God as the emperor to whom Babylon and the other nations bow. The writer of Isa 45 draws on general ideas of imperial rule that also form foundations for Roman practice. The question of the extent to which option (2) is present (Christianity follows Rome) carries substantial significance for the politics of interpretation. Many strands of church doctrine, from the time of Constantine onward, have seen Christ and the monarch (or state) as parallel powers, each with their own appointed sphere (although with the monarch ultimately subject to Christ). Such a theology of the state draws on perceived parallels between descriptions of Christ's position and those of earthly rulers, especially the Roman emperor. It is also noteworthy that study of the comparison between christological and imperial terminology was prominent in German scholarship of the early twentieth century but seems to have stopped rather suddenly.[59] One imagines that political considerations played a role in this. It is striking that when the topic reappeared, with scholars such as Wengst and Georgi, it was in the form of Paul's Christology radically opposing that of the state.

As explained above, options (2), (3), and (4) are all variants of the idea that Christians drew on Roman terminology. The distinctive points about options (3) and (4) are that Christian use of Roman terminology results from either Roman conflict with Christianity (e.g., persecution) or Christian conflict with Rome (e.g., opposition to Augustan eschatology). In Phil 2:9–11 there is probably a combination of (3) and (4). Paul reacts to persecution of the Christians by placing Jesus above the symbolic head of the persecutors (whether Roman or Greek). This offers security and encourages continued allegiance to Jesus. Paul also wants to assert a way of life, involving humility and mutual concern, that goes against the status-related norms of Greco-Roman life. By placing Christ above the symbolic head of Greco-Roman society, Paul reinforces the value and authority of Christ's norms of behavior over against those of society.[60]

We can draw these two strands together (reaction to persecution and assertion of Christian norms) by saying that Paul remaps society. Philippian society marginalizes the Christians. Paul moves them to the center. He does this first by moving Christ to the center of authority (2:6–11), then by moving the Christians to a key position in 2:15–16: "blameless children of god in the midst of a crooked and depraved generation, among whom you shine like stars, having the role of life in the world [ἐν κόσμῳ λόγον ζωῆς ἐπέχοντες]."[61]

59. Oakes, *Philippians*, 129–31.
60. Oakes, *Philippians*, 201–10.
61. The parallel between Phil 2:15 and Dan 12:3 suggests "shine like stars" as a translation

Paradoxically, Paul goes on to give the Christians a place in a state in the heavens (3:20). However, this does not preclude a central place in the world. Philippian citizens of Rome were also the leading people in Philippi.

Conclusion

Having set out options and basic data, then having looked at 1 Thessalonians and Philippians, we can see a pattern emerging. When Paul evokes Rome in these letters, Christianity does conflict with Rome. Christology and eschatology, in particular, conflict with Roman ideology. However, Paul does not seem to be wishing, as such, for Rome's overthrow. He is not writing anti-Roman polemic. Neither is he aiming specifically at preventing participation in the imperial cult.

Instead, he is redrawing the map of the universe. The marginalized Christians are brought near to the center. The center itself is occupied by Jesus, whose crucifixion had marginalized him as far as it was possible to do. In thus reorganizing space, and consequently the outcome of time, Paul decenters Rome. He decenters its earthly power and the security it offers. He decenters the emperor and the imperial family. In doing this he is inevitably doing away with the imperial cult. However, this does not seem to be a particular emphasis of his. It has already gone in any case along with all the other idols from which the Thessalonians had turned.

Philippians 2:6–11 springs (in its epistolary context at least) out of the concerns of 1:27–2:4. It then heads toward 2:12–18, where remapping the Philippian

---

of φαίνεσθε ὡς φωστῆρες. Ἐν κόσμῳ could be taken with that phrase and would hence mean "in the universe." However, it sits nicely with λόγον ζωῆς ἐπέχοντες. Study of contemporary lexical usage suggests that this phrase is unlikely to mean "holding firmly to the word of life." It might possibly mean "holding forth the word of life." However, λόγον + genitive + ἐπέχω is more likely to be a first-century development of the phrase λόγον + genitive + ἔχω. This phrase describes the relation in which something stands. To take an example from ca. 200 CE, Alexander of Aphrodisias writes: ἡ γὰρ δυὰς ὕλης ἐν αὐτοῖς ἐπέχει λόγον ("for among the Ideas the dyad has the role [logos] of matter"); Alexander of Aphrodisias, *On Aristotle's Metaphysics*, vol. 1, trans. W. E. Dooley (Ithaca, NY: Cornell University Press, 1989), A6.988a7. Λόγον ζωῆς ἐπέχοντες probably means something like "playing the role [i.e., having the function] of life" or "holding the position of life." For the full argument, see Peter Oakes, "Quelle devrait être l'influence des échos intertextuels sur la traduction? Le cas de l'epître aux Philippiens (2,15–16)," in *Intertextualités: La Bible en échos*, ed. Daniel Marguerat and Adrian Curtis (Geneva: Labor et Fides, 2000), 251–87, building on the work of F. W. Field, *Otium Norvicense* (Oxford, 1881), 3:118–19.

Christians' location in the world is a central concern (2:15–16). The whole argument of the letter then heads for 3:20–21, where the climactic statement of remapping is made.

Philippians remaps both space and time. First Thessalonians concentrates on time, although, in doing so, it too clearly remaps the power structures of the universe. In each letter, Paul strengthens the suffering Christians by emphasizing that the universe is not as it appears. The Christians have a secure place close to the real central power. They should therefore encourage one another.

Simon Price describes the Roman imperial cult in the Greek East as being an expression of the place that Greeks gave to Roman power in their universe: a great translocal, divine force on a par with that of the Hellenistic monarchs.[62] Paul rearranges this universe.

---

62. Price, *Rituals and Power*, 235, 238–39, 247–48.

8 | CHRISTIAN ATTITUDES TO ROME AT THE TIME OF PAUL'S LETTER

An avenue of study of Paul's Letter to the Romans that scholars have scarcely explored is the implication of the letter being written to Christians in Rome. Peter Lampe has investigated what the letter may tell us about the Roman Christians,[1] but that is using Romans to study history rather than using history to study Romans as a whole. Many scholars have investigated the possible reasons for the writing of the letter and quite a number of the suggestions have related to the situation of the Roman church or churches. However, the suggestions have rarely been intrinsically related to Rome itself. The issues involved are often ones that could have arisen in other cities. Wolfgang Wiefel's proposed reasons for the letter do relate to its setting at Rome but his study involves only very specific issues, namely, Claudius's expulsion of the Jews and Roman anti-Jewish sentiment.[2] He does not attempt to draw in more general characteristics of the city or attitudes to it.

In this chapter, I want to make an initial proposal for a framework for study of Romans as a letter written to a community specifically in Rome. My proposal is that we should try to construct a list of Christian attitudes to Rome at the time of the letter. When we study Romans, we could then use the list as a pool of possible, specifically Roman, issues that might inform our exegesis of any part of the letter.

How should we construct such a list? One avenue would be biographi-

---

1. Peter Lampe, *Christians of Rome in the First Two Centuries*, trans. J. Larrimore Holland and Michael Steinhauser (London: Burns & Oates, 2000); cf. Andrew D. Clarke, "Jew and Greek, Slave and Free, Male and Female: Paul's Theology of Ethnic, Social, and Gender Inclusiveness in Romans 16," in *Rome in the Bible and the Early Church*, ed. Peter Oakes (Carlisle: Paternoster; Grand Rapids: Baker, 2002), 103-25.

2. Wolfgang Wiefel, "The Jewish Community in Ancient Rome and the Origins of Roman Christianity," in *The Romans Debate*, ed. Karl P. Donfried (Peabody, MA: Hendrickson, 1991), 85-101.

cal, seeing the issue as being about Paul's experiences and hence attitudes. A problem with this approach is that our textual base is then limited. Many important issues will happen not to arise in Pauline (or Lukan) texts. Instead, we will follow a route of trying to model general attitudes of Christians at this time. That raises a much wider set of possible issues for study of the letter. Paul would have shared many of the general Christian attitudes to Rome. He will also have needed to take into consideration the attitudes of other Christians as he wrote.

In the late 50s, Christianity was a provincial religious movement rooted in Jewish beliefs, practice, and history. This gives three natural dimensions to a model of Christian attitudes to Rome. First, Christian attitudes to Rome would be attitudes of provincials to the imperial power. Even the Christian community at Rome would mainly have consisted of immigrants who would still be provincial in status and outlook. Second, Christian attitudes to Rome would to a considerable extent be Jewish attitudes to Rome, attitudes shaped by Jewish experience of Roman power and by the relationship between Jewish theology and perception of Rome. Third, Christian attitudes to Rome would stem from a range of issues particular to early Christianity, such as the social practices of Christian communities and aspects of Christology and eschatology.

There is a range of sources for understanding each of these three dimensions. For provincial issues, the main sources are inscriptions and the writings of provincial authors, including Jewish and Christian ones. We can also use Roman authors such as Cicero, who reflect on the relations between Rome and provincial life. The sources for Jewish issues are well known, especially Josephus, Philo, and the Dead Sea Scrolls, but also aspects of New Testament texts. For Christian issues we need to consider particularly the sources prior to the letter to the Romans. We can certainly use 1 Thessalonians, Galatians, and 1–2 Corinthians. I think that 2 Thessalonians also belongs in this period. There are also the early traditions in the Gospels and in the Acts of the Apostles.

We need a principle of selection among this mass of data. Probably the most appropriate principle to use for an initial study such as this one is to look for the attitudes that were most prevalent and most significant among provincials, Jews, and Christians. There is no obvious method for extracting this from our disparate sources. The best plan is probably for me to suggest a tentative list based on my own impressions from reading a variety of sources. If the approach of this chapter did prove useful in the exegesis of Romans, it would then be worth trying to sharpen up the list of attitudes further.

The list of Christian attitudes to Rome that I have arrived at is the following (in no particular order except that I would suggest that the first was probably the dominant attitude): awe, appreciation, resentment, contempt, denial of ultimate authority, and expectation of overthrow.

PROVINCIAL ATTITUDES

The main provincial attitude to Rome must have been one of awe, as Rome was immense in prestige, power, and wealth. The city of Rome was also very great in population, but the relation in population between Rome and Ephesus, Alexandria, or Antioch was only a factor of between three and five—the other cities would also have seemed enormous—whereas the prestige, power, and wealth of Rome outweighed that of any other city by an incalculable amount. Rome could blow on Ephesus and it would collapse. Rome had so much prestige and power that an itinerant Jewish preacher who was able to claim citizenship of the city was accorded a radically different status, wherever he was in Mediterranean world.

"Their greatest grievance is that they are subject to taxation," writes Cicero.[3] Cicero points out that the Greeks had agreed to the taxation and that taxes are needed to pay for the armies that protect the "allies" (the Roman term for provincial subjects) from external attack and internal strife. Farmers generally paid what was notionally 10 percent of the value of their crops (it was calculated on expected, rather than actual, yields), and they would have paid additional charges if the Romans had designated the land as property of Rome. Everyone paid, either directly or through increased prices, for indirect taxes such as *portoria*, the transit tax (typically 2.5 percent).[4] Historians tend to see the Early Principate as a period of fairly low taxation. The points of comparison are the depredations of the civil war periods of the first century BCE (alongside the exploitative role of the *publicani*, the Roman contracting companies, in the province of Asia in that period) and the heavy and often arbitrary demands made on provincial money during the chaos of the third century CE. However, in an ancient economy, in which most people existed close to or below the breadline, taxation was bound to be resented. Three particular problems were common. First, taxation frequently required a substantial move into cash transaction. Peasant subsistence was disturbed by the

3. Cicero, *Letters to his Brother Quintus* 1.1, in *Roman Civilization: Selected Readings*, vol. 1: *The Republic and the Augustan Age*, 3rd ed., trans. N. Lewis and M. Reinhold (New York: Columbia University Press, 1990), 380-84.

4. Andrew Lintott, *Imperium Romanum: Politics and Administration* (London: Routledge, 1993), 74-85.

necessity to raise money, usually by selling crops in unfavorable market conditions at harvest time. Second, finding the money to pay tax often involved borrowing it, frequently from the tax collector. This greatly increased the cost and often generated a cycle of indebtedness.[5] Third, whether taxes were collected by *publicani* or local organizations, exploitation was common.

Attitudes to the *pax Romana* are positive in most of the preserved sources. That these accurately reflect the general picture is shown by the Romans' ability to withdraw almost all their troops from most provinces that were away from the empire's border. Even in long-established provinces, people would have been aware that the Augustan Peace underwrote better economic conditions than would otherwise have prevailed. The Romans also underwrote (and had sometimes created) the stratified social system that was everywhere present. However, it would seem unlikely that people generally perceived social inequality as being due to imperial control. The one exception could be in Roman colonies and their vicinity. Most provincials would not have experienced Roman judicial action at firsthand. As Cicero reminds Quintus, the Romans delegated most day-to-day government to local "councils of the aristocracy."[6] A limited number of people would have encountered the Roman governor's action to suppress disorder. He could take such action anywhere in his province. His *imperium* overrode any consideration of whether any city was technically free (as Thessalonica was). The lightness of touch that Rome seems to have exercised in direct judicial action in most Mediterranean provinces in the first century suggests that the dominant attitude to the *pax Romana* and its implementation was, on balance, more appreciative than resentful.

The prestige and power of Rome were most strikingly reified in the offering of cult to the goddess Roma, to some governors (during the Republic), and to emperors and their families. As Simon Price argues, in the hellenized East this represented the people viewing Rome as a power that was beyond the scope of normal *polis* experience but that related in some way to the norms of Greek culture.[7] Rome was located among the gods.

5. Douglas E. Oakman, "The Countryside in Luke-Acts," in *The Social World of Luke-Acts: Models for Interpretation*, ed. Jerome H. Neyrey (Peabody, MA: Hendrickson, 1991), 151–79 at 157–58.

6. Cicero, *Letters to Quintus* 1.1.

7. S. R. F. Price, *Rituals and Power: The Roman Imperial Cult in Asia Minor* (Cambridge: Cambridge University Press, 1984).

Jewish Issues

We can divide the issues broadly into Jewish experience and Jewish theology. In 57 CE, Jewish current experience varied from place to place. Judea was under a Roman governor, Antonius Felix. Various northern and eastern areas of Israel were under an "allied king" (i.e., a client king), Agrippa II. The *pax Romana* was probably a key enabling factor in the existence of Jewish Diaspora communities in Alexandria, Antioch, and many other cities. Judaism had a number of legal privileges, but Roman writing indicates widespread anti-Jewish feeling.

Where did this leave Jewish attitudes? Josephus sees Felix's period of office (52–ca. 59 CE) as a time when resistance activity in Judea became widespread.[8] Popular resentment against Rome must have been increased during the rule of his predecessor, Ventidius Cumanus, whose incompetence and bloody actions ended in trial at Rome and exile.[9] In the Diaspora, Claudius's expulsion of Jews (or possibly Jewish Christians) at some point in the 40s probably caused anti-Roman feeling.[10] Memory of Claudius's intervention restraining Greek attacks on Jews in Alexandria presumably somewhat assuaged this resentment, especially if his command to act "kindly toward the Jews"[11] acted as a precedent for effective protection of Jewish communities across the Diaspora at this period. However, even in the same letter there is a threat, if Jews disobey various commands, that sounds deep-rootedly hostile: "I will move against them as if they were raising up some common plague for the inhabited world."[12] Among Diaspora Jews, there was probably a mixture of appreciation of and resentment toward Rome. In Israel, resentment probably predominated.

This resentment was reinforced (as the rhetoric of the Jewish War was to show) by a theological claim to political independence. Roman control of Israel was an offense to Jewish theology, an offense that was probably felt afresh in 44 CE when Judea returned to Roman governance after Agrippa I's brief Jewish rule. Alongside resentment was systemic Jewish disbelief in the entire religious world that structured Roman social and political attitudes and actions. Jews did have an element of *pietas*, in that they honored their forbears, but everything else, from augurs to imperial cult, was viewed, despite its an-

---

8. Josephus, *Jewish War* 2.13 §§250–70.

9. Lester L. Grabbe, *Judaism from Cyrus to Hadrian* (London: SCM, 1994), 440.

10. Grabbe, *Judaism*, 397–99.

11. Robert Sherk, *The Roman Empire: Augustus to Hadrian* (Cambridge: Cambridge University Press, 1988), no. 43 line 83.

12. Sherk, *Roman Empire*, no. 43 lines 99–100.

tiquity and evident global political effectiveness, as contemptible—I think that is not too strong a word, given most surviving Jewish rhetoric on the subject. Jewish theological ethics then extended this contempt into a further field, that of morality. Jews viewed certain aspects of Roman behavior with strong disapproval, especially the exposure of infants and sexual practice. In the latter area, disapproval certainly progressed to contempt. Wisdom of Solomon 13–14 is a good example of such negative rhetoric on both cults and morality.

CHRISTIAN ISSUES

Paul's collection for the "saints in Jerusalem," which was nearing completion at the time of the letter, shows that, at this period, even the Christian communities who might be thought of as most independent of Israel still had a strong orientation toward issues in the land. It therefore seems reasonable to model general Christian attitudes at this period as including the Jewish ones above.

Up to this period, Christians' experience of Rome, as Christians, was probably rather limited. Paul had certainly faced trouble from Roman magistrates at Philippi (1 Thess 2:2; Acts 16:20–23), but had almost certainly received support from the proconsul of Achaia (Acts 18:12–16). To the Romans involved, these were interactions with Jews. For the Christians they were beginnings of a history of dealings with Rome. However, by the mid-50s, the experience was probably too limited to have had a strong influence on attitudes to Rome. The possible exception to this was Claudius's expulsions after the rioting "at the instigation of Chrestus."[13] However, even if "Chrestus" means Christus and most of those expelled were Jewish Christians, the incident is still seen by Roman sources as a Jewish one, and even the Christians would have realized that Roman judicial action in response to rioting was not action against Christians as a religious group. In terms of their experience as Christians, I would expect attitudes to Rome in the mid-50s to have been fairly unformed and neutral.

The effects of Christian theology were a different matter. Christians adopted the negative attitudes to Rome inherent in Jewish theology but sharpened two elements of it. The first was Jewish theological denial of the full extent of Roman *imperium*. God's authority limited that of Rome. Christians sharpened this by making Christ the ultimate human-divine authority figure,

13. Suetonius, *Claudius* 25.4.

thus usurping the Augustan role.[14] They also adopted social practices that transgressed norms supported by Roman authority. This happened in various aspects of house-church life, from the mere fact of regularly meeting together irrespective of Roman regulation of associations, through the formation of fictive kinship groups that cut across household lines, to the challenge that the practice of prophecy represented to household authority structures. Rome generally did not interfere in the lives of people under its authority. However, Rome's *imperium* meant their claim that whatever they wanted should be done, in any sphere, with no limitation. From the early days of the Christian movement, "to listen to God, not people" (cf. Acts 4:19) was a fixed attitude.

Christians also sharpened the force of Jewish eschatology. They were not the only Jewish group to do so: the Qumran community wrote at length about the coming overthrow of the *Kittim*. In Paul's teaching at least, forceful eschatological material was already well entrenched by the time of Romans. The expectation of the overthrow of the current world order—which was the Roman world order—is expressed in 1 Thess 5:3, which promises destruction for those who say *pax et securitas* ("peace and security").[15] If 2 Thessalonians is from this period as well, the warnings are even more explicit. More broadly, the overthrow of the Roman order is implicit in the widespread teaching about the triumphant return of Christ, particularly given the roots of this teaching in the Jewish idea of the coming decisive intervention of God to reshape the life of the world. The full expression of Christian expectation of the overthrow of Rome, seen in the book of Revelation, was unlikely to have developed yet. However, an expectation of overthrow was inherent in Christian theology from its very beginnings.

Conclusion

This is a very strange mixture of attitudes to Rome. If, as suggested, Christians at this period held a combination of the main attitudes of provincials and

14. Peter Oakes, *Philippians: From People to Letter*, SNTSMS 110 (Cambridge: Cambridge University Press, 2001), 129–74; Peter Oakes, "God's Sovereignty over Roman Authorities: A Theme in Philippians," in *Rome in the Bible and the Early Church*, ed. Peter Oakes (Carlisle: Paternoster; Grand Rapids: Baker, 2002), 126–41, included as chap. 10 of the present volume.

15. See the substantial defense of this reading by Christoph vom Brocke, *Thessaloniki— Stadt des Kassander und Gemeinde des Paulus*, WUNT 125 (Tübingen: Mohr Siebeck, 2001), 167–85.

Jews, and also attitudes specific to Christians, then our brief survey suggests the following: awe at Rome's prestige, power, and wealth; appreciation of Roman peace, economic prosperity, partial protection of Diaspora communities, and laws permitting Jewish practice; resentment at taxation, occupation of Israel, and poor governing of Judea; contempt for Roman religious beliefs and certain aspects of morality; denial of ultimate authority; and expectation of overthrow.

Awe, appreciation, resentment, contempt, denial of ultimate authority, expectation of overthrow. It would be interesting to use these six as a grid, assessing the possible presence of each in each passage in Romans.

A glance at the letter itself immediately raises the issue of whether Rom 13:1–7 shows the list to be deficient. Where in the list is respect for Roman authority? One could see it as part of appreciation. This would view 13:1–7 as essentially pragmatic, seeing Paul as supporting most of the emperor's exercise of authority because it had proved, in the main, beneficial. A second place to look is at awe. For most provincials, this awe issued in religious reverence for Rome. Jews and Christians stopped short of worshiping Rome, but they must have still felt awe at the city's power. One solution to this conundrum of status was to conclude that Rome had a special status, given by God, over the world. This kind of view can be traced far back in the Hebrew Bible. However, it clearly forms a tension with the expectation of Rome's overthrow. In fact, it might be particularly interesting to study Romans within the framework of that tension (a tension that is also a feature of New Testament theology more broadly). However, another effect that use of the list has on the study of 13:1–7 is to make us think seriously about whether there is anything like it prior to the letter. The evidence is thin and ambiguous. The encouragement to social conformity in 1–2 Thessalonians needs to be considered alongside the negative description of secular judges in 1 Cor 6.

Our list is clearly partial and open to improvement. However, it does appear that attempts to describe Christian attitudes to Rome in such a way are likely to offer fruitful avenues for study of Paul's letter.

9 | A State of Tension: Rome in the New Testament

Richard Cassidy has made an interesting suggestion about Paul's attitudes to Rome. Cassidy suggests that Paul viewed Rome in positive terms when he wrote Rom 13 but that his subsequent experience, especially his imprisonment, made him negative about Rome by the time he wrote Philippians.[1] The elegance of this suggestion lies in its defusing of an apparent Pauline contradiction by appeal to a palpably reasonable process: anyone would be likely to be embittered against the authorities by a long period of imprisonment.

The difficulty with Cassidy's thesis is that the Pauline contradiction that Cassidy is trying to deal with is implicitly present in the letter to the Romans itself (and, I would also argue, in Philippians).[2] In particular, the criticism directed against the idolatrous world in Rom 1:18-32 is so comprehensive that it condemns the Roman system of thought and authority at its core.

In fact, many writers have noted elements of Paul's implied critique of Roman authority. Their consequent move has been to argue that an apparently positive passage, such as Rom 13:1-7, must be essentially tactical or, in fact,

1. On Rom 13:1-7, Cassidy writes: "Paul's position in these verses is one of virtually unqualified support for the authorities of the Roman Empire." Cassidy further expresses this as "the startling level of affirmation and support that Paul affords to the existing authorities." In describing the contrast with Philippians, Cassidy writes: "A dramatic shift occurs in Paul's outlook between Romans and Philippians. In effect, Philippians contains a critical perspective regarding the Roman authorities that Romans simply does not possess"; Richard J. Cassidy, *Paul in Chains: Roman Imprisonment and the Letters of St. Paul* (New York: Crossroad, 2001), 18, 5.

2. For discussion of Philippians in relation to Rome (although not on this particular issue), see Peter Oakes, *Philippians: From People to Letter*, SNTSMS 110 (Cambridge: Cambridge University Press, 2001), esp. chap. 5; Peter Oakes, "God's Sovereignty over Roman Authorities: A Theme in Philippians," in *Rome in the Bible and the Early Church*, ed. Peter Oakes (Carlisle: Paternoster; Grand Rapids: Baker, 2002), 126-41, included as chap. 10 of the present volume.

rather negative. Some writers have suggested that the passage merely promotes a survival strategy of conforming behavior.[3] Others have seen Paul as wishing to sound positive because of suspicion that he was disloyal.[4] Yet others have argued that the underlying idea is the restriction of Rome's authority, since it is a provisional institution and fundamentally not of divine nature.[5]

I would suggest that, although such points have some validity, the attempt by these writers and Richard Cassidy to remove the tension between positive and negative comments on Rome in Paul's writings is unnecessary. Paul's writings represent a pattern seen in the New Testament as a whole: a pattern of fundamental tension inherent in early Christian attitudes to Rome.

In preparing a 2003 article I began thinking about how to model the attitudes of Christians to Rome at the time of Paul's letter sent to the city.[6] At that period (the late 50s), Christianity was a provincial religious movement rooted in Jewish beliefs, practice, and history. This suggested that it would be illuminating to model Christian attitudes as a combination of prominent aspects of provincial, Jewish, and distinctively Christian (e.g., christological) attitudes to Rome.

Looking at provincial evidence gave me a list of three prominent attitudes: awe at Rome's prestige, power, and wealth; appreciation of the *pax Romana* for the stability and economic prosperity it brought; resentment at payment of taxes. My Jewish list contained: appreciation of Rome's (partial) protection of Diaspora communities and of laws permitting Jewish practice; resentment at occupation of Israel and recent poor governing of Judea; contempt for Roman religious beliefs and certain aspects of morality. Jews would also share the provincial attitudes above. Christians' experience of Rome, as Christians per se, was probably too limited at that period to have a great effect on Christian attitudes. However, Christian beliefs (in common with those of some other Jewish groups) sharpened certain elements of Jewish theology so as to produce

3. Richard A. Horsley and Neil Asher Silberman, *The Message and the Kingdom: How Jesus and Paul Ignited a Revolution and Transformed the Ancient World* (Minneapolis: Fortress, 1997), 191; J. Friedrich, W. Pöhlmann and P. Stuhlmacher, "Zur historischen Situation und Intention von Röm 13:1–7," *Zeitschrift für Theologie und Kirche* 73 (1976): 131–66 at 165.

4. Klaus Wengst, *Pax Romana and the Peace of Jesus Christ*, trans. J. Bowden (Philadelphia: Fortress, 1987), 82–83.

5. Oscar Cullmann, *The State in the New Testament* (London: SCM, 1957), 67; cf. Justin J. Meggitt, *Paul, Poverty, and Survival*, Studies of the New Testament and Its World (Edinburgh: T&T Clark, 1998), 185–86.

6. Peter Oakes, "Christian Attitudes to Rome at the Time of Paul's Letter," *Review and Expositor* 100 (2003): 103–11, included as chap. 8 in the present volume.

more emphatic attitudes of denying Rome's ultimate authority and expecting the overthrow of the Roman social and political system. This sharpening stemmed especially from fundamental Christian ideas about the authority of the Messiah and the advent of God's kingdom.[7]

In total, my list of expected Christian attitudes in the mid-50s had six broad elements: awe, appreciation, resentment, contempt, denial of ultimate authority, expectation of overthrow. My conclusion is that a list full of tension, such as this six-element list of attitudes, had deep and wide-spreading roots in the thought world of the earliest Christian writers.[8] Attempts to defuse such tension are likely to lose connection with these roots at some point.

To what extent is this conclusion about expected attitudes borne out by evidence of actual attitudes seen in the New Testament writings? Is tension inherent in each writing or, as Cassidy and others argue, do various books represent various elements of it? To what extent is there change over time or space in the nature of the tension? Is there ever resolution of the tension in favor of either its positive or negative pole?

To attempt to reach even provisional conclusions on these questions we must deal in some way with a substantial complicating factor. My previous model of attitudes was in principle a snapshot for the year 57 CE. If we move either backward or forward from this date, the picture changes.

CONTINUITIES AND DISCONTINUITIES IN ATTITUDE

In the years between Jesus's crucifixion and 57, provincial attitudes to Rome probably changed little. Caligula's eccentricity had only a limited general effect, and the solidity of Claudius's reign would have reestablished the impression of smoothly running Roman power and progress. After 57, Nero's decline was probably not a significant factor. He seems to have remained popular in the eastern half of the empire, where our interest lies. News of the catastrophic fire in 64 must have dented Rome's appearance of invulnerability. This must have been even truer of the "year of the four emperors," 69, and the difficulty that Rome had in suppressing the Jewish revolt (66–70). However, once the Flavian dynasty was installed and the revolt in the east put down, Rome's prestige and stability would have remained secure through to the end of the period of production of the New Testament writings. Although we know of some trouble

---

7. Oakes, "Christian Attitudes to Rome," 105–9.
8. Oakes, "Christian Attitudes to Rome," 110.

over taxation under Nero and of famines and some other calamities at other points in the first century, the provincial mixture of awe, appreciation, and resentment was probably relatively constant over the course of the century as a whole.

The same cannot be said of Jewish attitudes to Rome. The reign of Agrippa I (41–44), placed on the throne of Judea by an emperor who was his friend, probably represented a high point in Jewish attitudes to the Roman Empire. Direct Roman rule, the pattern for the rest of the period, was characterized by a long series of episodes of mismanagement, such as the string of problems under Ventidius Cumanus (48–52).[9] Such problems would primarily have annoyed Judean Jews, but Diaspora interest in the fate of Judea must have meant that bad governors affected attitudes in the Diaspora communities too. These communities owed their economic welfare to the *pax Romana*, but they also had their own difficulties in terms of periodic conflicts with other groups in the cities, most seriously in Alexandria in the late 30s. Jews blamed the Roman authorities for mismanagement of such conflicts (e.g., Philo, *Against Flaccus*).

There are, therefore, some potential sharp short-term variations in Jewish attitudes. However, for the purposes of our model it is probably worth simplifying all this to say that, up to the mid-60s, both Diaspora and Judean Jewish communities broadly held the combination of attitudes (appreciation, resentment, and contempt) described in the 57 CE model above.

The Jewish War changed that. Even if some Jews saw responsibility for the war as lying with certain hotheaded Jewish groups and saw Rome's crushing of the rebellion as political common sense (from a Roman viewpoint), the manner of Rome's action must have engendered great bitterness for a long time afterward. Rome killed thousands and enslaved far more. Rome demolished the temple and, indeed, the whole of Jerusalem. Rome gloried in its triumph over the Jews. There must have been great resentment at the JUDAEA CAPTA coins and, particularly, at the parading of the temple artifacts in Rome and their subsequent representation on the Arch of Titus. Most Jews would not have traveled to Rome, but many would have heard that a new architectural center point of the city was a depiction of the carrying off of the menorah. The war also saw fresh disturbances between some Diaspora communities and their neighbors, especially in Alexandria (Josephus, *Jewish War* 2.18.7–8 §§487–98).[10] Both in terms of Jewish experience of Rome and in terms of the offense to Jewish theology, postwar attitudes to Rome must have been very

9. Lester L. Grabbe, *Judaism from Cyrus to Hadrian* (London: SCM, 1994), 440.
10. Grabbe, *Judaism*, 439.

negative. Evidence for this is clear in apocalyptic texts such as 4 Ezra, 2 Baruch, and Sibylline Oracle 4, but it was surely also more generally true. Looking back at my list, Jewish attitudes to Rome must still have included awe, but appreciation had probably gone. Resentment and religious and moral contempt were still there. Jewish groups that particularly denied Roman authority or expected Rome's overthrow had largely been crushed, although apocalyptic writing continued to be produced, and more actively military groups reappear after the New Testament period. I would think that, between 70 CE and 100 CE, awe, resentment, and contempt were the predominant attitudes.

My method for arriving at specifically Christian attitudes in 57 was to look at the evidence up to that point; therefore I cannot distinguish between Christian attitudes in 57 and those prior to 57. Moving beyond 57, we have three major factors to consider: the first identifiable persecution of Christians as a distinct group, by Nero in 64; the Jewish War and its outcome; and the increasing separation of Christianity from Judaism.

The killing of Christians by Nero, and any further persecution by Roman authority figures in the remainder of the century, must have introduced a new element—that of resentment against persecution—into Christian attitudes to Rome. Christians' experience of Rome, as Christians, was no longer neutral. However, government action against Christians was not at all on the scale of government action against Jews. There is nothing like the mass slaughter and mass enslavement that Jews experienced during the war. Government persecution of Christians was probably not sufficiently widespread to extinguish all appreciation of the benefits of the *pax Romana*. Some such appreciation of the benefits that the authorities brought would generally have sat alongside resentment at stories of persecution.

The Jewish War and the increasing separation of Christians from Jews need to be taken together. The basic separation at this point is in experience. The war was a catastrophic trauma for Jews but not, to anything like the same extent, for most Christians. Conversely, the Neronian persecution and any aftermath of it affected Christians, not Jews. The experience-based attitudes to Rome of each community must have been becoming fairly independent of each other at this period. Whether Jews appreciated or resented Rome no longer directly affected Christian attitudes.

On the other hand, there is clearly still continuity in theological views about Rome between Jews and Christians. The texts of 4 Ezra, 2 Baruch, and Sibylline Oracle 4 show that at least certain groups of postwar Jews shared the expectation of Rome's overthrow by God that is also seen in Christian texts of the period. More broadly, Jews and Christians continued to hold basic theological views, such as contempt for Roman religious ideas, that they had shared since the earliest days of the Jesus movement.

Let us take the events of 64 together with those of 70 and try to characterize Christian attitudes in two periods, before and after 70. The overall list of expected attitudes is probably the same pre- and post-70: awe, appreciation, resentment, contempt, denial of ultimate authority, expectation of overthrow. However, this similarity masks two important differences. First, resentment now includes resentment against Roman persecution of Christians. Even if persecution was limited, stories of such events clearly circulated widely. Second, the post-70 Christian attitudes are more detached from Jewish attitudes than were the pre-70 ones. There is much continuity in theology, especially in apocalyptic texts, but the two groups' experiences of Rome are now rather divergent.

Let us now look at five test cases: 1 Thessalonians, Romans, Mark, Acts, and Revelation. These are five of the texts that tell us most about early Christian attitudes to Rome. Two of these are firmly pre-70. Mark probably dates from around 70 but certainly includes earlier traditions. Acts is usually seen as post-70, although some scholars place it in the 60s and, again, it includes earlier traditions. Revelation is almost universally seen as considerably later than 70. In fact, many scholars place it in the early second century. However, that does not affect our model of attitudes since, for our model, the end of the first century is not a sharp cutoff point.

The First Letter to the Thessalonians

First Thessalonians begins on a note of suffering. The Thessalonians have suffered (1:6; 2:14), as have Paul and his entourage, both in Thessalonica and Philippi (2:2, 17). However, unlike in 2 Thess 1:6–8, this does not lead into the issuing of apocalyptic warnings about the fate of the persecutors as such. They will get caught up in the trouble of 1 Thess 5:3, but there is no assertion there that the authorities, Greek or Roman, are destroyed because of their persecution of Christians. However, the rhetoric about suffering does imply a view of the social environment as hostile. Politically, in Thessalonica, that environment is one of Greek rule under Roman supervision. We should probably describe the attitude encapsulated by the rhetoric on suffering as being one of distrust and distance. However, this is directed essentially at the local society and authorities. It is not clear that we can yet draw Rome itself into its scope.

Jewish dismissal of the Greco-Roman religious system is clear in the fundamental description of conversion in 1:9: "You turned to God from idols to serve the living and genuine God." *Pietas*, right behavior toward ancestors and the gods, was central to the Romans' concept of their identity and of why their empire succeeded. For Paul to show contempt for gods (and hence ancestral traditions) as false, worthless things to be abandoned, meant contempt for Rome, even if he was a citizen. Of course, the Romans were used to Jewish denigration of the gods. However, for Paul to found predominantly gentile communities on that basis, as 1:9 implies, was going far further.

If 2:16c, "wrath has come upon them," is original to the letter, it could refer to some sort of Roman action that went against Jewish interests.[11] In that case, Paul would be responding to that action by giving it some sort of theological legitimation, rather than simply condemning it as one would expect a Jew of the time to do. Admittedly, Paul does not explicitly sanction the action that may lie behind 2:16. However, the rhetoric is more what one would expect of a post-70 attitude than a pre-70 one. Indeed, this argument has been used by some scholars to back the idea of the text being a post-70 interpolation.[12] However, the lack of text-critical evidence for interpolation makes one reluctant to accept the suggestion. From the point of view of this chapter, the interesting way to read the verse is as a possible sign of very early Christian development toward a kind of rhetoric, in relation to Rome's treatment of Judea, that became full blown once Christianity and Judaism moved further apart.

Paul urges the Thessalonian Christians to work and lead a quiet life, so as to seem respectable to outsiders (4:11–12). As with Rom 13, some scholars argue that this is a tactical, defensive measure. I agree that the practical imperatives of the Thessalonians' situation make it important. However, we should also see it as expressing a certain amount of respect for the Greco-Roman social status quo. Paul presents this as one in which quiet hard work can be expected to generate adequate income (1 Thess 4:12). There is nothing directly about Rome here but I think we should see a corollary of this passage as being that Paul does appreciate the socioeconomic system sustained by the *pax Romana*. One can contrast this with Rev 18 in which the Roman economic system is seen as working for the benefit of people such as merchants rather than that of ordinary people such as the Christians.

11. Abraham J. Malherbe, *The Letters to the Thessalonians: A New Translation and Commentary*, Anchor Yale Bible 32B (New York: Doubleday, 2000), 178, gives several possibilities, such as the killing of thousands of Jews in 49 CE (citing Josephus, *Jewish Antiquities* 20.5.2 §102; 20.5.3–4 §§112–17; *Jewish War* 2.12.1 §§225–27).

12. Most notably, B. A. Pearson, "1 Thessalonians 2:13–16: A Deutero-Pauline Interpolation," *Harvard Theological Review* 64 (1971): 79–94 at 82–84.

The text of 1 Thess 4:13–5:11 presents an event that changes the world order. We do not see Rome crashing down in flames. This is not the book of Revelation. However, the parousia in 1 Thessalonians is bound to be seen as overthrowing the Roman order. The apocalyptic language of commands, archangels and trumpets in 4:16 signals an intervention by God to change the world radically, to end the present age. The political overtones[13] of the description of Christ's return in 4:15–17 suggest Christ taking up some position of great authority. Above all, the destruction in 5:3 must sweep away the current system.

How specifically this relates to Rome depends on the interpretation of εἰρήνη καὶ ἀσφάλεια ("peace and safety"), *pax et securitas* (5:3). Abraham Malherbe is skeptical about political readings of this. He takes the slogan as summarizing the view of false teachers at Thessalonica, with Paul characterizing their message both in terms of the false prophets of Jeremiah's day who cried "Peace!" (Jer 6:14; 8:11) and of the Epicurean promise of "security" (Epicurus, *Principal Doctrine* 14).[14] A weakness in Malherbe's suggestion lies in the need to draw the two terms from different spheres. Christoph vom Brocke has given a robust defense of Ernst Bammel's drawing of both terms from the slogans of Roman politics.[15] Because this is a single sphere of discourse, this suggestion would, in principle, be stronger than that of Malherbe even if, in politics, the terms never occurred together. The popular spread of the terminology, seen especially in Claudius's PACI AUGUSTAE coins and the SECURITAS AUGUSTI ones of Nero, was also far wider than that of the Epicurean usage. The terms do, in fact, sometimes occur together. Velleius sees Tiberius as having restored *Asiae securitatem, Macedoniae pacem* (Velleius Paterculus 2.98.2). A first-century BCE inscription at Troas celebrates Pompey's restoration of εἰρήνη καὶ τὴν ἀσφάλειαν.[16] Klaus Wengst and Holland Hendrix give further examples.[17]

I doubt whether Paul is thinking specifically of the Roman authorities as

13. Karl Donfried, "The Cults of Thessalonica and the Thessalonian Correspondence," *NTS* 31 (1985): 336–56 at 334.

14. Malherbe, *Thessalonians*, 292, 304.

15. Ernst Bammel, "Ein Beitrag zur paulinischen Staatsanschauung," *Theologische Literaturzeitung* 85 (1960): 837–40; Christoph vom Brocke, *Thessaloniki—Stadt des Kassander und Gemeinde des Paulus*, WUNT 125 (Tübingen: Mohr Siebeck, 2001), 167–85.

16. Elmar Schwertheim, "Forschungen in der Troas im Jahre 1988," *Araştirma Sonuçlari Toplantisi* 7 (1990): 229–32 at 230. For all the above references see vom Brocke, *Thessaloniki*, 177–79.

17. Wengst, *Pax Romana*, 19, 21; H. L. Hendrix, "Archaeology and Eschatology at Thessalonica," in *The Future of Early Christianity: Essays in Honor of Helmut Koester*, ed. B. A. Pearson (Minneapolis: Fortress, 1991), 113–14.

those who say "peace and safety." In the context of the letter it looks more likely to be the general non-Christian population of Thessalonica.[18] Cocooned by the Roman peace, they assume that nothing will disturb their lives, a state that Paul characterizes as "sleep"—in an ironic juxtaposition to the state of the Christian dead (5:6-7; cf. 5:10). This illusory peace will be swept away by the arrival of the Lord "like a thief in the night" (5:2). This is bound to involve the Roman system being overthrown along with its *pax*. Paul seems to have Thessalonians rather than Romans at the center of his focus in 5:3, but he does seem to expect Rome's overthrow.

In 1 Thessalonians, Paul does not directly write about Rome. However, several of the points that he makes indicate attitudes that he has toward Rome. The advice to live quietly and work, and the confidence that this will avoid dependence, suggest confidence in the Greco-Roman socioeconomic order. However, the concern about suffering implies a picture of the surrounding society as hostile. His view may be that hostility toward Christians is a bad element in a generally beneficent system. There is no indication of resentment directed against Rome on this account, nor on account of harsh Roman treatment of Jews, if that is what is behind 2:16. There is clear contempt for the Greco-Roman religious system. There is expectation of the overthrow of the current world order but, although Roman political language is used, attention is not drawn to Rome as a particular power to be done away with. Paul's attitudes to Rome implied by the text lie broadly across the range that we are using.

THE LETTER TO THE ROMANS

Several scholars working on Romans are currently studying a wide range of material that may relate to Rome. I too have interests in this area. At present, I want to reinforce my comments on the tension between 1:18-32 and 13:1-7. Roman writers would regard Paul's combination of views as bizarrely paradoxical. They would agree that Rome was God's servant (13:4; Roman writers are happy to use monotheistic language in this kind of context, for example, Seneca, *On Benefits* 4.32.3), but they would see the center point of that service as being the maintenance of *pietas*. Rome's other good actions, such as praising good people and punishing the bad (Rom 13:3-4) would be seen as outwork-

18. Cf. vom Brocke, *Thessaloniki*, 184-85.

ings of this *pietas*. But in Rom 1 Paul sees Roman *pietas* as the very cause of all immorality (1:21–32)!

Paul shows appreciation of Rome's judicial role. He even shows a kind of awe in giving Rome the distinction of being God's servant in this way. Yet Paul displays contempt for Roman religion and aspects of Roman moral behavior. We must not bracket off this religious contempt as though Paul were criticizing only an incidental part of Roman life. From the taking of auguries before Senate meetings, to the Fetial Law (a complex system of ideas and ritual actions that governed warfare), to the religious role of the paterfamilias, to the way in which the imperial cult expressed provincial loyalty, religion lay at the heart of the functioning of the Roman Empire.[19] The tension inherent in Paul's view is powerfully illustrated in the incomprehension of Roman officials in many of the later martyr accounts. To honor Rome while dishonoring Rome's gods was a contradiction in terms. Paul inherited this contradiction as part of his Judaism. For gentile converts to Christianity it must have seemed very strange. Surely, they might think, if Rom 1 shows that Greco-Roman life is a progress from idolatry to immorality, Rom 13 should say that the Roman authorities serve demons. The authorities' very operation is by means of idolatry. How does God suddenly come into the equation? There is a tension in early Christian thought here.

There is, of course, a biblical pattern to all this. Figures like Nebuchadnezzar could be seen as God's instruments even though Babylonian religious beliefs were still attacked. Something of the tension that was present in early Christian attitudes to Rome was also present in earlier Israelite attitudes to other dominant political powers.

THE GOSPEL OF MARK

"Your manner of life must not be like that of those who are regarded as ruling the gentiles." If we paraphrase Mark 10:42–44 in this way we can see a sharp potential critique of the Roman model of rule.[20] Furthermore, the thing that will arrive in the temple is "the abomination of desolation" (13:14). That this is an allusion to Daniel's portrayal of the awful events under Antiochus Epiphanes (Dan 9:27; 11:31; 12:11) makes it very pointed. Mark also gives us our first view of Pontius Pilate. His administration of justice is clearly unfair and

19. Meggitt, *Paul, Poverty, and Survival*, 118.
20. Wengst, *Pax Romana*, 56.

brutal. Mark makes no attempt to signal that Pilate's actions are not typical of Roman governors.

On the other hand, a climactic theological assertion in the book is given to a centurion: "Truly this man was a son of God" (Mark 15:39). This is a Roman executioner being given a key positive role! There is also the question and answer in the temple. Jesus looks at the head of the emperor on a denarius and says, "Give the things of Caesar to Caesar and the things of God to God" (12:15–17). Jesus's reference to the denarius and the use of καί[21] in 12:17 make it difficult to follow Richard Horsley and N. A. Silberman in seeing the reference to God as effectively nullifying that to Caesar.[22] Mark's Jesus is supporting economic cooperation with the Romans.

In between those negative and positive points, some ambiguous issues raise far-reaching questions. Should we link to Rome the use of the term "gospel" (1:1) or the expression "son of God" (1:1; 5:7; 15:39)? Should we read anything into the demons being called "Legion" (5:9)?[23] How indicative of the nature of Rome should we see Pilate's behavior as being?

If Mark's Gospel is written during the momentous events of the 60s, either in Rome or near Judea, we might tend to expect a direct engagement with the issue of Roman power and Rome's attitudes. It could possibly be that the engagement stares us in the face. We take the general structure of Mark for granted, but it may be that we should see the long description of Jesus's passion as carrying an extended comment on the interaction between innocence and Roman power. Moreover, the hinge of the gospel is the revelation at Caesarea Philippi of Jesus's messiahship, a revelation that is immediately tied into a passage that culminates in an implied call to the reader to be willing to face martyrdom (8:31–38).

But such a reading cannot be completely convincing. The elaborate inter-actions of the week of the passion are mainly played out between Jesus and various Jewish groups, or between Jesus and his disciples. Politically, Mark is tantalizing. So many elements could be read in relation to Rome, but the prominence of other issues makes one wonder whether many of these elements point another way. For example, how much should be read in terms of a more cosmic conflict?—although, in turn, the cosmic conflict could, of course, relate to politics.

21. R. T. France, *The Gospel of Mark*, New International Greek Testament Commentary (Grand Rapids: Eerdmans, 2002), 469.

22. Horsley and Silberman, *Message and the Kingdom*, 84.

23. Gerd Theissen, *Miracle Stories of the Early Christian Tradition* (Edinburgh: T&T Clark, 1983), 255.

Mark's attitude to Rome is more a puzzle than a clear tension. However, we can see aspects of our model of attitudes. The course of the discussion on paying tax depicts Rome's ability to impose its economic and iconographic system on God's people. There is an element of awe implied here. There is, however, no obvious appreciation of the *pax Romana*. On the contrary, the portrayal of Pilate implies resentment at the rule of this governor at least. The prophecy of the events of 70 CE also conveys deep resentment at the way in which the attackers will behave. There is considerable stress on allegiance to the authority of Jesus being more important than that of those who might promise "life" and "the whole world" (8:35–36). His arrival with his father's glory and the holy angels (8:38) presumably represents the end of the present order. Mark does think about Rome—and the implied attitudes are generally negative. However, in the appreciation of the potential openness of the centurion at the cross, and in the instruction to give Caesar whatever is properly his, I still get a sense of the thought world of 1 Thessalonians. The call is radical but with a pervasive strand of quietism. Any book that can say "give to Caesar the things that are Caesar's" cannot be wholly on the negative side of the equation in relation to Rome. I think we can see enough to conclude that the tension that we are considering is at work in Mark's Gospel, although its effects are enigmatic.

THE BOOK OF ACTS

The ground here is very well worn. Steve Walton has surveyed various approaches and argued persuasively that Luke maintains a stance of critical distance toward Rome. Luke will effectively commend Rome when it does well but is always aware that it may do badly.[24] This is not quite the same as the tension that I am arguing for, although the two approaches can coexist. If Luke holds a mixture of positive and negative attitudes to Rome (my view) then one would expect him to evaluate Rome's actions and judge them as good or bad (Walton's view). By contrast, if Luke held a firmly negative view of Rome, one would expect him to prejudge all of Rome's actions as negative.

Roman officials abound. Cornelius the Italian centurion is a very positive character (Acts 10). Even before conversion to Christianity he is described as "devout and Godfearing" (10:2). His actions in Acts 10 play an important

---

24. Steve Walton, "The State They Were In: Luke's View of the Roman Empire," in *Rome in the Bible and the Early Church*, ed. Peter Oakes (Carlisle: Paternoster; Grand Rapids: Baker, 2002), 1–41 at 33–35.

positive role in the forward movement of Luke's story. The governor Sergius Paulus is also presented positively. He is "intelligent" and open to Christianity (13:6–12). Gallio judges in favor of the Christians (18:12–16), although the description of his lack of concern about the synagogue ruler being beaten up in front of him could carry a note of censure (18:17). The centurion in the shipwreck behaves well (27:32, 43). The chief magistrate on Malta is generous to Paul (28:7). The conditions of Paul's imprisonment at Rome seem very favorable (28:30–31).

Felix is an ambiguous character but, on balance, seems negative for Luke. Felix conducts an orderly hearing and certainly does not jump to conclusions! However, the ensuing two-year hiatus is clearly a scandal and, although his desire to talk repeatedly with Paul would look positive in itself, it becomes negative in Luke's note that Felix's motive is the hope for bribery (24:26). Festus is also ambiguous but does not have the obvious negative edge that Felix has. At the instigation of Paul's opponents among the Jewish authorities, Festus tries to resolve Paul's case (25:2–5). Festus's desire to "do the Jews a favor" inclines him to send Paul to Jerusalem (25:9). Luke's reader knows that this would lead to an ambush, but Luke's Festus is clearly not complicit in this. In any case, Paul solves Festus's problem by appealing to Caesar. The hearing involving Agrippa and Berenice, prior to Paul being sent to Rome, shows Festus as generally reasonable, although his outburst at Paul (26:24) suggests some intemperance.

Another ambiguous case of Roman behavior is the conduct of the troops who arrest Paul. They stop him being beaten by the mob in the temple court (21:32) but immediately chain him (21:33). Surprisingly, the tribune then permits Paul to deliver a speech to the crowd (21:40). When this ends in chaos, the tribune orders the flogging and questioning of Paul (22:24) but cancels the order in alarm on discovering Paul's Roman citizenship (22:29). The tribune then organizes a hearing before the Sanhedrin. His motive is the positive one of wanting to understand the case properly (22:30). He then intervenes again to rescue Paul at the end of that meeting (23:10). Finally, the tribune listens to the report of the plot against Paul and takes careful steps to preserve his life and refer his case to the governor (23:19–33).

The final example is the negative one of the behavior of the Roman authorities at Philippi. In response to charges of un-Roman teaching and to clamor from the forum mob, they peremptorily order the heavy beating and close imprisonment of Paul and Silas (16:20–24). Discovering the next morning that they had illegally beaten Roman citizens, the magistrates show fear and some servility (16:35–39). They compound the bad impression by tacitly reinforcing their original unjust action by asking Paul to leave Philippi (16:39).

This incident stretches Klaus Wengst's argument that Luke depicts Rome and its representatives "in an explicitly favourable light."[25] His view of the Philippi narrative is that Luke was faced with an unavoidable negative incident and toned down the magistrates' violence by appeal to points such as their lack of understanding.[26] On the contrary: Luke's narrative seems designed to highlight the arbitrariness and violence of the magistrates. They themselves tear off the apostles' clothes (contra NRSV, etc.) and order a particularly heavy beating and unnecessarily onerous imprisonment (16:22–23).

Looking through the series of incidents involving Roman officials in Acts leads to the conclusion that they are portrayed in varying ways, both positive and negative. This tells against views, such as that of Wengst, in which Luke is seen as attempting to portray Rome in a uniformly positive light. It would fit the opinion of Oscar Cullmann and others who see Luke as portraying a range of officials whose character and behavior varies. This view can be close to that of Wengst because the variation can be read in terms of some officials properly representing Rome, while others slip from the generally high standards that Luke sees Rome as having.

However, it may be that we should look at this evidence differently. We could read the officials as uniformly representing Rome, but a Rome that was, in Luke's eyes, a paradoxical mixture of good and bad. Felix's love of bribery was as much a part of the common behavior of Roman governors as was Gallio's dismissal of the case against Paul. Luke knew that Rome was like that. As Walton argues, Luke could see Rome (itself) as acting sometimes well and sometimes badly. As I would put it, this is simply the converse of Luke having a view of Rome in which there is tension between appreciation and resentment. The evidence in Acts does not show Luke's Rome as wholly positive. Luke's Rome is a mixture of efficiency, openness, justice, cruelty, and corruption.

THE BOOK OF REVELATION

Surely there is no paradox and tension here? Surely the attitudes to Rome are purely on the negative side—resentment, contempt, denial of ultimate authority, expectation of overthrow—without a hint of awe or of appreciation of the *pax Romana*?

The negative aspects of Revelation's attitude to Rome scarcely need docu-

25. Wengst, *Pax Romana*, 90.
26. Wengst, *Pax Romana*, 95–96.

menting. There is impassioned resentment at persecution, and the persecution is laid specifically at Rome's door (Rev 17:6; 18:20, 24). There is resentment at the nature of the Roman Empire. Rome "corrupted the earth" (19:2). The repeated emphasis on Rome's luxury (17:4; 18:3, 7, 11–14, 16) presumably implies an idea of economic exploitation of the empire. The long list of traded goods probably implies this too, especially since the list ends with slaves (18:11–13). Contempt for Rome is most graphically shown by the depiction of the city as a drunken, bejeweled prostitute riding a beast (17:3–6). There is more specific moral contempt in references such as those to luxury and the slave trade. A major thrust of the book of Revelation as a whole is to persuade its hearers not to submit to certain aspects of Roman authority. This is shown particularly by the insistence on refusing to receive the mark of the name of the beast (14:11). Expectation of Rome's overthrow in Revelation needs no documenting.

On the positive side of our list of attitudes, the writer of Revelation expresses awe at Rome's wealth and power. Rome glitters "with gold, precious stones, and pearls" (18:16). The list of goods of which Rome is the principal buyer is long and detailed (18:11–13). "Was there ever a city like this great city?" cry the seafarers (18:17–18). The angel calls Rome "the great city that has sovereignty over the kings of the earth" (17:18). The writer seems genuinely struck by the extent of Rome's riches and might. This stands in some tension with the derision expressed in the depiction of the prostitute on the beast. The seer holds together awe and contempt.

The writer also describes the Roman Empire as bringing economic benefits. "The merchants of the earth grew rich" (18:3). They sold the goods in the list of 18:11–13. Shipowners too became wealthy (18:19). However, the crucial point is that the writer of Revelation does not identify himself or his community as benefiting from these economic gains. The writer represents a group that sees itself as standing outside the benefits that many other people in the empire are enjoying. If we compare Luke's Roman Empire with that of Revelation, the Roman Empire of Revelation is a more exploitative place for most of its inhabitants. However, the greater structural difference between Luke and Revelation is that, for Revelation, Christians are not able to benefit from aspects of the empire that bring good to some subjects.

There is no tension in the seer's outlook between appreciation and resentment of the empire, even though the seer understands that the empire brings benefit to some people. There is no tension in the writer's assessment of whether Rome is good or bad. It is bad. The only tension in the attitudes in Revelation is probably between awe at "the great city" and derisive contempt at "the prostitute." One could certainly argue that in Revelation the tension between positive and negative elements in the evaluation of Rome is resolved in favor of the negative. However, even here there is the occasional air of the awestruck provincial, gaping at the splendor of the city. One might even say that it is the positive element of awe that lends sharpness to the negative catalogue of Rome's faults and impending disaster.

CONCLUSION

Horsley and Silberman, in their book *The Message and the Kingdom*, present early Christian attitudes to Rome as a trajectory, from the radical Jesus and Paul to the accommodating Luke. I agree that there are trajectories in operation. Two that we have noted in this chapter are the changing attitudes toward Rome's action in Judea and the changing place of persecution as a factor in Christian attitudes. However, the argument of this chapter is that, alongside any trajectories in attitudes, there is a fundamental and persistent element of tension between positive and negative factors within Christian attitudes to Rome. A corollary of this is that scholars' depictions of trajectories have generally been overplayed by ignoring the constant factor of tension.

The New Testament texts differ in the topics that they address and hence in the ways in which some of these topics relate to attitudes to Rome. This means that the nature of the indicators of attitude to Rome vary from text to text. However, the clues in each text add up to an element of tension. In 1 Thessalonians there is a tension indicated by the combination of Paul's confidence in his prescription of quietism and his apocalypticism with regard to *pax et securitas*. In Romans there is a tension in the depiction of Rome's relationship to God. The state, whose government is driven by an idolatry that inevitably produces moral degradation, is also God's servant for praising the good and punishing the bad. In Mark there is tension between a Caesar to whom his due must be rendered and a Caesar whose arrival in the temple is like the "abomination of desolation" of Antiochus Epiphanes. In Acts there is a tension evidenced by the range of behavior of the many Roman authority figures in the book. Even in the book of Revelation, where the moral evaluation of Rome is wholly negative, there is evidence of tension between awe at Rome's power and contempt at its corruption and at its ignominious fate.

Our sixfold model of expected early Christian attitudes to Rome—awe, appreciation, resentment, contempt, denial of ultimate authority, expectation of overthrow—is far from being the only list that could be made. However, it is a useful checklist for considering New Testament texts. None of the texts, except maybe the book of Revelation, discuss Rome explicitly enough to give us direct evidence of the presence or absence of every one of the six factors. However, in many of the texts there are enough clues to suggest that such a list of expected attitudes is not too far from a list of actual attitudes. There seems to be sufficient evidence to suggest that tension, such as that existing between elements of that list, is present in Christian attitudes to Rome in all of the New Testament.

10 | God's Sovereignty over Roman Authorities: A Theme in Philippians

Paul sits in a Roman prison, waiting for trial on a capital charge. He writes to his close friends at Philippi, who are suffering at the hands of fellow towns-people and Roman colonial magistrates. It is little surprise that he writes the letter that he does: a letter whose body begins with an assertion that the gospel flourishes despite Roman imprisonment, a letter that ends by highlighting the establishment of a Christian group among the people at the very heart of the Roman Empire. Paul's letter to the Philippians assures its hearers that God is sovereign over the Roman authorities under whom they are suffering. By doing this, Paul encourages them to stand firm for the gospel.[1]

In my book *Philippians: From People to Letter*, I argued that Paul presented himself as a model of the right attitude to have under suffering.[2] I think that we can be more specific about a major component of his attitude, namely confidence in God's sovereignty over his imprisonment. I also suggested that Christ was presented in such a way that he relativized the Roman emperor. The point of this was to relativize the social imperatives that opposed the unity Paul wanted in the Philippian church.[3] However, it is clear that the presentation of Christ also strongly implies God's sovereignty over the Roman authorities. If we take this sovereignty as a theme, it binds together the two types of passage: about Paul and about Christ. This theme is also highly relevant for the suffering Philippian church.

---

1. I would like to thank Sean Winter and Todd Klutz for their helpful comments on this chapter.

2. Peter Oakes, *Philippians: From People to Letter*, SNTSMS 110 (Cambridge: Cambridge University Press, 2001), chap. 4.

3. Oakes, *Philippians*, chaps. 5–6.

Paul's Situation and the Philippians' Situation

Paul

Paul is "in chains" (1:7), either literally or in the broader sense of being under arrest. He is in constant contact with "the Praetorium" (1:13). As J. B. Lightfoot argues, this expression usually refers to the Praetorian Guard at Rome.[4] Paul seems to be under military arrest.[5] He is also facing the possibility of execution. He writes of "my eager expectation and hope that I will in no way be brought to shame but . . . Christ will be glorified in my body, whether through life or through death" (1:20; cf. 1:21; 2:17; 3:10).

Lightfoot's argument supports the traditional view, that Paul is at Rome, writing in the early 60s. This is reinforced by the existence of a significant number of Christians among "Caesar's household" (4:22): the slaves, freedmen, and freedwomen who formed the bulk of the imperial civil service. There were far more of these at Rome than elsewhere. The counterargument that Rome is too far from Philippi for the speed of journeys presupposed by the letter is not persuasive. We have little basis for estimating the time between the events that frame the necessary journeys: Epaphroditus's arrival at Paul's location (4:18) and his return to Philippi. However, even if Paul is at Ephesus or Caesarea, the important point is that his imprisonment is under the Roman authorities.

The Philippians

The Philippian Christians have been suffering for their faith. Paul writes that they will undoubtedly receive salvation (1:28) "because it has been granted to you, on Christ's behalf, not only to believe in him but also to suffer for his sake" (1:29). Paul then likens their suffering to his: they are "having the same struggle that you saw me face and now hear of me facing" (1:30; cf. 1:7; 2:17-18; 3:17-18; 4:9). What they saw him face at Philippi was "suffering and ill treatment" (1 Thess 2:2), almost certainly at the hands of the authorities (Acts

4. J. B. Lightfoot, *Saint Paul's Epistle to the Philippians* (London: Macmillan, 1885), 99–102. This conclusion, as opposed to the alternative view that the term refers to a building such as a governor's palace, is strengthened by the next words, "and to all the others," referring to people rather than a place; see Peter T. O'Brien, *Commentary on Philippians*, New International Greek Testament Commentary (Grand Rapids: Eerdmans, 1991), 93.

5. Brian Rapske, *The Book of Acts and Paul in Roman Custody*, The Book of Acts in Its First Century Setting 3 (Carlisle: Paternoster; Grand Rapids: Eerdmans, 1994), 28–32.

16:19–39). What they now hear of him facing is what has just been described in Phil 1:12–26: Roman imprisonment on a capital charge.

We should not conclude that the Philippians were all in prison. This would be alien to Roman penal practice,[6] and, in any case, opposition to Christians could not have taken such an organized form at such an early point. On the other hand, it is implausible that "those who oppose" the Philippian Christians (and are in danger of "panicking" them; 1:28) are, say, merely Jewish or gentile false teachers. The Philippians' suffering is tangible, is in some way comparable to Paul's, and, as the rhetoric of the letter implies at several points, could lead to death (Paul uses himself and Christ as models of the right attitude for facing this: 1:20–23; 2:8; 2:17–18; 3:10–11). In a moderate-sized Roman colonial country town, halfway through the first century, the most likely form that "suffering on behalf of Christ" would take is trouble, of various kinds, from non-Christian relatives, neighbors, and other associates, exacerbated by occasional judicial punishment brought about when Christians become a focus of disturbances. I argue in *Philippians: From People to Letter* that the most prevalent long-term suffering would be economic. First-generation Christians had abandoned the gods of their family, trade, and city to join a new, unknown Jewish sect. The perception of this as insulting, disloyal, and shameful would lead to the breaking of many economically vital relationships, both within and beyond the family. This effect would be reinforced once some Christians were publicly perceived as troublemakers.[7] This all fits Paul's passionate plea for practical mutual support among the Christians (2:1–4): "each of you looking not to your own interests but rather[8] to those of others" (2:4). It also fits his reinforcement of this plea with the example of Christ Jesus, who underwent the deepest possible loss of status and stayed obedient through the worst possible suffering (2:6–8). For suffering first-generation Christians, the economic rearrangement needed for mutual support and survival was socially disturbing and dangerous.[9]

---

6. See Rapske, *Book of Acts and Paul in Roman Custody*, 16–20, on the complexities of this issue.

7. Oakes, *Philippians*, 89–96. The book also provides discussion of the views of scholars whose approaches differ from those of this chapter.

8. This translation of the word καί is offered by Markus Bockmuehl, *The Epistle to the Philippians* (London: A&C Black, 1997), 113–14.

9. Oakes, *Philippians*, 99–102, 188–201.

THE SOVEREIGNTY OF THE GOSPEL OVER PAUL'S IMPRISONMENT (PHIL 1:12–26)

The beginning of the body of a letter is a key point for understanding its central concern. Paul turns immediately to asserting the progress of the gospel in his imprisonment. As Loveday Alexander argues, it is unsurprising that in a "family letter" (or, as Gordon Fee and others describe it, a "letter of friendship"), such as Philippians, the first main topic involves telling the recipients about the sender's situation.[10] However, it is unusual for Paul to do this, even in a letter to close friends (1 Thessalonians) or when he is in prison (Philemon). Moreover, Paul does not tell the Philippians much news about his situation itself. His interest is in the gospel. In Phil 1:12–26 Paul makes a series of points that demonstrate that the gospel is sovereign over every aspect of his imprisonment. The interests of the gospel determine everything that happens or can happen. All those involved in Paul's situation are simply subject to these interests.

Roman Chains Cannot Bind the Gospel (Phil 1:12–14)

The Philippian Christians are in danger of buckling under their suffering and not standing firm for the gospel faith (cf. 1:27–29). Paul's first response to this is to show that the gospel flourishes under pressure from the Roman authorities. He expects this to be a surprise to his hearers: note μᾶλλον ("rather") in 1:12. The ways in which it happens are also surprising. First, Paul sees the spread, among Roman authorities, of the knowledge that he is suffering for Christ as itself being great progress for the gospel (1:13). Second, his imprisonment has made other Christians trust more in the Lord and tell the gospel more boldly (1:14).

The first of these redefines the experience of any Philippians who have been punished by magistrates and have become publicly known as troublemaking Christians. Paul reverses Roman social expectations by giving such notoriety a positive, rather than negative, value.[11] The news of Christ's lordship and salvation needs to be spread, and their troubles inevitably spread it! Attempts by the Roman authorities to clamp down on the gospel will intrinsically have

---

10. Loveday Alexander, "Hellenistic Letter-Forms and the Structure of Philippians," *JSNT* 37 (1989): 87–101 at 92, 95; Gordon D. Fee, *Paul's Letter to the Philippians*, New International Commentary on the New Testament (Grand Rapids: Eerdmans, 1995), 2–4.

11. Rapske, *Book of Acts and Paul in Roman Custody*, 298.

the opposite effect because they make it more widely known—and known in places, such as the Praetorium, that it might otherwise never penetrate. The second method of progress, of encouraging others to speak, is not so inevitable. Paul's declaration that the gospel is flourishing around him is probably intended to reveal to the Philippians that this is possible and, hence, to encourage them to see the faithful suffering of their fellow Christians at Philippi (and of Paul at Rome) as being a ground for deepened trust in the Lord and therefore a motive for bolder evangelism, despite the authorities. The suffering engenders a kind of faithfulness that can enable boldness.

Attempts to Prejudice Paul's Trial Promote the Gospel (Phil 1:15–18a)

Further surprises follow. Paul now unpacks his statement about Christians in Rome speaking the word boldly, and the first comment he makes is that some of them are doing it out of envy and as a form of strife (1:15). He admits that some preach out of good will and love (1:15–16), but his focus is on those who "proclaim Christ" from selfish ambition, "thinking to stir up trouble for my chains" (1:17). These Christians regard Paul negatively. Maybe they disagree with aspects of his views or practice. Or perhaps they see his arrival in Rome as something of a threat. They engage in evangelism but do so in a way calculated (as Paul sees it) to cause him trouble. Presumably, the point at which such trouble would take effect would be at his forthcoming trial. The evangelism might prejudice the outcome. I suppose that something like the painting of Christian graffiti in prominent places would be the kind of activity that might have that consequence.[12] Paul sees their activity, interprets it as aggression toward him, and still rejoices because some sort of extra evangelistic work is going on (1:18). Paul laughs, because even his Christian opponents' aim to cause trouble for his trial has become a cause of increased proclamation of the gospel.

Why put this in the letter? The most likely reason is that a related problem worries the Philippians. Since some Christians at Philippi are suffering, it would seem possible that the church there would be worried about trouble that continued evangelism might stir up for the sufferers. Paul's comments would then be particularly apposite: he rejoices in the spread of the gospel even if it is actually done deliberately to stir up trouble for him. On that basis, fear of

---

12. For the range of types of graffiti that could adorn a Roman town, see Jo-Ann Shelton, *As the Romans Did: A Sourcebook in Roman Social History*, 2nd ed. (Oxford: Oxford University Press, 1998), 98–99.

the consequences for suffering church members should certainly not prevent the Philippians from seeking to proclaim the gospel.

Even Paul's Execution Would Glorify Christ (Phil 1:18b–21)

Not only do Paul's imprisonment and the troublemaking tactics of his opponents cause the spread of the gospel, but he is confident that even in his death he would glorify Christ (1:20). The bases he gives for this confidence are particularly relevant for the Philippians since they are not special to him as an apostle but are ones they already have, namely their own prayers and the help of the Holy Spirit (1:19). These give Paul an "eager expectation and hope" of the glorification of Christ through Paul's death. The apostle describes this outcome as his σωτηρία ("salvation"). The echo of Job 13:16 in the phrase suggests that the word might have a connotation of "vindication" here. A possible meaning of σωτηρία that could fit here is "preservation of character (as a Christian)."[13] Probably a confidence of salvation in the sense of life after death would also flow from this (cf. Phil 2:8–9; 3:10–11).

Even if the Roman authorities go to the limit of their judicial powers, the gospel is still there, waiting to be honored as Christ is magnified. The Philippians need not fear suffering, because the sharpest form it could take would still glorify Christ and bring their salvation.

The Gospel Overrules the Roman Judicial Process (Phil 1:22–26)

In 1:22–26 Paul weighs the question of whether his trial will result in execution or release. Astonishingly, neither the court, the judge, the witnesses, the evidence, nor the Roman authorities in any form make any appearance. The sole arbiter of the outcome of Paul's trial is the gospel and its priorities.

This all comes as a surprise because, in 1:20–21 Paul seems to have been writing the more conventional things that one might expect a courageous and faith-filled potential martyr to write: "I am confident that I will die in a way that glorifies Christ; life is for Christ and death is gain." However, in 1:22–23 the apostle slides into an ambiguous rhetorical conversation in which he acts as though it is his choice how the trial ends. He weighs up the options and decides in favor of dying. But this is not the end of the matter. In 1:24–25 it

---

13. See the discussion of Epictetus, *Discourses* 4.1.163–67, in Peter Oakes, "Epictetus (and the New Testament)," *Vox Evangelica* 23 (1993): 39–56 at 42–43.

becomes clear that his choice is not actually what decides the outcome. Rather, the deciding factor is what benefits the Philippians. Paul knows what this is, so he knows what the outcome of his trial will be!

The furthering of the gospel, in this case among the Philippians, determines the outcome of the Roman judicial process. The Roman authorities have no say in the matter. We can probably add to this an implication of 1:16. Paul writes: κεῖμαι ("I am put here" or "I am destined") for the defense of the gospel. This refers either to his imprisonment as a whole or to his trial in particular. In either case, an implication is that it is God who determined that the imprisonment should happen. God determines both the imprisonment and the outcome. God is sovereign over the Roman authorities and all that they do to Paul.

THE SOVEREIGNTY OF CHRIST OVER ROMAN SOCIETY (PHIL 1:6; 2:9–11; 3:20–21)

In the letter to the Philippians, far more than in any other letter, Paul ties his hearers' experience to his and calls on them to imitate his attitudes and actions: "In my chains and in the defense and confirmation of the gospel you are all sharers with me in grace" (1:7); "having the same struggle that you saw me face and now hear of me facing" (1:30); "be imitators of me . . . and look at those who live according to the pattern you have in us" (3:17); "the things you learned and received and heard and saw in me—put these things into practice" (4:9). The things Paul presents in the letter, that the Philippians could imitate, are his attitude to his imprisonment and, in Phil 3, his willingness to lose privileges and face suffering. It is almost certain that Paul describes his views on his imprisonment to the suffering Philippians in order for them to adopt the views as their own. This conclusion is further strengthened by the way in which Paul also uses Christ as a model (2:5). In fact, not only does the apostle's christological material reinforce his modeling of suffering; it also elevates the idea of God's sovereignty over the Roman authorities to a far higher level.

We now move to passages in which no one would doubt that sovereignty is asserted. These are the description of Christ's accession to universal authority in 2:9–11 and the references to his final triumph, both in 3:20–21 and more broadly in the "day of Christ" texts such as 1:6. Paul draws the Philippians' attention to the sovereignty of Christ in a marked manner—and in ways reminiscent of the Roman emperor.

The Isaianic Triumph of God, in Christ, over the Roman Empire (and Everywhere Else) (Phil 2:9–11)

Either Paul adopted 2:9–11 because he sees it as being relevant to the Philippians or, more probably, he wrote it himself for the occasion.[14] The passage is a rewriting of the Septuagint of Isa 45:23: ἐμοὶ κάμψει πᾶν γόνυ καὶ ἐξομολογήσεται πᾶσα γλῶσσα τῷ θεῷ ("to me every knee shall bow and every tongue shall confess to God"). This rewriting of the Isaiah text is radical in several directions. The most startling is the replacing of God by Jesus as the figure bowed down to. The confession then consists of acknowledgement that Jesus Christ is Lord. The Isaiah passage is among the most emphatically monotheistic in Scripture. In a vision intended for the exiles in Babylon, God sits on his throne and calls "those from the end of the earth" to turn to him and be saved (Isa 45:22). He declares the uselessness of idols (45:20) and hence his uniqueness as savior (45:21) and God: "I am God, and there is no other" (45:22). Paul sees this gathering and submission before God's throne as being fulfilled in Jesus. More particularly, it is fulfilled in Jesus's accession to universal sovereignty.

Paul clearly does not see this as a negation of the Isaianic vision. He makes God the chief actor in the scene (Phil 2:9) and the ultimate recipient of glory through what happens (2:11).[15] Christ's accession to authority is the actualization of God's sovereignty.[16] If we can pick up the earlier element in Isa 45, Christ's accession also actualizes God's salvation. (If this element is there, then Paul would presumably have seen "those from the end of the earth" as fulfilled in the gentiles gathered in through the Christian mission.) Christ's accession to authority is the actualization of God's sovereignty over the nations, such as Babylon, who imposed their authority on Israel.

However, the second aspect of the rewriting of Isaiah is that Jesus's sovereignty is not only over the nations but over the whole universe. This is part of a consistent pattern of extremes in Phil 2:6–11. Christ moves from the highest status possible to the lowest (2:6–7). He suffers the worst death possible (2:8). He is given the highest name possible and the widest authority possible (2:9–10).

14. Oakes, *Philippians*, 207–10.

15. Contra David Seeley, "The Background of the Philippians Hymn (2:6–11)," *Journal of Higher Criticism* 1 (Fall 1994): 49–72; online at daniel.drew.edu/~doughty/jhcbody .html#reviews.

16. Richard J. Bauckham, "The Worship of Jesus in Philippians 2:9–11," in *Where Christology Began: Essays on Philippians 2*, ed. Ralph P. Martin and Brian J. Dodd (Louisville: Westminster John Knox, 1998), 128–39 at 121.

The third aspect of rewriting is the depiction of the accession of the figure to the Isaianic throne. The throne is not timelessly occupied but comes to be occupied. Along with this change comes a reference to the reason why this person comes to occupy the throne (note "therefore" in 2:9). This also functions as a legitimation of the authority of the one on the throne.

To some extent these changes could be seen simply as further implications of the core change of Jesus being on God's throne. This is especially so since the narrative needs to have a link to get from Jesus's death to his universal authority. However, neither description nor legitimation of the process of Jesus gaining authority is a normal feature of New Testament discourse. The explanation of these unusual features is probably to be found in the parallel process that happens in 3:20-21 (see below) where ideas about the parousia are rewritten in a form that deliberately evokes ideas about the Roman emperor.

Once the parallel process in 3:20-21 is seen, and the broader Roman references in Philippians are noted, then 2:9-11 too begins to look evocative of the Roman emperor. Jesus can be seen both to take on the central function of the emperor and to have his authority legitimated in a way familiar from Roman imperial ideology.

The function that Jesus takes on is the bringing of universal submission to a single head. This was consistently presented to the Roman provinces as the central benefit brought by the emperor. He alone could make the world function rationally and peacefully by bringing it under a single authority. For example, Philo writes of Augustus: "Who reclaimed every state to liberty, who led disorder into order. . . . He was also the first and the greatest and the common benefactor in that he displaced the rule of many and committed the ship of the commonwealth to be steered by a single pilot. . . . 'It is not well that many lords should rule.'"[17]

Jesus achieves everything that the emperor does in this but goes beyond him by doing it for the entire universe, including even the world of the dead.

The legitimation that supports Jesus's authority is the moral one of demonstrating both lack of self-interest and concern for others. He chose not to exploit his equality with God (2:6),[18] a decision whose consequence was that

17. Philo, in *On the Embassy to Gaius* 147-49, trans. F. H. Colson, Loeb Classical Library (London: Heinemann, 1962). See Oakes, *Philippians*, 160-65; cf. E. Faust, *Pax Christi et Pax Caesaris: Religionsgeschichtliche, traditionsgeschichtliche und sozialgeschichtliche Studien zum Epheserbrief* (Freiburg: Universitätsverlag; Göttingen: Vandenhoeck & Ruprecht, 1993), esp. 475.

18. R. W. Hoover, "The Harpagmos Enigma: A Philological Solution," *Harvard Theological Review* 64 (1971): 95-119; N. T. Wright, *The Climax of the Covenant: Christ and the Law in Pauline Theology* (Edinburgh: T&T Clark, 1991), 62-90.

he became like people (twice in 2:7). Moral legitimation of the emperor's rule was a central plank of the public presentation of imperial ideology. Concern for others and lack of self-interest were particularly prominent in such legitimation. Seneca writes: "God says: 'Let these men be kings because their forefathers have not been, because they have regarded justice and unselfishness as their highest authority, because, instead of sacrificing the state to themselves, they have sacrificed themselves to the state.'"[19]

How might a depiction of Christ acceding to an authority beyond that of the Roman emperor help the Philippians? Essentially, it remaps the universe. Just as, later, 2:15-16 remaps Philippian society, moving the Christians from a despised, peripheral place to the core position of light and life, so 2:9-11 moves a crucified Jew to the center of authority, relegating all competing authorities to places beneath him. In particular, the emperor and, hence, the Philippian authorities and Philippian society as a whole are relegated to a lower place. The immediate effects of this reinforce Paul's call to act for practical unity in the way shown by Christ's willingness to lose status and suffer obediently. The world has changed: it is now under Christ. Therefore Christ's imperatives of unity outweigh society's imperatives of cautious status preservation. Conversely, the security that Christ now offers outweighs that offered by society. As Paul implies in 2:12 the apparently suicidal path of unity and suffering is actually the way to bring about their individual and corporate salvation (cf. 3:10-11).[20]

Leaving these points aside, the key implication of 2:9-11 for this chapter is the simpler one that it places Christ above the Roman authorities. The enthronement of Christ brings about God's sovereignty over them. The Philippian Christians can with confidence stand firm because the one they follow is in authority over the colonial magistrates.

My reading of 2:9-11 has links with that of Dieter Georgi. The sharpest point of difference is that he sees the verses as comparable to an emperor's apotheosis after death, whereas I see them as comparable to an enthronement.[21] Christ is now in the position of reigning, rather than receiving reward for his past reign. Gordon Fee sees a contrast with "lord Nero" in 2:9-11: the Christians have refused to participate in the imperial cult and God's exaltation

19. Seneca, *On Benefits* 4.32.2, in *Moral Essays*, vol. 3: *De Beneficiis*, trans. J. W. Basore, Loeb Classical Library (Cambridge: Harvard University Press, 1935). See Oakes, *Philippians*, 154-60.

20. Oakes, *Philippians*, 204-7.

21. Dieter Georgi, *Theocracy in Paul's Praxis and Theology*, trans. D. E. Green (Minneapolis: Fortress, 1991), 73.

of Christ vindicates their action.[22] I agree with many of Fee's general points about encouraging suffering Christians,[23] and I agree that 2:9–11 does relativize the imperial cult. However, I see little evidence that the imperial cult itself is the key problem at Philippi. Richard Horsley argues that every presentation of the emperor is entangled with the imperial cult since that was the essential form of imperial ideology.[24] However, a writer can still make points about the emperor other than cultic ones. The emperor stands at the head of a social order and an authority structure. The overall content of Philippians suggests that these, rather than cultic issues per se, are more likely to be the target of 2:9–11 when interpreted as part of the letter.

To return to the question of authorship of 2:9–11, the familiarity of Isa 45:23 to Paul is seen from his use of it in Rom 14:11. Indeed, his straightforward interpretation of it there in terms of the judgment seat of God emphasizes how unusual is his handling of it in Philippians. This could act as evidence of the non-Pauline origin of 2:9–11. However, the overall pattern of "Roman" texts in Philippians, and the pertinence of 2:6–8 to the Philippians' circumstances, suggest to me that 2:9–11 is composed especially to help the Philippians in their situation.

The Triumphant Return of the Lord Jesus Christ (Phil 3:20–21; 1:6)

In announcing the submission of every creature to Jesus, Phil 2:9–11 is intrinsically political. If anything, 3:20–21 is still more sharply political because its explicit aim is to realign current allegiance. Also, the parallels between Christ and the Roman emperor are unmistakable. The Philippian Christians belong to a state elsewhere.[25] It is a place from which a "savior" who is the "lord" will come to rescue them. This transforming rescue will happen "in accordance with the power that enables him also to subject all things to himself." The Christians are like members of a colony such as Philippi, defended from a distance by the ruler of the city to which they ultimately belong. Moreover, their belonging to that city defines their ethics. Almost every element of this recalls Rome and the emperor.[26]

Citizenship (although not using that word) of heaven is contrasted with

22. Fee, *Philippians*, 31–32, 197.

23. Fee, *Philippians*, 222–23.

24. Richard A. Horsley, ed., *Paul and Empire: Religion and Power in Roman Imperial Society* (Harrisburg, PA: Trinity, 1997), 4, 17, 21, 22.

25. Cf. Horsley, *Paul and Empire*, 140.

26. Oakes, *Philippians*, 138–45.

citizenship on earth, which leads to a mind focused on earthly things (3:20; cf. 3:19). This must have evoked the idea of the Roman citizenship that was held by many of the people of Philippi, including, no doubt, a significant number of the Christians. Roman citizenship was supposed to define one's ethics.[27] Paul proclaims heavenly citizenship that implies different ethics. For Christian Roman citizens this relocates their place of primary allegiance. For probably most of the Philippian Christians, who are not Roman citizens,[28] Paul announces a citizenship that surpasses the citizenship of Rome and Philippi, which they are prevented from attaining. One effect of this is to put all the Christians in Philippi on a level with each other. This could itself help Paul's call for unity in the church.

Philippians 3:20-21 holds a structurally important place in the letter. The chapter break after it is misleading. Paul's announcement of Christ's use of his universal authority to return to rescue his people forms the final climax of his main message to the Philippians. He concludes, with a great rhetorical flourish: "Thus, my beloved and longed-for brothers and sisters, my joy and my crown, in this way stand firm in the Lord, my beloved ones" (4:1). The promise of Christ's triumphant return caps the argument. In fact, at the ends of previous sections too Paul tended to lead the argument to that return, with references to "the day of Christ" (1:10; 2:16). A key element of the apostle's call for the Philippians to stand firm is his teaching of Christ's final sovereignty, a sovereignty that will be used to rescue his people. Again, this fulfils a central function of the Roman emperor. If the emperor's key function toward the *provinces* was the bringing of universal submission to a single head, his key function toward the *Roman people* was to be the one who would save them from their enemies and from internal trouble.[29]

The Christians have a better citizenship than that of Rome, defended by a stronger savior than that of Rome. On this basis, the Philippian church can confidently stand firm under their sufferings, assured of Christ's final sovereignty.

27. Cicero, *On the Laws* 2.2.5.

28. Oakes, *Philippians*, 62-63.

29. Jean Béranger, *Recherches sur l'aspect idéologique du Principat* (Basel: Reinhardt, 1953), 254-78; Oakes, *Philippians*, 138-45.

CONCLUSION

Paul remaps the universe and consequently remaps both Philippian society and the future. Rome, the emperor, and even Jupiter are replaced in the positions of decisive authority by Christ. Paul urges the Philippians to look at their world and see a new reality: to look even at imprisonment and other suffering and see, even in those settings, the reality of God's sovereignty. Paul urges them to look at the future and see it as the implementation and final fulfillment of Christ's sovereignty. This rounded presentation of God's sovereignty over the authorities everywhere, from the apostle's prison to the courts of the universe, gives a firm basis for Philippian courage and steadfastness on behalf of the Christian gospel.

Sources

1. "A House-Church Account of Economics and Empire" (not previously published).

2. "Nine Types of Church in Nine Types of Space in the Insula of the Menander." Pages 23–58 in *Early Christianity in Pompeian Light: People, Texts, Situations*. Edited by Bruce W. Longenecker. Minneapolis: Fortress, 2016.

3. "Methodological Issues in Using Economic Evidence in Interpretation of Early Christian Texts." Pages 9–34 in *Engaging Economics: New Testament Scenarios and Early Christian Reception*. Edited by Bruce W. Longenecker and Kelly D. Liebengood. Grand Rapids: Eerdmans, 2009.

4. "Economic Approaches: Scarce Resources and Interpretive Opportunities." Pages 72–91 in *Studying Paul's Letters: Contemporary Perspectives and Methods*. Edited by Joseph A. Marchal. Minneapolis: Fortress, 2012.

5. "Urban Structure, Patronage, and the Corinthian Followers of Christ." Pages 178–93 in *Understanding the Social World of the New Testament*. Edited by Dietmar Neufeld and Richard E. DeMaris. London: Routledge, 2009.

6. "Jason and Penelope Hear Philippians 1:1–11." Pages 155–64 in *Understanding, Studying, and Reading: New Testament Essays in Honour of John Ashton*. Edited by Christopher Rowland and Crispin H. T. Fletcher-Louis. Sheffield: Sheffield Academic Press, 1998.

7. "Re-mapping the Universe: Paul and the Emperor in 1 Thessalonians and Philippians." *JSNT* 27 (2005): 301–22.

8. "Christian Attitudes to Rome at the Time of Paul's Letter [to the Romans]." *Review and Expositor* 100 (2003): 103–11.

9. "A State of Tension: Rome in the New Testament." Pages 75–90 in *The Gospel of Matthew in Its Roman Imperial Context*. Edited by John Riches and David Sim. London: T&T Clark, 2005.

10. "God's Sovereignty over Roman Authorities: A Theme in Philippians." Pages 126–41 in *Rome in the Bible and the Early Church*. Edited by Peter Oakes. Carlisle: Paternoster; Grand Rapids: Baker Academic, 2002.

Bibliography

Adams, Edward. *The Earliest Christian Meeting Places: Almost Exclusively Houses?* The Library of New Testament Studies 450. London: Bloomsbury T&T Clark, 2013.

———. "Placing the Corinthian Common Meal." Pages 22–37 in *Text, Image, and Christians in the Graeco-Roman World.* Edited by A. C. Niang and C. Osiek. Eugene, OR: Pickwick, 2012.

Alexander of Aphrodisias. *On Aristotle's Metaphysics,* vol. 1. Translated by W. E. Dooley. Ithaca, NY: Cornell University Press, 1989.

Alexander, Loveday. "Hellenistic Letter-Forms and the Structure of Philippians." *JSNT* 37 (1989): 87–101.

Alföldy, Geza. *The Social History of Rome.* Totowa, NJ: Barnes & Noble, 1985.

Allison, Penelope M. *The Insula of the Menander at Pompeii,* vol. 3: *The Finds: A Contextual Study.* Oxford: Clarendon, 2006.

———. *Pompeian Households: An Analysis of the Material Culture.* Monograph 42. Los Angeles: Cotsen Institute of Archaeology at UCLA, 2004.

Ando, Clifford. *Imperial Ideology and Provincial Loyalty in the Roman Empire.* Berkeley: University of California Press, 2000.

Andringa, William van. *Quotidien des dieux et des hommes: La vie religieuse dans les cités du Vésuve à l'époque romaine.* Rome: École française de Rome, 2009.

Ascough, Richard S. *Paul's Macedonian Associations: The Social Context of Philippians and 1 Thessalonians.* WUNT 161. Tübingen: Mohr Siebeck, 2003.

Bagnall, Roger S., and Bruce W. Frier. *The Demography of Roman Egypt.* Cambridge: Cambridge University Press, 1994.

Balch, David L. "The Church Sitting in a Garden (1 Cor. 14:30; Rom. 16:23; Mark 6:39–40; 8:6; John 6:3, 10; Acts 1:15; 2:1–2)." Pages 201–35 in *Contested Spaces: Houses and Temples in Roman Antiquity and the New Testament.* Edited by D. L. Balch and A. Weissenrieder. WUNT 285. Tübingen: Mohr Siebeck, 2012.

Balch, David L., and Carolyn Osiek, eds. *Early Christian Families in Context: An Interdisciplinary Dialogue.* Grand Rapids: Eerdmans, 2003.

Bammel, Ernst. "Ein Beitrag zur paulinischen Staatsanschauung." *Theologische Literaturzeitung* 85 (1960): 837–40.

Bang, Peter F., Mamoru Ikeguchi, and Harmut Ziche. *Ancient Economies, Modern Methodologies: Archaeology, Comparative History, Models, and Institutions.* Bari: Edipuglia, 2006.

Barron, Caroline. "Letter of Vespasian to the Town Councillors of Sabora (*CIL* II,1423)." judaism-and-rome.org/letter-vespasian-town-councillors-sabora-cil-ii-1423. Accessed 22 Oct 2019.

Batten, Alicia. "Brokerage: Jesus as Social Entrepreneur." Pages 167–77 in *Understanding the Social World of the New Testament.* Edited by Dietmar Neufeld and Richard E. DeMaris. London: Routledge, 2010.

Bauckham, Richard J. "The Worship of Jesus in Philippians 2:9–11." Pages 128–39 in *Where Christology Began: Essays on Philippians 2.* Edited by Ralph P. Martin and Brian J. Dodd. Louisville: Westminster John Knox, 1998.

Beard, Mary, John North, and Simon Price. *Religions of Rome,* vol. 1: *A History.* Cambridge: Cambridge University Press, 1998.

Beare, F. W. *A Commentary on the Epistle to the Philippians.* New York: Harper, 1959.

Belo, Fernando. *A Materialist Reading of the Gospel of Mark.* Maryknoll, NY: Orbis, 1981.

Béranger, Jean. *Recherches sur l'aspect idéologique du Principat.* Basel: Reinhardt, 1953.

Berry, Joanne. "Household Artefacts: Towards a Re-interpretation of Roman Domestic Space." Pages 183–95 in *Domestic Space in the Roman World: Pompeii and Beyond.* Edited by Ray Laurence and Andrew Wallace-Hadrill. Journal of Roman Archaeology Supplement 22. Portsmouth, RI: Journal of Roman Archaeology, 1997.

Bingen, Jean, Adam Bülow-Jacobsen, et al. Duke Databank of Documentary Papyri, accessible via the Perseus website: perseus.tufts.edu.

Bockmuehl, Markus. *The Epistle to the Philippians.* London: A&C Black, 1997.

Bookidis, Nancy. "Religion in Corinth: 146 BCE to 100 CE." Pages 141–64 in *Urban Religion in Roman Corinth: Interdisciplinary Approaches.* Edited by Daniel Schowalter and Steven J. Friesen. Cambridge: Harvard University Press, 2005.

Bourdieu, Pierre. *Zur Soziologie der symbolishen Formen.* 2nd edition. Frankfurt: Suhrkamp, 1983.

Braund, D. "Function and Dysfunction: Personal Patronage in Roman Imperialism." Pages 137–52 in *Patronage in Ancient Society.* Edited by Andrew Wallace-Hadrill. London: Routledge, 1989.

Brocke, Christoph vom. *Thessaloniki—Stadt des Kassander und Gemeinde des Paulus*. WUNT 125. Tübingen: Mohr Siebeck, 2001.

Caird, G. B. *Paul's Letters from Prison: Ephesians, Philippians, Colossians, Philemon*. New Clarendon Bible. Oxford: Oxford University Press, 1976.

Carney, Thomas. *The Shape of the Past: Models and Antiquity*. Lawrence, KS: Coronado, 1975.

Carter, Warren. *Matthew and Empire: Initial Explorations*. Harrisburg, PA: Trinity, 2001.

———. *The Roman Empire and the New Testament: An Essential Guide*. Nashville: Abingdon, 2006.

Cassidy, Richard J. *Paul in Chains: Roman Imprisonment and the Letters of St. Paul*. New York: Crossroad, 2001.

Cassirer, Ernst. *Philosophie der symbolischen Formen*, vol. 3: *Phänomenologie der Erkenntnis*. Gesammelte Werke 13. Edited by J. Clemens. Darmstadt: WBG, 2002. Originally 1929.

Chow, John K. *Patronage in Corinth: A Study of Social Networks in Corinth*. JSNTSup 75. Sheffield: JSOT Press, 1992.

Clarke, Andrew D. "Jew and Greek, Slave and Free, Male and Female: Paul's Theology of Ethnic, Social, and Gender Inclusiveness in Romans 16." Pages 103–25 in *Rome in the Bible and the Early Church*. Edited by Peter Oakes. Carlisle: Paternoster; Grand Rapids: Baker, 2002.

———. *Secular and Christian Leadership in Corinth: A Socio-Historical and Exegetical Study of 1 Corinthians 1–6*. Arbeiten zur Geschichte des antiken Judentums und des Urchristentums 18. Leiden: Brill, 1993.

Clarke, John R. *Art in the Lives of Ordinary Romans: Visual Representation and Non-elite Viewers in Italy, 100 BC–AD 315*. Berkeley: University of California Press, 2003.

———. *The Houses of Roman Italy, 100 BC–AD 250: Ritual, Space, and Decoration*. Berkeley: University of California Press, 1991.

Collange, Jean-François. *The Epistle of Saint Paul to the Philippians*. Translated by A. W. Heathcote. London: Epworth, 1979.

Collart, Paul. *Philippes, ville de Macédoine: Depuis ses origines jusqu'à la fin de l'époque romaine*. Paris: Ecole Française d'Athènes, 1937.

Crook, Zeba A. *Reconceptualising Conversion: Patronage, Loyalty, and Conversion in the Religions of the Ancient Mediterranean*. Beihefte zur Zeitschrift für die neutestamentliche Wissenschaft 130. Berlin: de Gruyter, 2004.

Cullmann, Oscar. *Christ and Time: The Primitive Christian Conception of Time and History*. Translated by Floyd V. Filson. London: SCM, 1950.

———. *The State in the New Testament*. London: SCM, 1957.

DeFelice, John. "Inns and Taverns." Pages 474–86 in *The World of Pompeii*. Edited by J. J. Dobbins and P. W. Foss. London: Routledge, 2007.

Deissmann, Adolf. *Light from the Ancient East: The New Testament Illustrated by Recently Discovered Texts of the Graeco-Roman World*. Translated by L. R. M. Strachan. London: Hodder & Stoughton, 1927.

———. "Das Urchristentum und die unteren Schichten." Pages 8–28 in *Die Verhandlungen des neunzehnten Evangelisch-sozialen Kongresses*. Edited by Wilhelm Schneemelcher. Göttingen: Vandenhoeck & Ruprecht, 1908.

Della Corte, Matteo. *Case ed abitanti di Pompei*. 3rd edition. Naples: Faustino Fiorentino, 1965.

———. "Epigrafi della via fra le isole VI e X della Reg. I." *Notizie degli scavi* (1929): 455–76.

———. "Pompei: Iscrizioni dell' isola X della Regione I." *Notizie degli scavi* (1933): 277–331.

Dinbabin, Katharine M. D., and William J. Slater. "Roman Dining." Pages 438–66 in *Oxford Handbook of Social Relations in the Roman World*. Edited by Michael Peachin. Oxford: Oxford University Press, 2011.

Donfried, Karl. "The Cults of Thessalonica and the Thessalonian Correspondence." *NTS* 31 (1985): 336–56.

Duling, Dennis C. "Matthew as Marginal Scribe in an Advanced Agrarian Society." *Hervormde Teologiese Studies* 58 (2002): 520–75.

Duncan-Jones, R. *The Economy of the Roman Empire: Quantitative Studies*. 2nd edition. Cambridge: Cambridge University Press, 1982.

Dunn, James D. G. *Romans 9–16*. Word Biblical Commentary 38B. Grand Rapids: Zondervan, 1988.

Eisenstadt, S. N., and Louis Roniger. *Patrons, Clients, and Friends: Interpersonal Relations and the Structure of Trust in Society*. Cambridge: Cambridge University Press, 1984.

Elia, Olga. "Pompei: Relazione sullo scavo dell'Insula X della Regio I." *Notizie degli scavi* 12 (1934): 264–344.

Elliott, John H. *Social Scientific Criticism of the New Testament*. London: SPCK, 1995.

Elliott, Neil. *Liberating Paul*. Maryknoll, NY: Orbis, 1994.

Faust, E. *Pax Christi et Pax Caesaris: Religionsgeschichtliche, traditionsgeschichtliche und sozialgeschichtliche Studien zum Epheserbrief*. Freiburg: Universitätsverlag; Göttingen: Vandenhoeck & Ruprecht, 1993.

Fee, Gordon D. *Paul's Letter to the Philippians*. New International Commentary on the New Testament. Grand Rapids: Eerdmans, 1995.

Field, F. W. *Otium Norvicense*, vol. 3. Oxford, 1881.

Fishwick, Duncan. *The Imperial Cult in the Latin West*, vol. 2.1. Leiden: Brill, 1991.

France, R. T. *The Gospel of Mark*. New International Greek Testament Commentary. Grand Rapids: Eerdmans, 2002.

Freyne, Sean. *Galilee from Alexander the Great to Hadrian, 323 BCE to 135 CE*. Wilmington, DE: Glazier, 1980.

Friedrich, J., W. Pöhlmann, and P. Stuhlmacher. "Zur historischen Situation und Intention von Röm 13:1–7." *Zeitschrift für Theologie und Kirche* 73 (1976): 131–66.

Friesen, Steven J. "Poverty in Pauline Studies: Beyond the So-called New Consensus." *JSNT* 26 (2004): 323–61.

Garnsey, Peter. *Cities, Peasants, and Food in Classical Antiquity: Essays in Social and Economic History*. Edited by Walter Scheidel. Cambridge: Cambridge University Press, 1998.

Garnsey, Peter, and Richard Saller. *The Roman Empire: Economy, Society, and Culture*. London: Duckworth, 1987.

Gellner, Ernest. *Nations and Nationalism*. 2nd edition. Oxford: Blackwell, 2006.

Georgi, Dieter. *Theocracy in Paul's Praxis and Theology*. Translated by D. E. Green. Minneapolis: Fortress, 1991 (German 1987).

Gnilka, Joachim. *Der Philipperbrief*. Herders Theologischer Kommentar zum Neuen Testament 10.3. Freiburg: Herder, 1968.

Goodman, Martin. *Mission and Conversion: Proselytizing in the Religious History of the Roman Empire*. Oxford: Clarendon, 1994.

Grabbe, Lester L. *Judaism from Cyrus to Hadrian*. London: SCM, 1992. Reprinted in one volume, 1994.

Greene, Kevin. "Archaeological Data and Economic Interpretation." Pages 109–36 in *Ancient Economies, Modern Methodologies: Archaeology, Comparative History, Models, and Institutions*. Edited by Peter F. Bang, Mamoru Ikeguchi, and Hartmut Ziche. Bari: Edipuglia, 2006.

———. *The Archaeology of the Roman Economy*. London: Batsford, 1986.

Hanson, K. C., and Douglas E. Oakman. *Palestine in the Time of Jesus: Social Structures and Social Conflicts*. 2nd edition. Minneapolis: Fortress, 2008. Originally 1998.

Harland, Philip A. *Associations, Synagogues, and Congregations: Claiming a Place in Ancient Mediterranean Society*. Minneapolis: Fortress, 2003.

Harris, Marvin, and Orna Johnson. *Cultural Anthropology*. 5th edition. Boston: Allyn & Bacon, 2000.

Harrison, J. R. "Paul and the Imperial Gospel at Thessaloniki." *JSNT* 25 (2002): 71–96.

Harvey, David. *The Condition of Postmodernity: An Enquiry into the Origins of Cultural Change*. Oxford: Blackwell, 1989.

Hawthorne, G. F. *Philippians*. Word Biblical Commentary 43. Grand Rapids: Zondervan, 1983.

Heers, Jacques. *Family Clans in the Middle Ages: A Study of Political and Social Structure in Urban Areas*. Translated by B. Herbert. Amsterdam: North-Holland, 1977.

Hendrix, H. L. "Archaeology and Eschatology at Thessalonica." Pages 113–14 in *The Future of Early Christianity: Essays in Honor of Helmut Koester*. Edited by B. A. Pearson. Minneapolis: Fortress, 1991.

Hoover, R. W. "The Harpagmos Enigma: A Philological Solution." *Harvard Theological Review* 64 (1971): 95–119.

Hope, Valerie. "A Roof over the Dead: Communal Tombs and Family Structure." Pages 69–88 in *Domestic Space in the Roman World: Pompeii and Beyond*. Edited by Ray Laurence and Andrew Wallace-Hadrill. Journal of Roman Archaeology Supplement Series 22. Portsmouth, RI: Journal of Roman Archaeology, 1997.

Horden, Peregrine, and Nicholas Purcell. *The Corrupting Sea: A Study of Mediterranean History*. Oxford: Blackwell, 2000.

Horrell, David G. "Domestic Space and Christian Meetings at Corinth: Imagining New Contexts and the Buildings East of the Theatre." *NTS* 50 (2004): 349–69.

Horrell, David G., and Edward Adams, eds. *Christianity at Corinth: The Quest for the Pauline Church*. Louisville: Westminster John Knox, 2004.

Horsley, Richard A. *Covenant Economics: A Biblical Vision of Justice for All*. Louisville: Westminster John Knox, 2009.

———. "Unearthing a People's History." Pages 1–20 in *Christian Origins*. Edited by Richard A. Horsley. A People's History of Christianity 1. Minneapolis: Fortress, 2005.

Horsley, Richard A., ed. *Christian Origins*. A People's History of Christianity 1. Minneapolis: Fortress, 2005.

———, ed. *Paul and Empire: Religion and Power in Roman Imperial Society*. Harrisburg, PA: Trinity, 1997.

Horsley, Richard A., and N. A. Silberman. *The Message and the Kingdom: How Jesus and Paul Ignited a Revolution and Transformed the Ancient World*. Minneapolis: Fortress, 1997.

Horster, Marrieta. "Primary Education." Pages 84–100 in *The Oxford Handbook of*

Social Relations in the Roman World. Edited by Michael Peachin. Oxford: Oxford University Press, 2011.

Houlden, J. L. *Paul's Letters from Prison.* Pelican New Testament Commentary. Harmondsworth: Penguin, 1970.

Huttunen, Pertti. *The Social Strata in the Imperial City of Rome: A Quantitative Study of the Social Representation in the Epitaphs Published in the Corpus Inscriptionum Latinarum VI.* Oulu, Finland: University of Oulu Press, 1974.

Jashemski, Wilhelmina F. *The Gardens of Pompeii: Herculaneum and the Villas Destroyed by Vesuvius.* 2 vols. New Rochelle: Caratzas, 1979, 1993.

Jashemski, Wilhelmina F., and Frederick G. Meyer, eds. *The Natural History of Pompeii: A Systematic Survey.* Cambridge: Cambridge University Press, 2002.

Jewett, Robert. *Romans: A Commentary.* Hermeneia. Minneapolis: Fortress, 2007.

Johnson, Terry, and Chris Dandeker. "Patronage: Relation and System." Pages 219–41 in *Patronage in Ancient Society.* Edited by Andrew Wallace-Hadrill. London: Routledge, 1989.

Judge, Edwin A. "The Decrees of Caesar at Thessalonica." *Reformed Theological Review* 30 (1971): 1–7.

———. *The Social Pattern of the Christian Groups in the First Century: Some Prolegomena to the Study of New Testament Ideas of Social Obligation.* London: Tyndale, 1960.

Kay, Nigel M. *Epigrams from the Anthologia Latina: Text, Translation, and Commentary.* London: Bloomsbury, 2013. Originally Duckworth, 2006.

Keppie, Lawrence. *Colonisation and Veteran Settlement in Italy, 47–14 B.C.* London: British School at Rome, 1983.

Klinghardt, Matthias. *Gemeinschaftsmahl und Mahlgemeinschaft: Soziologie und Liturgie frühchristlicher Mahlfeiern.* Texte und Arbeiten zum neutestamentlichen Zeitalter 13. Tübingen: Francke, 1996.

———. "A Typology of the Communal Meal." Pages 9–22 in *Meals in the Early Christian World: Social Formation, Experimentation, and Conflict at the Table.* Edited by Dennis E. Smith and Hal Taussig. New York: Palgrave Macmillan, 2012.

Kloppenborg, John S. *The Tenants in the Vineyard.* WUNT 195. Tübingen: Mohr Siebeck, 2006.

Kloppenborg, John S., and Stephen G. Wilson, eds. *Voluntary Associations in the Graeco-Roman World.* London: Routledge, 1996.

Lampe, Peter. *Christians of Rome in the First Two Centuries.* Translated by J. Larrimore Holland and Michael Steinhauser. London: Burns & Oates, 2000.

———. *From Paul to Valentinus: Christians at Rome in the First Two Centuries.*

Translated by M. Steinhauser. Edited by M. D. Johnson. Minneapolis: Fortress; London: T&T Clark, 2003.

Lane Fox, Robin. *Pagans and Christians in the Mediterranean World from the Second Century AD to the Conversion of Constantine*. Harmondsworth: Viking, 1986.

Laurence, Ray. *Roman Pompeii: Space and Society*. 2nd ed. London: Routledge, 2007. Reprinted 2010.

Lazer, Estelle. *Resurrecting Pompeii*. London: Routledge, 2009.

Lenski, Gerhard. *Power and Privilege: A Theory of Social Stratification*. New York: McGraw-Hill, 1966.

Lewis, N., and M. Reinhold, eds. *Roman Civilization: Selected Readings*, vol. 1: *The Republic and the Augustan Age*. 3rd edition. New York: Columbia University Press, 1990.

———. *Roman Civilization: Selected Readings*, vol. 2: *The Empire*. 3rd edition. New York: Columbia University Press, 1990.

Lightfoot, J. B. *Saint Paul's Epistle to the Galatians*. London: Macmillan, 1880.

———. *Saint Paul's Epistle to the Philippians*. London: Macmillan, 1885.

Ling, Roger. *The Insula of the Menander at Pompeii*, vol. 1: *The Structures*. Oxford: Clarendon, 1997.

Ling, Roger, and Lesley Ling. *The Insula of the Menander at Pompeii*, vol. 2: *The Decorations*. Oxford: Clarendon, 2005.

Lintott, Andrew. *Imperium Romanum: Politics and Administration*. London: Routledge, 1993.

Lohmeyer, Ernst. *Der Brief an die Philipper*. Göttingen: Vandenhoeck & Ruprecht, 1928.

Longenecker, Bruce W. "Exposing the Economic Middle: A Revised Economy Scale for the Study of Early Urban Christianity." *JSNT* 31 (2009): 243–78.

———. *Remember the Poor: Paul, Poverty, and the Greco-Roman World*. Grand Rapids: Eerdmans, 2010.

Longenecker, Bruce W., and Kelly D. Liebengood, eds. *Engaging Economics: New Testament Scenarios and Early Christian Reception*. Grand Rapids: Eerdmans, 2009.

Lopez, Davina C., and Todd Penner. "'Houses Made with Hands': The Triumph of the Private in New Testament Scholarship." Pages 89–118 in *Text, Image, and Christians in the Graeco-Roman World*. Edited by A. C. Niang and C. Osiek. Eugene, OR: Pickwick, 2012.

Mack, Joanna, and Stewart Lansley. *Poor Britain*. London: Allen & Unwin, 1985.

Mackie, G. V. *Early Christian Chapels in the West: Decoration, Function, and Patronage*. Toronto: University of Toronto Press, 2003.

Maiuri, Amadeo. *La Casa del Menandro e il suo tesoro di argenteria*. Rome: La Libreria dello Stato, 1933.

Malherbe, Abraham. *The Letters to the Thessalonians: A New Translation with Introduction and Commentary*. Anchor Yale Bible 32B. New York: Doubleday, 2000.

Malina, Bruce J. *The New Testament World: Insights from Cultural Anthropology*. 3rd edition. Louisville: Westminster John Knox, 2001.

———. *The Social World of Jesus and the Gospels*. London: Routledge, 1996.

Marchal, Joseph A. "'With Friends Like These . . .': A Feminist Rhetorical Reconsideration of Scholarship and the Letter to the Philippians." *JSNT* 29 (2006): 77–106.

Martin, Dale B. "Review Essay: Justin J. Meggitt, *Paul, Poverty, and Survival*." *JSNT* 84 (2001): 51–64.

McLaren, James S. "Jews and the Imperial Cult: From Augustus to Domitian." *JSNT* 27 (2005): 257–78.

Meeks, Wayne A. *The First Urban Christians: The Social World of the Apostle Paul*. 2nd edition. New Haven: Yale University Press, 2003.

Meggitt, Justin J. *Paul, Poverty, and Survival*. Studies of the New Testament and Its World. Edinburgh: T&T Clark, 1998.

Millett, Paul. "Patronage and Its Avoidance in Classical Athens." Pages 5–47 in *Patronage in Ancient Society*. Edited by Andrew Wallace-Hadrill. London: Routledge, 1989.

Mitchell, Alan C. "The Social Function of Friendship in Acts 2:44–47 and 4:32–37." *Journal of Biblical Literature* 111 (1992): 255–72.

Mitchell, Steven. *Anatolia: Land, Men, and Gods in Asia Minor*, vol. 1: *The Celts in Anatolia and the Impact of Roman Rule*. Oxford: Clarendon, 1993.

Morris, Ian. "The Early Polis as City and State." Pages 24–57 in *City and Country in the Ancient World*. Edited by John Rich and Andrew Wallace-Hadrill. London: Routledge, 1991.

Mosala, Itumeleng J. *Biblical Hermeneutics and Black Theology in South Africa*. Grand Rapids: Eerdmans, 1989.

Mouritsen, Henrik. *Elections, Magistrates, and Municipal Élite: Studies in Pompeian Epigraphy*. Analecta Romana Instituti Danici Supplement 15. Rome: "L'Erma" di Bretschneider, 1988.

Moxnes, Halvor. *The Economy of the Kingdom: Social Conflict and Economic Relations in Luke's Gospel*. Philadelphia: Fortress, 1988.

Murphy-O'Connor, Jerome. *St. Paul's Corinth: Texts and Archaeology*. 3rd edition. Good News Studies 6. Wilmington, DE: Glazier, 1983. Reprinted Collegeville, MN: Liturgical Press, 1990, 2002.

Nasrallah, Laura S. "Spatial Perspectives: Space and Archaeology in Roman Philippi." Pages 53–74 in *Studying Paul's Letters: Contemporary Perspectives and Methods.* Edited by J. Marchal. Minneapolis: Fortress, 2012.

Nasrallah, Laura S., and Elisabeth Schüssler Fiorenza, eds. *Prejudice and Christian Beginnings: Investigating Race, Gender, and Ethnicity.* Minneapolis: Fortress, 2009.

Neyrey, Jerome. *Render to God: New Testament Understandings of the Divine.* Minneapolis: Fortress, 2004.

Oakes, Peter. "Christian Attitudes to Rome at the Time of Paul's Letter." *Review and Expositor* 100 (2003): 103–11.

——. "Constructing Poverty Scales for Graeco-Roman Society: A Response to Steven Friesen's 'Poverty in Pauline Studies.'" *JSNT* 26 (2004): 367–71.

——. "Epictetus (and the New Testament)." *Vox Evangelica* 23 (1993): 39–56.

——. "God's Sovereignty over Roman Authorities: A Theme in Philippians." Pages 126–41 in *Rome in the Bible and the Early Church.* Edited by Peter Oakes. Carlisle: Paternoster; Grand Rapids: Baker Academic, 2002.

——. "Made Holy by the Holy Spirit: Holiness and Ecclesiology in Romans." Pages 167–83 in *Holiness and Ecclesiology in the New Testament.* Edited by Kent E. Brower and Andy Johnson. Grand Rapids: Eerdmans, 2007.

——. "Methodological Issues in Using Economic Evidence in Interpretation of Early Christian Texts." Pages 9–34 in *Engaging Economics: New Testament Scenarios and Early Christian Reception.* Edited by Bruce W. Longenecker and Kelly D. Liebengood. Grand Rapids: Eerdmans, 2009.

——. "Philippians: From People to Letter." DPhil thesis, Oxford University, 1995, supervised by N. T. Wright.

——. *Philippians: From People to Letter.* SNTSMS 110. Cambridge: Cambridge University Press, 2001.

——. "*Pistis* as Relational Way of Life in Galatians." *JSNT* 40 (2018): 255–75.

——. "Quelle devrait être l'influence des échos intertextuels sur la traduction? Le cas de l'epître aux Philippiens (2,15–16)." Pages 251–87 in *Intertextualités: La Bible en échos.* Edited by Daniel Marguerat and Adrian Curtis. Geneva: Labor et Fides, 2000.

——. *Reading Romans in Pompeii: Paul's Letter at Ground Level.* London: SPCK; Minneapolis: Fortress, 2009.

——. "Re-mapping the Universe: Paul and the Emperor in 1 Thessalonians and Philippians." *JSNT* 27 (2005): 301–22.

——. "Revelation 17.1–19.10: A Prophetic Vision of the Destruction of Rome." In *The Future of Rome: Roman, Greek, Jewish, and Christian Perspectives.*

Edited by Jonathan Price and Katell Berthelot. Cambridge: Cambridge University Press, 2020.

———. "A State of Tension: Rome in the New Testament." Pages 75–90 in *The Gospel of Matthew in Its Roman Imperial Context*. Edited by John Riches and David Sim. London: T&T Clark, 2005.

———. "Urban Structure and Patronage: Christ Followers in Corinth." Pages 178–93 in *Understanding the Social World of the New Testament*. Edited by Dietmar Neufeld and Richard E. DeMaris. London: Routledge, 2010.

Oakman, Douglas E. "The Countryside in Luke-Acts." Pages 151–79 in *The Social World of Luke-Acts: Models for Interpretation*. Edited by Jerome H. Neyrey. Peabody, MA: Hendrickson, 1991.

———. *Jesus and the Peasants*. Matrix: The Bible in Mediterranean Context 4. Eugene, OR: Cascade, 2008.

O'Brien, Peter T. *Commentary on Philippians*. New International Greek Testament Commentary. Grand Rapids: Eerdmans, 1991.

Økland, Jorunn. *Women in Their Place: Paul and the Corinthian Discourse of Gender and Sanctuary Space*. JSNTSup 269. London: T&T Clark, 2004.

Osiek, Carolyn, and David L. Balch. *Families in the New Testament World: Households and House Churches*. Louisville: Westminster John Knox, 1997.

Ostrow, Steven E. "The Topography of Puteoli and Baiae on the Eight Glass Flasks." *Studi di Storia Antica* 3 (1979): 77–140.

Painter, Kenneth S. *The Insula of the Menander at Pompeii*, vol. 4: *The Silver Treasure*. Oxford: Clarendon, 2001.

Parkin, Michael. *Economics*. 7th edition. Boston: Addison Wesley, 2005.

Parkin, Tim G. *Demography and Roman Society*. Baltimore: Johns Hopkins University Press, 1992.

Pearson, B. A. "1 Thessalonians 2:13–16: A Deutero-Pauline Interpolation." *Harvard Theological Review* 64 (1971): 79–94.

Perring, Dominic. "Spatial Organisation and Social Change in Roman Towns." Pages 273–93 in *City and Country in the Ancient World*. Edited by John Rich and Andrew Wallace-Hadrill. London: Routledge, 1991.

Peterson, E. "Die Einholung des Kyrios." *Zeitschrift für systematische Theologie* 7 (1929–30): 682–702.

Philo. *On the Embassy to Gaius*. Translated by F. H. Colson. Loeb Classical Library. London: Heinemann, 1962.

Pilhofer, Peter. *Philippi*, vol. 1: *Die erste christliche Gemeinde Europas*. Tübingen: Mohr, 1995.

———. *Philippi*, vol. 2: *Katalog der Inschriften von Philippi*. WUNT 119. Tübingen: Mohr, 2000.

Pitt-Rivers, Julian. *The Fate of Shechem or the Politics of Sex: Essays in the Anthropology of the Mediterranean*. Cambridge: Cambridge University Press, 1977.

Polanyi, Karl, et al. *Trade and Market in the Early Empires*. Chicago: Regnery, 1971.

Price, S. R. F. *Rituals and Power: The Roman Imperial Cult in Asia Minor*. Cambridge: Cambridge University Press, 1984.

Pudsey, April. *Sex, Statistics, and Soldiers: New Approaches to the Demography of Roman Egypt, 28 BC–259 AD*. Manchester: University of Manchester Press, 2007.

Rapske, Brian. *The Book of Acts and Paul in Roman Custody*. The Book of Acts in Its First Century Setting 3. Carlisle: Paternoster; Grand Rapids: Eerdmans, 1994.

Reed, Jonathan. *Archaeology and the Galilean Jesus*. Harrisburg, PA: Trinity, 2000.

Robbins, Lionel. *Essay on the Nature and Significance of Economic Science*. London: Macmillan, 1932.

Rodger, A. F. "Peculium." Page 1130 in *Oxford Classical Dictionary*. 3rd edition. Edited by S. Hornblower and A. Spawforth. Oxford: Oxford University Press, 1996.

Rohrbaugh, Richard L. "Methodological Considerations in the Debate over the Social Class Status of Early Christians." *Journal of the American Academy of Religion* 52 (1984): 519–46.

———. "The Pre-industrial City in Luke-Acts: Urban Social Relations." Pages 125–49 in *The Social World of Luke-Acts*. Edited by Jerome H. Neyrey. Peabody, MA: Hendrickson, 1991.

Romano, David Gilman. "Urban and Rural Planning in Roman Corinth." Pages 25–59 in *Urban Religion in Roman Corinth: Interdisciplinary Approaches*. Edited by Daniel Schowalter and Steven J. Friesen. Cambridge: Harvard University Press, 2005.

Saller, Richard P. "Patronage and Friendship in Early Imperial Rome: Drawing the Distinction." Pages 49–62 in *Patronage in Ancient Society*. Edited by Andrew Wallace-Hadrill. London: Routledge, 1989.

Salmon, E. T. *Roman Colonization under the Republic*. London: Thames & Hudson, 1969.

Scheid, John. "Genius." Page 630 in *Oxford Classical Dictionary*. 3rd edition. Edited by S. Hornblower and A. Spawforth. Oxford: Oxford University Press, 1996.

Scheidel, Walter, Ian Morris, and Richard Saller, eds. *The Cambridge Economic History of the Greco-Roman World*. Cambridge: Cambridge University Press, 2007.

Schowalter, Daniel. "Seeking Shelter in Roman Corinth: Archaeology and the

Placement of Paul's Communities." Pages 327–41 in *Corinth in Context: Comparative Studies on Religion and Society*. Edited by Steven Friesen, Daniel Schowalter, and James Walters. Leiden: Brill, 2010.

Schowalter, Daniel, and Steven J. Friesen, eds. *Urban Religion in Roman Corinth: Interdisciplinary Approaches*. Cambridge: Harvard University Press, 2005.

Schwertheim, Elmar. "Forschungen in der Troas im Jahre 1988." *Araştirma Sonuçlari Toplantisi* 7 (1990): 229–32.

Scott, James C. *Domination and the Arts of Resistance: Hidden Transcripts*. New Haven: Yale University Press, 1990.

Seeley, David. "The Background of the Philippians Hymn (2:6–11)." *Journal of Higher Criticism* 1 (Fall 1994): 49–72. daniel.drew.edu/~doughty/jhcbody.html#reviews.

Seneca. *Moral Essays*, vol. 3: *De Beneficiis*. Translated by J. W. Basore. Loeb Classical Library. Cambridge: Harvard University Press, 1935.

Sève, M., and P. Weber. "Un monument honorifique au forum de Philippes." *Bulletin de Correspondance Hellénique* 112 (1988): 467–79.

Shelton, Jo-Ann. *As the Romans Did: A Sourcebook in Roman Social History*. 2nd edition. Oxford: Oxford University Press, 1998.

Sherk, Robert. *The Roman Empire: Augustus to Hadrian*. Cambridge: Cambridge University Press, 1988.

Sjoberg, Gideon. *The Preindustrial City: Past and Present*. New York: Free Press, 1960.

Smith, Dennis E. *From Symposium to Eucharist: The Banquet in the Early Christian World*. Minneapolis: Fortress, 2003.

———. "The Greco-Roman Banquet as a Social Institution." Pages 23–33 in *Meals in the Early Christian World: Social Formation, Experimentation, and Conflict at the Table*. Edited by Dennis E. Smith and Hal Taussig. New York: Palgrave Macmillan, 2012.

———. "The House Church as Social Environment." Pages 3–21 in *Text, Image, and Christians in the Graeco-Roman World*. Edited by A. C. Niang and C. Osiek. Eugene, OR: Pickwick, 2012.

Smith, Dennis E., and Hal Taussig, eds. *Meals in the Early Christian World: Social Formation, Experimentation, and Conflict at the Table*. New York: Palgrave Macmillan, 2012.

Soja, Edward W. *Postmodern Geographies: The Reassertion of Space in Critical Social Theory*. London: Verso, 1989.

Stegemann, Ekkehard W., and Wolfgang Stegemann. *The Jesus Movement: A So-*

cial History of Its First Century. Translated by O. C. Dean Jr. Minneapolis: Fortress, 1999.

Stewart, Eric C. "Social Stratification and Patronage in Ancient Mediterranean Societies." Pages 156–66 in *Understanding the Social World of the New Testament.* Edited by Dietmar Neufeld and Richard E. DeMaris. London: Routledge, 2010.

Still, Todd D. *Conflict at Thessalonica: A Pauline Church and Its Neighbours.* JSNTSup 183. Sheffield: Sheffield Academic Press, 1999.

Talbert, Charles H. *Matthew.* Paideia Commentaries on the New Testament. Grand Rapids: Baker Academic, 2010.

Theissen, Gerd. *Miracle Stories of the Early Christian Tradition.* Edinburgh: T&T Clark, 1983.

———. *The Shadow of the Galilean: The Quest of the Historical Jesus in Narrative Form.* Translated by J. Bowden. Minneapolis: Fortress, 1987.

———. *The Social Setting of Pauline Christianity: Essays on Corinth.* Translated by John H. Schütz. Edinburgh: T&T Clark; Philadelphia: Fortress, 1982.

———. "The Social Structure of Pauline Communities: Some Critical Remarks on J. J. Meggitt, *Paul, Poverty, and Survival.*" JSNT 84 (2001): 65–84.

———. *Sociology of Early Palestinian Christianity.* Translated by J. Bowden. Philadelphia: Fortress, 1978. UK edition: *The First Followers of Jesus.* London: SCM, 1978. German original: *Soziologie der Jesusbewegung.* Munich: Kaiser Verlag, 1977.

Thompson, John B. *Ideology and Modern Culture: Critical Social Theory in the Era of Mass Communication.* Cambridge: Polity Press, 1990.

Touratsoglou, Ioannis. *Die Münzstätte von Thessaloniki in der römischen Kaiserzeit (32/31 v. Chr. bis 268 n. Chr.).* Antike Münzen und geschnittene Steine 12. Berlin: de Gruyter, 1988.

Turner, Seth. "The Interim, Earthly Messianic Kingdom in Paul." JSNT 25 (2003): 323–42.

Velleius Paterculus. *Historiae Romanae.* Translated by F. W. Shipley. Loeb Classical Library. London: Heinemann; Cambridge: Harvard University Press, 1924.

Wallace-Hadrill, Andrew. "*Domus* and *Insulae* in Rome: Families and Housefuls." Pages 3–18 in *Early Christian Families in Context: An Interdisciplinary Dialogue.* Edited by David L. Balch and Carolyn Osiek. Grand Rapids: Eerdmans, 2003.

———. *Houses and Society in Pompeii and Herculaneum.* Princeton: Princeton University Press, 1994.

———. "Patronage in Roman Society: From Republic to Empire." Pages 63–87 in

Patronage in Ancient Society. Edited by Andrew Wallace-Hadrill. London: Routledge, 1989.

Wallace-Hadrill, Andrew, ed. *Patronage in Ancient Society*. London: Routledge, 1989.

Walton, Steve. "The State They Were In: Luke's View of the Roman Empire." Pages 1–41 in *Rome in the Bible and the Early Church*. Edited by Peter Oakes. Carlisle: Paternoster; Grand Rapids: Baker, 2002.

Weissenrieder, Annette. "Contested Spaces in 1 Corinthians 11:17–33 and 14:30: Sitting or Reclining in Ancient Houses, in Associations, and in the Space of *Ekklēsia*." Pages 59–107 in *Contested Spaces: Houses and Temples in Roman Antiquity and the New Testament*. Edited by D. L. Balch and A. Weissenrieder. WUNT 285. Tübingen: Mohr Siebeck, 2012.

Wengst, Klaus. *Pax Romana and the Peace of Jesus Christ*. Translated by J. Bowden. Philadelphia: Fortress, 1987. German original: *Pax Romana, Anspruch und Wirklichkeit: Erfahrungen und Wahrnehmungen des Friedens bei Jesus und im Urchristentum*. Munich: Kaiser Verlag, 1986.

Whittaker, C. R. "The Poor in the City of Rome." Pages 1–25 in *Land, City, and Trade in the Roman Empire*. Edited by C. R. Whittaker. Variorum. Aldershot: Ashgate, 1993.

Wiefel, Wolfgang. "The Jewish Community in Ancient Rome and the Origins of Roman Christianity." Pages 85–101 in *The Romans Debate*. Edited by Karl P. Donfried. Peabody, MA: Hendrickson, 1991.

Winter, Bruce W. *Divine Honours for the Caesars: The First Christians' Responses*. Grand Rapids: Eerdmans, 2015.

———. "Roman Law and Society in Romans 12–15." Pages 67–102 in *Rome in the Bible and the Early Church*. Edited by Peter Oakes. Carlisle: Paternoster; Grand Rapids: Baker Academic, 2002.

———. *Seek the Welfare of the City: Christians as Benefactors and Citizens*. First-Century Christians in the Graeco-Roman World. Carlisle: Paternoster; Grand Rapids: Eerdmans, 1994.

Wright, N. T. *The Climax of the Covenant: Christ and the Law in Pauline Theology*. Edinburgh: T&T Clark, 1991.

———. *Jesus and the Victory of God*. London: SPCK, 1996.

———. *What Saint Paul Really Said*. Oxford: Lion, 1997.

Index of Modern Authors

Adams, Edward, 31–32, 36, 51–52, 61, 74
Alexander, Loveday, 184
Alföldy, Geza, 82–85
Allison, Penelope M., 6–7, 37, 49, 73, 98
Ando, Clifford, 146
Andringa, William van, 15, 52
Ascough, Richard S., 9, 11, 78, 108, 138

Bagnall, Roger S., 12, 76–77
Balch, David L., 31–32, 38, 44–46, 50, 52, 61, 76
Bammel, Ernst, 171
Bang, Peter, 66
Barron, Caroline, 16
Batten, Alicia, 9, 78
Bauckham, Richard J., 188
Beard, Mary, 15, 17
Beare, F. W., 129
Belo, Fernando, 96
Béranger, Jean, 192
Berry, Joanne, 73
Bingen, Jean, 77
Bockmuehl, Markus, 183
Bookidis, Nancy, 120
Braund, D., 111
Brocke, Christoph vom, 141–42, 151, 162, 171–72
Bülow-Jacobsen, Adam, 77

Caird, G. B., 129
Carney, Thomas, x
Carter, Warren, 4, 139
Cassidy, Richard J., 164–66
Chow, John K., 117, 121
Clarke, Andrew D., 44, 75, 91–93, 119, 156
Clarke, John R., 38, 86–87
Collange, Jean-François, 131, 143
Collart, Paul, 142
Crook, Zeba A., 9
Cullmann, Oscar, 25, 165, 177

Dandeker, Chris, 111
DeFelice, John, 52–53
Deissmann, Adolf, 92, 137
Della Corte, Matteo, 37, 41, 73
Dinbabin, Katharine M. D., 24
Donfried, Karl, 146, 149, 171
Duling, Dennis C., 83
Duncan-Jones, Richard, 76
Dunn, James D. G., 57, 102, 130

Eisenstadt, S. N., 109, 111
Elia, Olga, 8, 37
Elliott, John H., 5
Elliott, Neil, 139

Index of Subjects

apantēsis (meeting), 149–50
apocalyptic, 26, 150, 168, 171, 177–79
association, 9, 11, 46, 77, 81, 108, 138
Athens, 114–15

children, 9–10
church. *See* house church; tenement church
class, 65, 66, 69, 96–97, 116
Corinth, 35, 74, 80–81, 117–20
craftworker, 8–10, 17, 21, 73, 104–6
cult, 57–58, 113–14, 115–16, 120–21, 140, 143, 147, 161, 169–70, 173; domestic, 9, 15, 25, 51. *See also* Rome: imperial cult

ecclesiology, 104–8
economics: definition, 67–68, 93–95; economic evidence, 72–82, 98; economic issues facing house churches, 4–14, 19–23; economic scale, 87–89, 93; embedded economy, 66–67; precariousness, 10–14, 21, 124. *See also* poverty: poverty scale
elite, 24, 29, 48, 56, 83–88, 95, 108, 109–21
Erastus, 74–75, 119
eschatology, 26, 139, 143, 148, 162, 171–72

family, 12, 20, 78, 106; size of, 12, 77

Gaius, 118–19

hidden transcript, 4, 25–26
homeless people, 13–14, 18–19, 21, 23
honor, 15, 47, 79, 92, 106–7, 109, 111–14, 147, 173
house church, 36n12, 48–50; size of, 43, 44–45, 48, 50, 54. *See also* models: model craftworker house church
household, 106–7; size of, 77

idol meat, 120–22
Insula of the Menander, 6, 37–39; House I.10.1, 48–51; House I.10.2–3 (bar), 15, 51–54; House I.10.4, 15, 16, 17 (House of the Menander), 14–16, 38, 42–48, 57–60; House I.10.6 (workshop), 54; House I.10.7 (workshop, House of the Cabinetmaker, *Casa del Fabbro*), 6–8, 55–57, 73, 105, 118
intersectionality, 95
itinerant preachers, 3, 20–21, 99–101

Jesus Christ, authority of, 25, 139–40, 143, 148, 161–62, 187–92
Jewish war against Rome, 167–68

217

INDEX OF ANCIENT SOURCES